Praise for Stephen Plumb's

NOTABLE NEW YORK:
The West Side
& Greenwich Village

*A Walking Guide to the Historic Homes
of Famous (and Infamous) New Yorkers*

"This is just the kind of book I love. Clear, concise facts, logically organized, packed with information I never knew. What a treat to discover someone who loves the details of the city to share them with us all. It's easy to use because of the handy maps and compact enough to take out on the streets with a bagel and a can of Dr. Brown's Cel-Ray Soda. Can't wait for the East Side volume.
—*Bill Morgan*, Author of *The Beat Generation in New York: A Walking Tour of Jack Kerouac's City*

"..readers can now visit the homes of Mark Twain, Lenny Bruce, Thomas Edison, Bob Dylan, and Babe Ruth. Plumb's lively anecdotes engage the reader and make the book a pleasure to read from cover to cover. This excellent supplement to travel guides to New York City is recommended..."
— *Library Journal*

"Stephen Plumb's... splendid book has opened my eyes to a fascinating parade of people and places; an olio of architecture and anecdote; and a delightful diversion from the usual deathly dull guidebook. The starting point is people — the cloyingly good, the outrageously bad, the embarrassingly public, the reclusively private, and even those I never realized had ever lived here. Stephen Plumb has put a human face on otherwise faceless buildings, and enlivened our understanding of the many smaller neighborhoods that make up Manhattan's West Side. And he's given us a lighthearted and charming read in the process. Thank you, Stephen.
—*Andrew Alpern*, Author of *New York's Fabulous Luxury Apartments*

Praise for

THE STREETS
WHERE THEY LIVED

"If you are planning a visit to New York City, *The Streets Where They Lived*...will offer a different perspective. It's a walking guide to the present or former residences of movie and stage personalities, artists and journalists, as well as nearly 400 other celebrities. Also included are distinctive hotels and apartments."
—*Los Angeles Times*

"The book, which covers Manhattan in eight different sections, is a mini-history of the city and interesting to read even if you don't set out to see the city in a good, comfortable pair of walking shoes."
—*Gale Shufelt, Schenectady Sunday Gazette*

"The book remains a delightful tour guide, equally suitable for locals and visitors."
—Denise Perry Donavin,
—*Booklist*

"The 36 tours can each be walked in 15 minutes to an hour
— unless you become too entranced
to tear yourself away that quickly."
—Theodora Nelson, T*ravel-Holiday Magazine*

"Folks who like to walk the sidewalks of New York will also like *The Streets Where They Lived* by Stephen W. Plumb ...Start reading it and you can't stop."
—Dave Wood, *Minneapolis Star Tribune*

NOTABLE NEW YORK

The East Side

A Walking Guide to the Historic Homes
of Famous (and Infamous) New Yorkers

STEPHEN W. PLUMB

MARLOR PRESS, INC.
SAINT PAUL, MN

NOTABLE NEW YORK
The East Side

A Walking Guide to the Historic Homes
of Famous (and Infamous) New Yorkers

A MARLIN BREE BOOK

Copyright 2006 by Stephen W. Plumb
Maps by Stephen W. Plumb
Cover design by Theresa Gedig
Maps designed by Gary Swanson

ISBN -13: 978-1-892147-12-7
ISBN -10: 1-892147-12-2

Printed in the United States of America
Distributed to the book trade by Independent Publishers Group, Chicago
First Edition

Library of Congress Cataloging-in-Publication Data

Plumb, Stephen W., 1942-
Notable New York. The East Side : a walking guide to the historic homes of famous (and infamous) New Yorkers / Stephen W. Plumb. -- 1st ed.
    p. cm.
"A Marlin Bree book"--T.p. verso
Includes bibliographical references and index
ISBN-13: 978-1-892147-12-7
ISBN-10: 1-892147-12-2
    1. Historic buildings -- New York (State) -- New York -- Guidebooks. 2. Dwellings -- New York (State) -- New York -- Guidebooks. 3. New York (N.Y.) -- Buildings, structures, etc. -- Guidebooks. 4. Upper East Side (New York, N.Y.) -- Tours. 5. Midtown Manhattan (New York, N.Y.) -- Tours. 6. Lower East Side (New York, N.Y.) -- Tours. 7. New York (N.Y.) -- Tours. 8. Walking -- New York (State) -- New York -- Guidebooks. 9. New York (N.Y.) Biography -- Miscellanea. I. Title. II. Title: East Side, a walking guide to the historic homes of famous (and infamous) New Yorkers.

F128.37.P63 2006
917.47'10444--dc22   2006046319

MARLOR PRESS, INC.
4304 Brigadoon Drive
Saint Paul, MN 55126

For

Wendy Adamson

BOOKS
BY
STEPHEN PLUMB

NOTABLE
NEW YORK
The East Side

A Walking Guide to the Historic Homes
of Famous (and Infamous) New Yorkers
(Marlor Press Spring 2006)

NOTABLE
NEW YORK
The West Side
& Greenwich Village

A Walking Guide to the Historic Homes
of Famous (and Infamous) New Yorkers
(Marlor Press Fall 2006)

THE STREETS
WHERE THEY LIVED

A Walking Guide to the Residences
of Famous New Yorkers
(Marlor Press Spring 1989)

CONTENTS

New York's East Side has been the home to countless notable and celebrated individuals. The second in a two-volume set, this volume covers the East Side, with the main dividing line (or western border) being Fifth Avenue in the north and Broadway in the south. With this guide, you can see the house, apartment or hotel where Hemingway, Hammett, Cather, Faulkner, Brecht, and O'Neil wrote; where Porter, Berlin, Rodgers, Arlen and Gershwin composed their music; where the Marx Brothers grew up; where Franklin and Eleanor Roosevelt were married; and where Buster Keaton performed in his first silent film.

Tour maps show where the Notable New Yorkers worked, played and loved. Each tour will take a walker anywhere from 15 to 90 minutes, depending on the number of places included in that particular tour and the pace. The text for each haunt, place or building tells something about the individual who stayed there and gives a brief history or description of the person's stay as well as why the person is notable. About 800 people are profiled at about 500 addresses in 30 short walking tours.

Since the turn of the last century, the Upper East Side has been the favorite residential area of Manhattan's wealthiest people. Its borders run from East 60th Street to East 102nd Street, and between Fifth Avenue and the East River. The Upper East Side has a rich and varied history and has been and continues to be the home of a great number of New York's most famous people—entertainers, writers, athletes and even criminals. At one time, Ernest Hemingway, Oscar Hammerstein II, Franklin and Eleanor Roosevelt, Dorothy Parker, Willa Cather, Danny Kaye and Gypsy Rose Lee called the Upper East Side home.

Midtown East stretches from East 40th Street to East 60th Street and between Fifth Avenue and the East River. Once a neighborhood of mansions and brownstones and the haunt of the wealthy, this area has such wonderful neighborhoods as Turtle Bay, Beekman Place, Tudor City and Sutton Place and has been the home for a number of important and colorful New Yorkers including Clare Boothe, Ed Sullivan, Toots Shore, William Paley, Audrey Hepburn, Greta Garbo, Howard Hughes and Johnny Carson.

195 SECTION THREE: MURRAY HILL AND SURROUNDINGS

Murray Hill became very fashionable in the mid-nineteenth century as affluent New Yorkers moved uptown, building mansions along Fifth, Madison and Park Avenues. It covers the area from East 28th to East 40th Street and between Third and Fifth Avenue. Although most of the great mansions are gone, a number of outstanding brownstones and carriage houses remain, keepsakes of this neighborhood's more elegant days—and reminders of the fact that Murray Hill was once the home of a number of prominent New Yorkers including Mrs. George Armstrong Custer, F. Scott and Zelda Fitzgerald, Katharine Hepburn, Dashiell Hammett, Harold Ross, Kate Smith, Robert Benchley, Eugene O'Neill and Veronica Lake.

212 SECTION FOUR: GRAMERCY PARK AND SURROUNDINGS

Gramercy Park, along with its surrounding streets, is one of New York's most charming neighborhoods and certainly one part of the city that has retained the look and feel of old New York. This section covers an area from East 15th to East 27th Street and between Broadway and First Avenue. Over the years it has been the home of countless prominent artists, writers, entertainers and businessmen including John Garfield, Edith Wharton, Eleanor Roosevelt, Humphrey Bogart, James Cagney, Thomas Edison, James Stewart, Henry Fonda, Cole Porter, Isadora Duncan and Theda Bara.

238 SECTION FIVE: EAST GREENWICH VILLAGE

The East Village represents the eastern extension of the West Greenwich Village that was covered in Volume One and occupies the area from Broadway to the East River and from Houston to East 14th Street. This neighborhood has been a magnet for the counterculture of the last century, attracting many artists, writers, poets, musicians and social radicals. Notable New Yorkers who called the East Village home include Diane Arbus, Lucky Luciano, George and Ira Gershwin, Emma Goldman, and James Fenimore Cooper.

INTRODUCTION

*New York is the concentrate of art and commerce and sport and
religion and entertainment and finance, bringing to a single arena the
gladiator, the evangelist, the promoter, the actor, the trader and the
merchant. It carries on its lapel the unexpungeable odor of
the long past, so that no matter where you sit...you feel the
vibrations of great times and tall deeds, of queer people
and events and undertakings.*

— **E.B. White**, *Here Is New York,* 1949

NO OTHER AMERICAN CITY has such a rich past—and present—
as New York City. This is true, in part, because it has been
the home of so many notable and amazing people. A visitor or resident can stand on practically any street in Manhattan
and feel engulfed by its colorful history.

This book, the second volume of a two-volume set, is an
attempt to capture some of that history by focusing on a large
number of the notable individuals who have inhabited the city's
many buildings. Specifically, it is a record of the places in New
York City where these famous people have lived in the last one
hundred and fifty years. It aims to guide the reader in a series of
short walking tours, street by street, to the actual houses, apartment buildings, hotels, and public places where they stayed. It
offers brief descriptions of the events that took place during
each person's residency at a particular address. This volume
covers the neighborhoods on the East side of Manhattan. An earlier volume, published in 2006, covered the West Side.

I have selected my group of people from various walks of life.
The reader will find on the following pages individuals who were
politicians, artists, musicians, playwrights, poets, actors,

comedians, novelists, criminals, journalists, and businessmen. Most of them lived in New York during the last century. All were individuals who were made famous by New York and, in turn, helped to make New York famous.

In presenting this list of New Yorkers, I must emphasize that it is very much a selective and subjective one. The more than five hundred people and addresses in this guide represent one person's choices made from a vast number of possibilities. These choices obviously reflect the author's personal interests, but I have made no attempt to be comprehensive. My aim, instead, has been to give a reader a flavor of the history of a selected number of Manhattan neighborhoods.

The terrible events of September 11th, 2001 are a reminder not only of the fragile nature of our day-to-day existence but also of the fragility of our physical surroundings—our very streets and homes and treasured landmarks—which we sometimes take for granted. In addition to their beauty and utility, these structures seem to have the power to evoke time and place and often embody the characters of those who erect and inhabit them. Edward Hopper, who during his long career captured New York life so memorably in his paintings and etchings, spent many hours observing people in their homes as he walked the city's streets and rode its elevated trains. "I like to look in windows and see people standing there in the light at night," he once said in an interview. In this act of voyeurism, he was doing what many of us do—consciously or not—as we too walk the streets of Manhattan. We look up at all those windows and imagine what has gone on behind them. What would these buildings say if their walls could talk?

This guidebook will provide you with a number of answers to that question. With it you can see where Hemingway, Hammett, Cather, Faulkner, Brecht, and O'Neill wrote, where Porter, Berlin, Rodgers, Arlen, and Gershwin composed their music, where Rothko, O'Keeffe, Warhol, de Kooning, Lichtenstein, and Avedon created their art, where the Marx Brothers grew up, where Franklin and Eleanor Roosevelt were married, and where Buster Keaton performed in his first silent film.

Most of the people described on the following pages have died or moved on. A number of their former residences have disappeared—victims of the wrecking ball. Yet, on block after block, you can still find, standing as memorials, many of the places they inhabited. Their spirits remain as a presence.

It's my hope that you meet a few of those spirits as you walk these streets.

MANHATTAN

THE EAST SIDE

IN FIVE
SECTIONS

Section 1: **UPPER EAST SIDE**

The area between Fifth Avenue
and the East River and from
East 60th Street to East 102nd Street

Section 2: **MIDTOWN WEST**

The area between Fifth Avenue
and the East River and from
East 40th Street to East 60th Street

Section 3: **MURRAY HILL**

The area between Fifth Avenue
and Third Avenue and from East
27th Street to East 40th Street

Section 4: **GRAMERCY PARK**

The area between Broadway and
First Avenue and from East 14th
Street to East 27th Street

Section 5: **THE EAST VILLAGE**

The area between Broadway and
the East River and from Houston
Street to East 14th Street

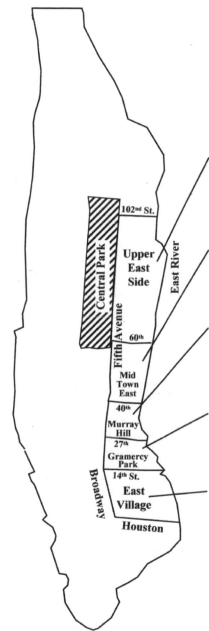

ABOUT
THIS
GUIDE

THIS GUIDE to the residences of famous New Yorkers is the second of a two-volume set. I have divided the island of Manhattan into two sections—east and west—and this second volume covers, roughly, the east side, with the main dividing line (or western border) being Fifth Avenue in the north and Broadway in the south. This book does not cover neighborhoods above 102nd Street or below Houston Street.

The guide is made up of five sections—the Upper East Side, Midtown East of Fifth Avenue, Murray Hill, Gramercy Park, and East Greenwich Village. Each section is divided into a number of short walking tours, twenty-nine in all. Each tour will take the walker anywhere from fifteen minutes to an hour to cover, depending on the number of places included in that particular tour and the pace that is chosen. A map accompanies each tour.

Each house, apartment, hotel, or other building in a tour is given a number corresponding to the same number on the tour map. The text entry for each building gives the name of the person who stayed there, the address, and a brief history or description of the person's stay, including relevant dates.

The emphasis of this guide is on people who lived or stayed at a place in the past although, in a few cases, the individual in question may still be in residency there.

All of the information in this book was found in standard biographies, newspaper and magazine accounts, and basic library reference books such as biographical dictionaries, city directories, and phone books. The most important of these books are cited in the bibliography. The book would be unnecessarily cumbersome if it included detailed references and footnotes. However, if any reader has questions or comments about anything written here, he or she may contact the author through his website *www.plumden.com* and he will be happy to respond and provide information.

Stephen W. Plumb
Author

THE UPPER EAST SIDE

*East 60th Street to East 102nd Street
and between Fifth Avenue and the East River.*

SINCE THE TURN OF THE LAST CENTURY, the Upper East Side has been the favorite residential area of Manhattan's wealthiest people. Its most famous section runs along Fifth Avenue and its related side streets, from the Sherry Netherland Hotel at 60th Street to the Carnegie mansion at 91st. Here, along the eastern border of Central Park, were once found block after block of the spectacular marble and brownstone houses that gave this stretch its name, Millionaires' Row. Most of these homes were built between 1880 and 1930 by the industrial barons and their followers who amassed their fortunes in the era after the Civil War. With the social changes wrought by the First World War, and the the economic pressures of the Great Depression, they became impractical and far too costly to be maintained by a single family. Now, the few of these residences that remain among the newer grand apartment buildings that replaced them have either been subdivided into multi-family occupancy or taken over by various learned societies, clubs, museums and foreign delegations.

The area east of Millionaires' Row was effectively divided into two distinct neighborhoods at the turn of the century, both containing different populations. The first, spanning Madison, Park, and Lexington Avenues, was basically middle class in composition. The second, which ran from Lexington to the East River, was a working class tenement neighborhood with a concentration of families of German, Irish, Italian, and Eastern European origin. Both of these areas have greatly changed in character since those days. After the First World War, middle class Park Avenue became a new magnet for the affluent and that famous street soon became a name synonymous with the rich as luxury high-rise apartment buildings, divided into elegant duplexes and triplexes, were constructed. In the last fifty years, those working class streets closer to the river have been transformed into an upper middle-class neighborhood as tenements and brownstones have either been renovated or torn down to make way for the many large modern apartments seen here today. The Upper East Side has a rich and varied history. It has been, and continues to be, the home of a great number of New York's most famous people.

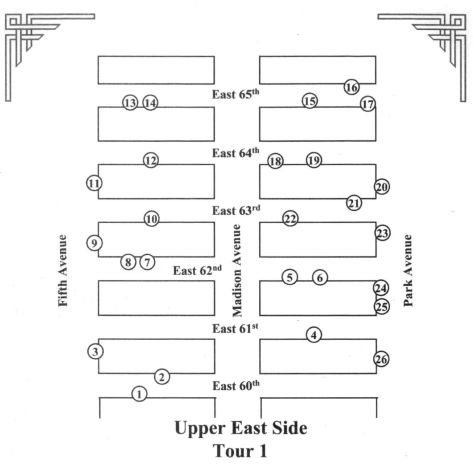

Upper East Side
Tour 1

TOUR 1

1/Alfred Stieglitz
14 East 60th Street between Fifth and Madison Avenue.

Photographer **Alfred Stieglitz** lived in a brownstone on this site as a young boy. He was seven years old when his wealthy parents bought the house in 1871 and moved in with their six children. The Upper East Side was relatively undeveloped in those days—Fifth Avenue was paved with cobblestones only as far north as 59th Street and, in the summers, residents had to contend with problems such as malaria and the stench of dead horses decaying in vacant lots.

Alfred Stieglitz

By 1900, Stieglitz's father had sold the house and moved the family but after his death in 1909, Stieglitz's mother, Hedwig, came back to this block and rented an apartment in this twelve-story building that was built on the site of the brownstone they once owned. She lived here until her death in 1922. After she died, the residence became the **Hotel Fourteen.**

Actress **Laurette Taylor,** famous as the star of Tennessee Williams's play *The Glass Menagerie*, lived at the Hotel Fourteen from 1934 until her death in 1946. She died in her suite here of a heart attack at age sixty-two.

Catholic philosopher **Teilhard de Chardin** lived in a room on the sixth floor of the hotel in 1954-55. It was his residence at the time of his death.

From 1940 to 1973, Hotel Fourteen was the location of the fabled **Copacabana** nightclub. It had a separate entrance numbered 10 East 60th Street. The Copa was one of the most glamorous meeting places in Manhattan and a spot where most of the top entertainers of that era performed, including **Martin and Lewis, Nat King Cole, Ella Fitzgerald, Frank Sinatra,** and **Jimmy Durante.**

2/Fanny Brice
15 East 60th Street between Fifth and Madison Avenue.

In 1927, soon after she divorced her first husband, gambler Nicky Arnstein, **Fanny Brice** moved to a large apartment in an elegant old brownstone on this site. The place later became part of the site for the office structure that stands here now. The location is next door to the **Metropolitan Club**, which occupies the corner of 60th Street and Fifth Avenue.

Brice was one of the biggest stars on Broadway at that time and her home featured a butler, a large, pine-paneled living room and simulated Chippendale furniture. One night she was visited by songwriter **Billy Rose**, who offered to write the material for her upcoming Palace Theater show. Not only did the show became another hit for her but soon Brice and Rose became a couple and they were married in February 1929.

3/Hotel Pierre
799 Fifth Avenue between 60th and 61st Street.

The **Pierre**, a landmark New York hotel, was built in 1929 on the site of the mansion owned by **Elbridge Gerry**, whose ancestor was one of the signers of the Declaration of Independence. The forty-story, Neo-Georgian building with its Italian marble floors and four-hundred rooms furnished with reproductions of English antiques was probably the city's top celebrity hotel in the 1930s—luminaries such as **Spencer Tracy, Gary Cooper,** and **Constance Bennett** stayed here whenever they were in town.

The hotel cost $15 million to build but the Depression took its toll on the Pierre and in 1938 it was put up for sale. **J. Paul Getty** bought it for $2,500,000—less than a fifth of its assessed value—and, as a member of the smart set, he was able to attract his playmates and their friends to the hotel, soon restoring its reputation.

The Pierre was heiress **Barbara Hutton's** favorite New York residence. She had suites on the thirty-sixth and later thirty-ninth floor. **Dashiell Hammett**, the detective novelist, started writing *The Thin Man* here in 1932 and when he ran up a bill that he couldn't pay, he disguised himself by wearing several layers of clothing, puffed out his cheeks to alter his face, and managed to sneak out without paying.

In 1938, while broke and coming off a drinking bout, **John O'Hara** wrote the first *Pal Joey* story (one of fourteen) here which later became the basis for the **Rodgers** and **Hart** musical. French film director **Rene Clair** lived in the hotel after coming to the United States to escape the German Occupation in the early 1940s.

In November 1940, after their wedding, **Lucille Ball** and **Desi Arnaz** moved to the Pierre for their honeymoon. They stayed for six weeks while Desi performed with his orchestra at the Roxy Theater. Actors **Robert Taylor** and **Barbara Stanwyck** also made the Pierre their home during the 1940s before their divorce.

Irene Mayer Selznick, wife of film producer **David Selznick** and daughter of of **MGM's Louis Mayer**, lived at the Pierre starting in 1945 after she separated from her husband. She bought up four suites on the tenth floor and combined them into one luxury apartment overlooking Central Park. Selznick, who is now best remembered for producing the stage version of *Streetcar Named Desire* in 1947, lived at the Pierre for forty-five years. She died in her bed here on October 11, 1990.

Greek shipping millionaire **Aristotle Onassis** always stayed at the Pierre when he was in town rather than in the apartment of his wife, **Jacqueline Kennedy Onassis**, who lived up Fifth Avenue at 85th Street (see this section, Tour 13, Number 6).

Composer **Richard Rodgers** lived in an eighteenth-floor suite at the Pierre during the last decade of his life. He died in his bed here on December 30, 1979. The marquees on Broadway went dark for one minute in his memory.

4/Leo Durocher

46 East 61st Street between Madison and Park Avenue.

In 1948, baseball's **Leo Durocher** was living in a house on this site with his wife, actress **Lorraine Day.** He was managing the **Brooklyn Dodgers.** One day his boss **Branch Rickey**, unhappy with the way he was handling the team, suggested that Durocher should quit and go to work for the rival **New York Giants.** Soon after, Durocher met with Giants owner **Horace Stoneham** in his home here and agreed to become the manager of the Giants.

In 1951, Durocher's new team won its first pennant in fourteen years after **Bobby Thomson's** dramatic home run at the Polo Grounds beat the Dodgers in the National League playoff. In 1954, though underdogs to the Cleveland Indians, Durocher's Giants won the World Series.

Across the street at 41 East 61st is the site of the home of songwriter **Vernon Duke** who wrote the music for such standards as *April in Paris, Autumn in New York,* and *I Can't Get Started (With You).*

5/Vincent Astor

34 East 62nd Street between Madison and Park Avenue.

Vincent Astor was one of New York's richest men. In 1912, as a college student, he inherited $87 million after his father **Colonel John Jacob Astor IV** went down with the *Titanic.*

The younger Astor, close friend of **Franklin D. Roosevelt,** had a passionate interest in the subject of espionage. In the late 1920s, he along with a circle of friends rented an apartment in this five-level brownstone where they set up a mail drop and installed an unlisted telephone. They formed a tight little society called **The Room** and met secretly here each month to trade gossip and informal information about foreign affairs and the spy business. Its members included **Kermit Roosevelt, Nelson Doubleday, Winthrop Aldrich,** and **Marshall Field**—all prominent New Yorkers whose elevated professional and social status placed much valuable information at their disposal.

When Franklin Roosevelt became president in 1933, Astor and his friends passed on whatever information they had gathered to the new chief, who liked to get reports about the activities of foreign powers through private channels and personal friends. The Room (the name was later changed to the Club) continued to report its findings to the president right up to the time of America's entry in World War II.

On July 10, 2006, the house here on 62nd Street was totally destroyed by a gas explosion.

Theodore Roosevelt

6/Henry Hardenbergh and Theodore Roosevelt
40 East 62nd Street between Madison and Park Avenue.

A three-bedroom apartment in this grand-looking nine-story building (built in 1910) was the home of one of New York City's most gifted and celebrated architects. **Henry Janeway Hardenbergh** designed some of New York's most distinguished landmark buildings including the old **Waldorf Astoria Hotel** (demolished in 1929), the **Plaza Hotel**, and **The Dakota** apartment house. He died at his home here on March 13, 1918 at the age of seventy-one. Hardenbergh didn't design this building, however; it was the work of another architect, **Alfred Joseph Bodker.**

At the southeast corner of 62nd Street and Madison Avenue is the site of a house once occupied by **Theodore Roosevelt.** The address was 689 Madison Avenue (the building here today is numbered 30 East 62nd Street) and it was owned by Roosevelt's sister, Bamie. Theodore and his second wife, **Edith Carow,** lived in it from 1895 to 1897 while he served as the city's police commissioner. Roosevelt became New York's governor in 1898 and moved to Albany. The Roosevelt house at this site was demolished in 1955.

7/Vanderbilt mansion
11 East 62nd Street between Fifth and Madison Avenue

This five-level Beaux-Arts style mansion was built at the turn of the last century by one of **Commodore Cornelius Vanderbilt's** granddaughters for her daughter **Edith Shepard** and husband **Ernesto Fabbri.** They lived here for twelve years before moving to France in 1912.

The **Johnson O'Connor Research Foundation** moved its offices here in 1943 and when they decided to sell it in 1997, they received the highest recorded price for a New York townhouse—twenty-one million dollars. The mansion now houses the permanent Japanese representative to the United Nations. When it was put on the market, architectural historians marveled at its wonderful condition. The huge mahogany-paneled dining room, ballroom with ornate plastered ceilings, and walk-in safes and coal bins hadn't been touched or modified in generations. "It's like the clock stopped here seventy years ago and never started up again," said the real estate agent who handled the sale of the property.

Hemingway's apartment

8/Ernest Hemingway

1 East 62nd Street near Fifth Avenue.

In the fall of 1959, **Ernest Hemingway**, wanting a place that would insure his privacy when he was in New York, rented a fourth-floor apartment in this building across from the **Knickerbocker Club**. He came with his fourth wife, **Mary Welsh.**

Hemingway was in poor physical and mental condition at the time. During the summer, he set up a card table in the corner of the living room to serve as an office and labored with great difficulty to write his Paris memoirs. The project took all of his energy but he managed to complete it while he stayed here; it later became the book *A Moveable Feast.*

Hemingway celebrated his sixty-fifth birthday in July 1960. He and Mary left New York for good in the fall to make one last trip to Spain. By October Ernest had returned to his home in Idaho. He committed suicide there on July 2, 1961. Mary kept the apartment on 62nd Street and at the end of her life, she lived alone here as an invalid, seldom going out. She died in 1986 at the age of seventy-eight.

9/Nelson Rockefeller and Richard Nixon

810 and 812 Fifth Avenue between 62nd and 63rd Street.

Nelson Rockefeller, with his first wife, **Mary Todhunter Clark**, lived on the top floors at 810 Fifth Avenue starting in 1934. The apartment was ultimately expanded to become a triplex of more than twenty rooms. The couple was living here when he became governor of New York in 1958.

When the Rockefellers separated in 1961, Mary got the top two floors including the penthouse terrace; Nelson retained the twelfth floor. After he married **Margaretta "Happy" Murphy** in 1963, Rockefeller expanded his residence by purchasing an apartment in the building next door at 812 Fifth Avenue and connecting the two places with a short flight of steps. He owned this very large expanded apartment until he died in 1979. In 1999, Mary's apartment at 810 went on sale for a stunning $19.5 million, and in 2000 sold for a still-impressive price of $16 million.

Former Vice President **Richard**

Nixon and his family lived in the fifth floor apartment here at 810 in 1963, soon after he lost his bid to be California's governor. He stayed here until he took over the **White House** in 1969 as the nation's thirty-seventh president. Coincidentally, Nixon and his neighbor, Nelson Rockefeller, were the two main contenders for the Republican Party's presidential nomination in 1968. While they competed for the nomination that year, they used different elevators in the building to reach their respective residences here.

10/Oscar Hammerstein II
10 East 63rd Street between Fifth and Madison Avenue

Hammerstein, with his wife, **Dorothy**, took an apartment in this five-floor brick house in 1948. It was the songwriter's last Manhattan home. He occupied it during the winter and lived at his farm in Doylestown, Pennsylvania, the rest of the time. He and **Richard Rodgers** wrote many of their most notable musicals while he lived here, including *South Pacific, The King and I, Flower Drum Song,* and *The Sound of Music.*

Hammerstein's daughter, Susan, married actor **Henry Fonda** in this house on December 28, 1950. Hammerstein died of cancer at his farm on August 23, 1960.

11/Al Smith
820 Fifth Avenue between 63rd and 64th Street.

Al Smith, who was elected New York governor four times and lost the

1928 presidential election as the Democratic candidate, took a large full-floor apartment in this building in 1936. He moved here from his former home in Greenwich Village, largely because this place was across the street from the **Central Park Zoo** and Smith was a passionate animal lover. He had been made an honorary superintendent of the zoo which gave him the privilege of visiting the animal houses whenever he wanted. The doormen here at 820 were used to seeing Smith walk out the front door at night and cross Fifth Avenue to the zoo to visit his animal friends. Whenever one of the tigers had a toothache or a hippo was sick, Smith would throw on a coat over his pajamas, put on his bedroom slippers, and hurry to the animal houses, where he sat up for the rest of the night with the troubled beast. Smith's day job in those days was president of the newly-built **Empire State Building.** He died while he resided in this apartment on October 4, 1944.

12/James Gould Cozzens
18 East 64th Street between Fifth and Madison Avenue.

The Pulitzer Prize-winning novelist rented an apartment in this five-level town house in 1935 with his wife, **Bernice Baumgarten.** Their main home was at a farm in Lambertville, New Jersey but Bernice, a successful literary agent, had an office in New York City. Cozzens published his ninth novel *Men and Brethren* while he lived here but he spent much of his time working on short stories; he was awarded the **O'Henry Prize** for the best story of 1936.

13/Moss Hart
4 East 65th Street near Fifth Avenue.

The Broadway playwright and director, who collaborated with **George S. Kaufman** on such hit plays as *Once in a Lifetime, You Can't Take It With You,* and *The Man Who Came To Dinner,* moved to a large duplex apartment in this building in the early 1940s. He was still a bachelor and was now attempting to work on his own for the first time without Kaufman. In 1941, his play *Lady in the Dark,* with music by **Kurt Weill,** was his first solo writing effort. In 1943, he wrote another one, this time a story about the Air Force called *Winged Victory.* Hart was living in this apartment when he courted and married actress/singer **Kitty Carlisle** in 1946.

14/James J. Hill
8 East 65th Street near Fifth Avenue.

Hill, the entrepreneur who built the **Great Northern Railroad** which stretched from St. Paul to Seattle and was completed in 1893, made this five-story limestone mansion his New York home. He purchased it in 1906 for $422,000 and lived here until his death in 1916, although Hill's home base remained in Minnesota.

Hill had been spending more time in New York since 1901 when he joined **J.P. Morgan** and **E.H. Harriman** in forming the gigantic **Northern Securities Company** which com-

bined three railroads. The new company was declared to be in restraint of trade and broken up by the Supreme Court in 1904. Hill's mansion here is now the **Pakistani Mission to the United Nations.** It is numbered 6 through 12 East 65th Street.

15/Marilyn Miller
46 East 65th Street between Madison and Park Avenue.

Marilyn Miller, one of the greatest musical comedy stars in Broadway's history, was living in this red brick house in 1936 when she died, tragically, of a brain infection. She had recently completed a long-running performance in **Irving Berlin's** acclaimed musical *As Thousands Cheer.* Miller had lived here with her third husband, **Chester O'Brien.** She was only thirty-eight at the time of her death.

16/Franklin and Eleanor Roosevelt
49 East 65th Street between Madison and Park Avenue.

This six-story brick and limestone townhouse was built in 1907 by **Sara Delano Roosevelt** as a wedding present for her newly-married son and his young wife. The mother lived next door at Number 47 and **Franklin** and **Eleanor** moved into Number 49 in the fall of 1908. The drawing and dining rooms of the two houses opened onto each other, there was a connecting door on the fourth floor, and they had a common vestibule. These architectural features allowed Sara to assert her dominance over the household.

Franklin and Eleanor Roosevelt

Franklin Roosevelt

On their first evening in the new house, Eleanor broke down in tears, proclaiming to her husband that she was unhappy at the prospect of living here in such close proximity to her mother-in-law.But they stayed in this house over the next twenty-five years. Franklin began his political career soon after they moved here; he was elected to the New York State Senate in 1910. In August 1921, he became afflicted with polio and it was here, in the fourth-floor front bedroom, that he began his long convalescence. Roosevelt was elected governor of the state in 1928.

The Roosevelts moved to the **White House** after he became president in 1933. Sara lived in Number 47 here until her death in 1941.

Nearby **Hunter College** took over the property in 1943 and utilized it as a student center until 1992 after which it stood empty for ten years.

In 2003, **City University of New York** made plans to spend $15 million to renovate it as the home of a public policy institute. It opened in 2006.

17/Jimmy Walker

610 Park Avenue at 65th Street (entrance on 65th Street) (southwest corner).

Jimmy Walker, New York's flamboyant and notorious mayor from 1925 to 1932, moved to a suite here at **Mayfair House** in 1928. It was called the **Mayfair** in those days.

Walker had recently separated from his wife, **Janet**, and spent most of his time in the company of his girlfriend, showgirl **Betty Compton.** He lived in this building until 1932 when, amid accusations of corruption, he was forced to resign his office.

He immediately left for Europe where he and Compton were married.They remained overseas for the following three years.

The Mayfair, built in 1925 to the designs of architect **James E.R.**

Jimmy Walker

Carpenter, replaced a house that was owned by the brother of photographer Alfred Stieglitz. The address was 60 East 65th Street. Between 1920 and 1924, Stieglitz and his companion, artist **Georgia O'Keeffe** lived there. Because they were not yet married and were living in the house of Alfred's relatives, they occupied rooms on separate floors. **Franklin** and **Eleanor Roosevelt** lived directly across the street (see number 16 above).

18/Charles Evans Hughes and Fanny Brice

32 East 64th Street at Madison Avenue (southeast corner).

Charles Evans Hughes was one of the most prominent American citizens of the early twentieth century, serving as New York's governor from 1906 to 1910 and later as both U.S. Secretary of State and U.S. Supreme Court Justice.

In 1916, he was the Republican Party's candidate for president and lost a close election to **Woodrow Wilson**. After his defeat, Hughes moved into this grandly neo-Italianate-style apartment house, the ten-story **Verona,** where he lived for the next five years. During that time, he returned to the private practice of law.

He left New York in 1921 for Washington D.C., after he was appointed Secretary of State by **President Warren Harding.** Note the plaque about Hughes at the front entrance.

Fanny Brice, with her new husband **Billy Rose,** moved to a large apartment in this same building in 1929. The place was the scene of numerous show business parties at which many of the top celebrities of Broadway—**Ziegfeld, George M. Cohan, Noel Coward,** and **Cole Porter**—could be found, some of whom stayed all night and were still singing, drinking, and talking in the morning when Brice's children were taken to school.

Brice and Rose lived here until they divorced in 1938. Soon after, Fanny moved permanently to California.

19/Cass Gilbert

42 East 64th Street between Madison and Park Avenue.

Architect **Cass Gilbert** moved to this five-story white stone house in 1913. It was soon after his most famous New York work—**The Woolworth Building**—opened. At the time it was built, the Woolworth was the tallest building in the world. Gilbert lived at 42 East 64th until the

1920s. His main home was in Ridge-field, Connecticut.

20/Edward R. Murrow
580 Park Avenue between 63rd and 64th Street.

Murrow was probably America's best known broadcast journalist from the time he covered the European theater of action in World War II for CBS Radio until he left television in 1961.

In 1950, he acquired an apartment in this **J.E.R. Carpenter**-designed building and lived in it for the next decade with his wife, **Janet**, and young son, **Casey**. The previous owner had convinced herself that the Korean War would bring destruction to New York and Murrow was able to buy the place for only $30,000.

During the 50s, he hosted such weekly shows as *Person to Person* and *See It Now* for **CBS Television**. On the latter program, on March 9, 1954, Murrow presented a critical expose of red-baiter, **Senator Joseph McCarthy**. The broadcast was one of the most powerful documentaries in television history and began the demise of the country's most danger-ous demagogue.

Murrow left New York for Washington in 1961 when **President Kennedy** asked him to head the **U.S. Information Agency**. Murrow died in 1965.

21/Maxwell Parrish
49 East 63rd Street between Madison and Park Avenue.

The artist was forty-eight years old and already famous when he spent the winter of 1918-19 in this beauti-ful white stone building with the below-street-level entrance.

Parrish was married but he enjoyed spending his winters alone with his work; his wife, **Lydia Austin**, usual-ly stayed in Georgia during the cold months.

By this time in Parrish's career, he was becoming one of the most repro-duced artists in history. His 1922 painting *Daybreak* became a pop icon of the 1920s, selling more than 200,000 prints. It was estimated that one out of every five American homes had a Parrish print on its wall.

Parrish died in 1966 at the age of ninety-five at his longtime home in Cornish, New Hampshire.

Dorothy Parker

22/Dorothy Parker and Walter Lippmann
28 East 63rd Street between Madison and Park Avenue.

The Art Deco-style **Lowell** apartment hotel opened in 1926. **Dorothy Parker** moved here in 1932 from her suite at the **Algonquin Hotel.** It was a low period in her life—she had tried to commit suicide a few months earlier. As a result of her depression, she had written very little in the past year and she was flat broke.

The **Lowell** management seemed glad to have her as a tenant; the resulting publicity offset the fact that Parker often missed paying her rent. Gradually she began to write again.

In 1934, while living here, she met actor **Alan Campbell** and they soon moved together into a new apartment on East 52nd Street (see Section Two, Tour 5, Number 3).

In 1970, political columnist **Walter Lippmann,** then eighty-one years old, leased an apartment at the Lowell. He came with his second wife, **Helen Byrne Armstrong.** Lippmann had retired from his long-time writing job at the *Washington Post* in 1967; by that time his attacks on **President Lyndon Johnson's** Vietnam War policies had made him an unlikely hero of the American Left.

Lippmann suffered a heart attack in 1973 while living at the Lowell and he died in December 1974 at age eighty-five.

23/Willa Cather
570 Park Avenue at 63rd Street (southwest corner).

Willa Cather, age fifty-eight, took a large apartment in the rear of this building with her lifelong companion, **Edith Lewis**, in the fall of 1932. All of their windows faced the blank wall of the **Colony Club** just to the

Willa Cather

south of here.

Cather had recently published her novel *Shadow on the Rock.* The book was written at a difficult time in the author's life, following her father's death and the serious illness of her mother.

While Cather lived here, she wrote the popular *Lucy Gayheart* in 1935 and her last novel *Sapphira and the Slave Girl* in 1940.

This was Cather's last residence. She died in her apartment of a cerebral hemorrhage on the afternoon of April 24, 1947.

24/Danny Kaye
550 Park Avenue between 61st and 62nd Street.

The comedian and actor rented a ten-room apartment in this 1916 building next to the **Regency Hotel** in the early 1940s, soon after his marriage to **Sylvia Fine** who, throughout his career, served as his

Eddie Rickenbacker

From 1954 until 1963, World War I flying ace **Eddie Rickenbacker** lived in an elegant old apartment house that stood on this site until the existing **Regency Hotel** was built.

Rickenbacker had been serving as the general manager of **Eastern Airlines** and had turned that company into an industry leader but in 1959, as the company's business declined, he was forced to give up the top position. He retired from Eastern in 1963 and moved out of New York to a small ranch in Texas with his wife, **Adelaide**.

26/Adele Astaire
530 Park Avenue between 60th and 61st Street.

Adele Astaire, sister of **Fred**, and one half of the most famous dance team on the American stage during the 1920s, lived in this eighteen-story 1941 apartment building with her second husband, investment banker **Kingman Douglas**.

Adele quit the Astaire dance act in 1932 to marry a British lord, **Charles Cavendish**. When he died in 1944, she moved from Europe back to New York and married Douglas in 1947. The couple shared their apartment in this building until 1971 when they relocated to Arizona.

After Adele broke up the dancing partnership with her brother, Fred was temporarily shaken but he moved to Hollywood soon after and in 1933 he began a movie career that made him a legend.

In 1934, Astaire made his first film *Flying Down to Rio* with his new partner, **Ginger Rogers**.

personal director, writer, and coach. In 1941, Kaye was offered a leading role in **Moss Hart's** new play *Lady in the Dark.*

On opening night, he scored a hit when he rattled off in thirty-eight seconds the names of fifty Russian composers, strung together by lyricist **Ira Gershwin** for the tongue-twisting effect.

The show made Kaye a star and, by 1944, he was making movies, starting with *Up In Arms* and continuing with *The Kid from Brooklyn* and *The Secret Life of Walter Mitty.*

Kaye owned a home in Hollywood but he made this apartment his New York residence for many years.

25/Eddie Rickenbacker
540 Park Avenue between 61st and 62nd Street.

TOUR 2

1/Jean Herman
134 East 60th Street at Lexington Avenue (near southwest corner).

This solitary truncated remnant of a brownstone, huddled beneath a tall modern building, was the home of one of New York's more obstinate rent-controlled holdout tenants. The row house, built in 1865, had long since been subdivided into small apartments, one of which was occupied by **Jean Herman**, a stubborn woman who refused to move when a developer purchased her building in 1981 with plans to demolish it along with others in this block and build modern office towers.

The other tenants agreed to leave but Herman declined, even after she was offered $650,000.She continued to live alone in her two-room walk-up on the fourth floor of the building for the next eleven years. In 1987, the developer, Cohen Brothers Realty Corporation, blocked by the strong rent-control laws of the city, finally gave up on their plans to raze the building and constructed their skyscraper around it after lopping off the floors above hers and removing the entire rear portion of the building (her apartment faced only the front). Miss Herman surrendered her lease on the $200 apartment only in death. She passed away at age sixty-nine in 1992.

When a reporter asked Herman's brother why she turned town the lucrative offer to leave, he said: "She liked the publicity; she liked the neighborhood." Her attorney added two other reasons: "She had a principled opposition to what she perceived to be over-development. And she was eccentric."

2/Johnny Mercer
111 East 60th Street between Park and Lexington Avenue.

The great songwriter lived in this six-level brownstone in the 1930s and 40s with his wife, dancer **Ginger Meehan**. **Johnny Mercer** had his first big success in 1933 when he wrote the lyrics for the hit song *Lazy Bones* in collaboration with **Hoagy Carmichael**. Other standards followed, including *Goody Goody* (1936), *Jeepers Creepers* (1938), and *Day In Day Out* (1939). Mercer was living in this building in the early 40s when he and **Harold Arlen** wrote three classics: *Blues in the Night, One For My Baby,* and *That Old Black Magic*—all for the movies. In 1942, Mercer co-founded **Capitol Records** and became its first president and talent scout. By 1948, he had written more than 250 songs, sixty of which were hits.

3/Oscar Hammerstein II
126 East 61st Street between Park and Lexington Avenue.

Songwriter **Oscar Hammerstein** moved to this brownstone with his wife, **Dorothy,** in 1938.After he wrote the lyrics for the groundbreaking musical *Showboat* in 1928 with **Jerome Kern**, Hammerstein's career had gone into a downturn. He created a number of songs in the 1930s for plays that failed to become hits.

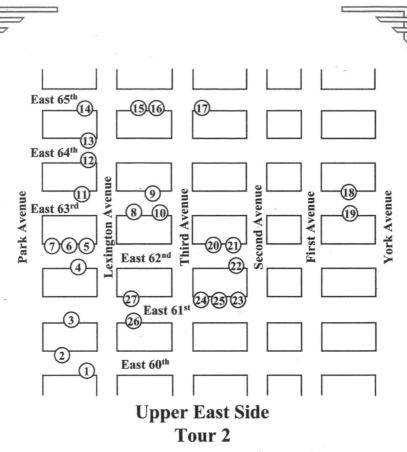

Upper East Side
Tour 2

1. Jean Herman
2. Johnny Mercer
3. Oscar Hammerstein II
4. Bennett Cerf
5. Charles Evans Hughes
6. Ethel Barrymore and Don Marquis
7. Ray Bolger
8. Barbizon Hotel
9. Gypsy Rose Lee
10. George S. Kaufman
11. Samuel Goldwyn
12. Claudette Colbert
13. Otto Preminger

14. Ethel Barrymore
15. Tennessee Williams
16. Richard Nixon
17. O.J. Simpson
18. Myrna Loy
19. Martha Graham
20. Eleanor Roosevelt
21. Weill and Lenya
22. Tallulah Bankhead
23. Walter Lippmann
24. Montgomery Clift
25. Montgomery Clift
26. Marilyn Monroe
27. Oscar Hammerstein II

However, while he lived at this address, he composed the lyrics for two of his most beautiful songs: *All The Things You Are* and *The Last Time I Saw Paris*, both written in collaboration with Kern. For the latter song, Hammerstein won an Academy Award in 1941. By 1943, Hammerstein had moved a block east of here to 157 East 61st Street (see number 27 below).

4/ Bennett Cerf
132 East 62nd Street between Park and Lexington Avenue.

This five-story gray house was the residence of **Random House** publisher **Bennett Cerf** and his second wife, **Phyllis Fraser**, from 1941 until his death in 1971. Cerf made publishing history in 1934 when he challenged the country's obscenity laws; the result was that U.S. Courts finally allowed him to publish **James Joyce's** novel *Ulysses* in this country for the first time. During the thirty years that he lived at this address, Random House, under Cerf's leadership, became the publisher of such best-selling authors as **James Michener, William Styron, Philip Roth, Truman Capote, Moss Hart,** and **Dr. Seuss.**

5/Charles Evans Hughes
129 East 62nd Street between Park and Lexington Avenue.

Hughes, who in his long career would serve as New York governor, Republican presidential candidate, and Supreme Court Justice, moved into this four-story house with his new bride, **Antoinette Carter**, in December 1888. He was twenty-six years old and had just entered into a law partnership with his father. Hughes's parents lived with them in this house; the rent was $1,200 a year. A year after they came, with the birth of a son, they moved to Brooklyn.

They returned to Manhattan in 1893, taking a house on the Upper West Side at 329 West End Avenue. Hughes became New York's governor in 1906 after defeating **William Randolph Hearst.**

6/ Ethel Barrymore and Don Marquis
125 East 62nd Street between Park and Lexington Avenue.

During the 1920s, this brownstone was the home of humorist and journalist **Don Marquis**. He was one of America's most popular columnists in the early decades of the last century. His most famous creations were the popular characters *Archy and Mehitabel*, both cockroaches—they first appeared in his column in the *New York Sun* in 1916.

Marquis rented an apartment on the second floor of this house to actress **Ethel Barrymore** in 1929 while she was acting in the Broadway production of *The Kingdom of God* in which she played a nun. The play received critical and popular acclaim. Barrymore's biographer **Margot Peters** reports that the actress was living beyond her means in those days and was perpetually short of cash. For several months Marquis received no rent and she successfully avoided all attempts to collect. She moved out a few months later. "Like all good

Barrymores," says Peters, "she was careless about bills, far too philistine a concern."

7/Ray Bolger
123 East 62nd Street between Park and Lexington Avenue.

After his memorable performance as the scarecrow in *The Wizard of Oz* in 1939, **Bolger** returned to New York to appear in a Broadway musical called *Keep Off the Grass*. He lived in this house during that period. The play didn't run very long but in 1942 he starred in **Rodgers** and **Hart's** *By Jupiter* and received rave reviews. In 1943, Bolger returned to Hollywood to continue his film career.

8/Barbizon Hotel
140 East 63rd Street at Lexington Avenue (southeast corner).

The twenty-two story **Barbizon** was once a well-known residential hotel for women, usually those with wealthy parents. It opened in 1927. Its owners sought to create an environment that reflected the values of the women's families—codes of conduct and dress were enforced, three references of respectability were required, and no men were allowed beyond the lobby floor. Among the Barbizon's most famous residents was actress **Grace Kelly**. She was one tenant who managed to bend the rules in 1947-48 while she pursued a modeling career and studied acting at the American Academy of Dramatic Arts. Not only did Kelly smuggle a few male friends above the ground floor but her Barbizon companions also remember the future princess, clad in brief underwear, performing exotic dances in the hallway, then slipping back into her room when the elevators opened.

A number of other famous women celebrities lived at the Barbizon while being introduced to New York. They include **Gene Tierney, Nanette Fabray, Lauren Bacall, Candice Bergen, Liza Minnelli,** and **Cloris Leachman.** Poet **Sylvia Plath** stayed here in 1963 when she was a *Mademoiselle* magazine guest editor from Smith College. She fictionalized the hotel as the Amazon in her book *The Bell Jar.*

In 2005, the Barbizon was converted into condominiums and changed its name to **Barbizon 63.**

9/Gypsy Rose Lee
153 East 63rd Street between Lexington and Third Avenue.

Gypsy Rose Lee, the "Queen of Burlesque" moved to this twenty-four-room stucco house in the early 1940s. The residence originally cost $300,000 to build but Lee paid only five figures for it. "It's all in eighteenth century French," she was quoted as saying, "with gold plumbing. Not just faucets, but faucets in the shape of dolphins, if you please." In 1941, Lee expanded on her notoriety as New York's most famous striptease artist by publishing a mystery novel called *The G-String Murders,* which became a best-seller. After that she wrote plays and began a movie career.

She moved to California late in her life and died there of lung cancer in 1970 at age fifty-six. In 1984, Lee's only son, **Erik,** discovered that his real father was film director **Otto Preminger.** It was a secret that his mother had kept from him all his life. Preminger was a neighbor of the Lee family; he lived just north of them at 129 East 64th Street (see number 13 below).

Across the street from 153 on this block, at 154 East 63rd Street, was the home of **Samuel Seabury,** the judge and attorney who conducted the famous 1931 investigation of corruption in New York City government which ultimately led to the resignation of **Mayor Jimmy Walker.** It was in the study of Seabury's house here on January 1, 1934, just after midnight,that **Fiorello La-Guardia** was sworn in as New York's ninety-ninth mayor.

10/George S. Kaufman

158 East 63rd Street between Lexington and Third Avenue.

The Broadway director and playwright **George S. Kaufman** lived in a penthouse apartment in this building with his wife, **Beatrice,** from 1929 until 1932. Earlier, it was the home of playgirl **Peggy Hopkins Joyce.** It was here that Kaufman began his collaboration with **Moss Hart** on *Once in a Lifetime.* For ten months in 1929 and 1930, they labored over the play in Kaufman's fourth-floor study, writing and re-writing, while silently tolerating each other's eccentricities.

The result was a smash hit on Broadway that launched Hart's career. The two went on to co-write seven other plays. Kaufman also completed three plays with other partners while he lived here—*The Band Wagon, Of Thee I Sing,* and *Dinner at Eight.*

11/Samuel Goldwyn

125 East 63rd Street between Park and Lexington Avenue.

In the 1920s, before he moved to Hollywood, film producer **Sam Goldwyn** had a bachelor apartment in this nine-story brick building. He had recently founded **Metro-Gold-wyn-Mayer.**

Goldwyn, who had a reputation as a womanizer, was once the victim of friend **Charlie Chaplin's** practical joke. Chaplin arranged a blind date for Goldwyn with a woman that he described as "rich and beautiful" and on the next evening Chaplin and the woman showed up here at Goldwyn's apartment to pick up the producer. Later, as the three made a carriage ride around Central Park, Goldwyn began to nuzzle his date, only to suddenly discover that "she" was his friend, Los Angeles theater-owner **Sid Grauman.**

12/Claudette Colbert

136 East 64th Street at Lexington Avenue (southwest corner).

In 1958, actress **Claudette Colbert** moved into a penthouse in this eleven-story building. At the time, Colbert was starring on Broadway in the play *The Marriage-Go-Round* with **Charles Boyer.** Her neighbor here was **Verna Hull** who was her best friend.

Besides living in the same building, the two traveled together and, because of their mutual interest in art, they painted together. In 1961, Colbert made her last movie, *Parrish*, and then bought a beachfront house in Barbados which became her main residence for the rest of her life.

13/Otto Preminger
129 East 64th Street near Lexington Avenue.

Movie director **Otto Preminger**, who will be remembered for such films as *Laura, Exodus,* and *The Man With the Golden Arm*, lived in this white stucco townhouse. His eight-bedroom home was noted for its large collection of modern art. It also featured a Zen garden with a seventeenth century fountain and a movie screening room with remote control projectors.

Preminger was known for his battles against movie censorship and blacklisting in the 1950s. He went to court twice successfully to defeat bans on his films, *The Moon is Blue*, a mild sex comedy, and *The Man With the Golden Arm*, which dealt with drug addiction. He made headlines in 1960 when he hired the blacklisted screenwriter **Dalton Trumbo** to work on his film *Exodus*. Preminger died in his home here of cancer in April 1986. In the summer of 2002, this house went on the market with an asking price of $12.95 million.

14/Ethel Barrymore
130 East 65th Street between Park and Lexington Avenue.

Ethel Barrymore was living in this five-story brownstone in 1919 with her millionaire husband **Russell Colt** and her three young children. Colt's great-uncle was **Samuel Colt**, the inventor of the six-shooter.

Barrymore was starring on Broadway at that time in the play *Declassee*. Her troubled marriage came to a crisis one night in the bedroom of their house here when she accused Colt of adultery; he responded by beating her brutally. The actress was confined to her bed for five days and, soon after, made the decision to divorce him. Barrymore, who was forty years old at the time, never married again.

15/Tennessee Williams
134 East 65th Street between Lexington and Third Avenue.

This elegant red brick building was the New York home of **Tennessee Williams** from 1957 to 1963. The playwright, who lived at this address with his lover, **Frank Merlo**, wrote the play *Suddenly Last Summer* in the study of his apartment here. It opened on Broadway in January 1958. Williams split his time between his flat on this street and his home in Key West, Florida. He was at the height of his fame and several of his best-known works, including *Sweet Bird of Youth* and *Night of the Iguana*, were produced while he lived here.

In September 1963 when Merlo died, Williams fell into a severe depression and stayed at this 65th Street apartment alone. "I went out just once every twenty-four hours, to a little grocery store around the corner on Lexington," he wrote in his memoirs, "to purchase a box of spaghetti. This was my sole and solitary meal each day, and I don't recall embellishing it with any kind of sauce." Williams moved away to 145 West 55th Street at the end of 1963.

16/Richard Nixon
142 East 65th Street between Lexington and Third Avenue.

After **Richard Nixon** was forced to resign as President in 1973, he tried unsuccessfully for a number of years to buy a co-op apartment in New York and finally purchased this twelve-room, four-level townhouse in early 1980. The building was erected in 1871 and had been the home of Supreme Court Justice **Learned Hand** for fifty-five years. Nixon paid $750,000 for it. The place was only five minutes away from daughter **Tricia's** apartment. Nixon worked on his book *The Real War* while he lived here; it was published in the summer of 1980. One of Nixon's neighbors was scholar and political enemy **Arthur Schlesinger** who lived across the backyard and who said that the ex-president was lucky to be living in such luxury "when he ought to be in the federal penitentiary." Nixon sold this house for $2.6 million in 1982.

17/O.J. Simpson
200 East 65th Street at Third Avenue (southeast corner).

O.J. Simpson bought a condominium in this huge **Bristol Plaza** complex in 1990. The price was $1.15 million. He was forced to sell it to raise cash during his financial difficulties following the trial that result-ed in his acquittal for the murder of his wife.

18/Myrna Loy
425 East 63rd Street between First and York Avenue.

Actress **Myrna Loy**, who gained fame as the breezy wife, **Nora Charles**, to **William Powell** (as **Nick**) in the 1934 hit movie *The Thin Man* made this high-rise building her New York home during the last years of her life. She lived in a comfortable, book-lined terrace apartment overlooking the East River. Loy, whose career in the movies spanned over fifty years, had been married and divorced four times and lived in this building alone.

In 1991, she won her only Academy Award, an honorary one, and spoke to the audience in Los Angeles via satellite from her apartment here. Her message was short: "You've made me very happy. Thank you very much." Loy died on December 15, 1993 at the age of eighty-eight.

19/Martha Graham
430 East 63rd Street between First and York Avenue.

Martha Graham, the dancer, choreographer and teacher who was the most notable exponent of Expressionist modern dance in this country, lived in these **Sutton Terrace** apartments during her last years. Graham's famous studio was just west of here at 316 East 63rd Street. Her flat in this building had walls covered with shelves of glass, backlit, and filled with carved rocks, porcelain, and blown glass from all over the world. She owned an **Alexander Calder** painting, a gift of the artist. Every nook and cranny was filled with tropical green plants in tubs.

By this time in her life, Graham was suffering from acute arthritis and various other debilitating afflictions. Still she continued to work, conducting dance rehearsals, raising money, giving interviews, and making TV appearances.she lived to the age of ninety-six and died in 1991.

20/Eleanor Roosevelt
211 East 62nd Street between Third and Second Avenue.

F.D.R.'s widow was sixty-eight years old when she moved from a suite at the **Park Sheraton Hotel** to an apartment in this five-level building with the stained-glass windows in 1953. Mrs. Roosevelt made the move because she needed more space; this larger apartment had a garden and allowed her to bring her dog into town from her country home in Hyde Park.

She had recently resigned from her position as United States delegate to the United Nations, a position she had held since her appointment by **President Truman** in 1948. She soon went to work for the American Association for the U.N. and became an unofficial ambassador at large, visiting countries throughout the world. Two of these trips were to the Soviet Union in 1957 and 1958. In 1954, while living in this apartment, she wrote the book *Ladies of Courage.* Mrs. Roosevelt purchased a house at 55 East 74th Street and moved there in 1958 (see this section, Tour 5, Number 17).

21/Kurt Weill and Lotte Lenya
231 East 62nd Street between Third and Second Avenue.

Weill and **Lenya** had fled Nazi Germany in 1935 and for two years, under a tight budget, lived in cheap hotels or with friends while they established themselves in America. Finally, in the fall of 1937, with money that Weill had earned as a movie composer in Hollywood, they could afford to rent an apartment—a duplex with terraces and a roof garden in this white stone building. Lenya, soon after moving in, made her American radio debut for CBS in a musical drama.

The couple lived on 62nd Street until the spring of 1941 when the sale of the film rights to the play **Lady in the Dark** (for which Weill wrote the music) allowed them to buy a large house outside New York City.

22/Tallulah Bankhead
230 East 62nd Street between Third and Second Avenue.

In 1956, **Tallulah Bankhead** bought this four-story townhouse with the red shutters. It had twelve rooms, six fireplaces, a latticed garden, and sycamore trees.

The actress, now fifty-four years old, was becoming increasingly dependent on alcohol and drugs and finding it difficult to get dramatic roles. After her unsuccessful attempt to revive the **Ziegfeld Follies,** she appeared around the city in cabarets and became a familiar figure as a guest on TV shows.

Bankhead sold this place to millionaire **Huntington Hartford** at a handsome profit in 1962 and moved to a condominium at 447 East 57th Street (see Section Two, Tour 4, Number 9).

23/Walter Lippmann
245 East 61st Street between Third and Second Avenue.

Political journalist **Walter Lippmann** lived in this four-story brownstone from 1929 to 1937 with his first wife, **Faye Albertson**. He began to write his famous *Today and Tomorrow* column for the *New York Herald Tribune* around this time; it appeared regularly for over thirty-five years and was eventually syndicated in more than two hundred newspapers.

In 1937, Lippmann led the attack against President Roosevelt's proposal to pack the U.S. Supreme Court and it was also in that year that he fell in love with **Helen Armstrong**, the wife of a close friend. It led to Lippmann's divorce from Albertson; he married Armstrong in 1938. Their actions caused a scandal in New York and the Lippmanns, feeling increasingly uncomfortable living in this city, soon moved to Washington D.C., where he lived until his retirement.

24/Montgomery Clift
209 East 61st Street between Third and Second Avenue.

By 1951, **Montgomery Clift** had become an established movie star and he gave up his forty-dollar-a-month walk-up at 127 East 55th Street for a spacious duplex apartment in this building. He lived here

for almost a decade. Clift was nominated twice for Academy Awards: in 1951 for *A Place in the Sun* and in 1953 for *From Here To Eternity*.

He was at the height of his career and only a few people knew how troubled he was. He was becoming increasingly dependent on alcohol and, in his bathroom in this building, he built a fourteen-foot-long medicine cabinet filled with drugs.

One night in 1956, during the filming of *Raintree County*, the actor smashed his car after a party and was almost killed. In early September 1959, a fire broke out here in Clift's apartment and he had to be rescued by firemen who broke in through the skylight. Clift was forced to find a new home (see number 25 below).

25/Montgomery Clift
217 East 61st Street between Third and Second Avenue.

Montgomery Clift purchased this spacious four-story brownstone in January 1960 soon after his previous home—just four doors to the west—was gutted in a fire (number 24 above). His new place had six baths, six fireplaces, and a large tree-filled garden. It was the same home that **Theodore Roosevelt** had given to his daughter, **Alice Longworth**, for her wedding. Critic **Clifton Fadiman** had lived here in the 1940s.

Soon after Clift moved in, he began work on **John Huston's** film *The Misfits,* written by **Arthur Miller** and co-starring **Marilyn Monroe** and **Clark Gable.** He followed that with a small part in **Stanley Kramer's** *Judgment at Nuremberg* before portraying Sigmund Freud in another

Montgomery Clift at 217 East 61st Street

Huston film. But by this time, the drinking and the drugs had taken their toll. Clift died in his home here of a heart attack on the morning of July 23, 1966. He was only forty-five years old.

26/Marilyn Monroe

164 East 61st Street between Third and Lexington Avenue.

This is the brownstone building where the characters played by **Marilyn Monroe** and **Tom Ewell** in the 1954 movie *The Seven Year Itch* lived.

When director **Billy Wilder** filmed the action here in an apartment leased by Twentieth Century Fox, a barricade was set up on both ends of the street to keep the large crowd of onlookers away. Still, the noise was so loud that Wilder had to shoot the scenes without sound which were later inserted in the studio. The movie, released in 1955, was not critically acclaimed but was very popular; it grossed over $5 million in its first year.

27/Oscar Hammerstein II

157 East 61st Street between Third and Lexington Avenue.

Songwriter **Oscar Hammerstein** lived in this five-level brownstone with his wife, **Dorothy**, from 1943 to 1948. A room on the second floor served as his study. By the time he had moved here, his musical play *Oklahoma!*, written in collaboration with **Richard Rodgers**, had become Broadway's biggest hit; it eventually ran for 2,212 performances.

Hammerstein followed it up by writing lyrics to the all-black musical *Carmen Jones* in 1943 as well as *Carousel* in 1945. By the time that he and Rodgers had completed work on their next production, *South Pacific* in 1948, the Hammersteins had moved again—this time just a few blocks away to 10 East 63rd Street (see this section, Tour 1, Number 10).

TOUR 3

1/Isak Dinesen

122 East 66th Street between Park and Lexington Avenue.

The Danish author of *Out of Africa* was seventy-three years old in January 1959 when she arrived in Manhattan for a lecture and readings tour. For much of the time during her visit, she stayed here at the **Cosmopolitan Club,** where she was made an honorary member. She gave a reading and speech here and received a stream of visitors—authors, agents, film producers and scholars. After her first appearance at the 92nd Street **YMHA's Poetry Center,** there was such a wild clamor for an encore that she was called back two more times.

Dinesen became the most sought-after dinner guest in Manhattan and many famous hostesses entertained her. She was eager to meet **Marilyn Monroe** and the person who organized their meeting, author **Carson McCullers,** claimed that, at one point in the evening, Marilyn and Dinesen danced together on a marble table. By the end of her visit to New York, Dinesen was exhausted and had to be hospitalized for a number of weeks. She returned to Denmark in April 1959.

2/Helena Rubinstein and Charles Revson

625 Park Avenue at 65th Street (northeast corner).

Madame Helena Rubinstein, the beauty salon operator and manufacturer of cosmetics, came to New York from Paris in 1914 and opened her first American salon soon after. Her business became fabulously successful. In the 1930s, she tried to rent an apartment here at 625 Park Avenue and when she was turned down for being Jewish, she bought the whole building.

Madame Rubinstein lived in the twenty-six-room triplex penthouse for thirty years and turned it into an open, airy, uncluttered space that housed her large and eclectic collection of art and jewelry, including rooms devoted to miniature furniture and murals painted for her by **Salvador Dali.**

After her death in 1965, another cosmetics entrepreneur, **Charles Revson** of **Revlon Inc.**, purchased her triplex for a bargain price of $390,000 and then spent over two years renovating the place at a cost of $3 million. Revson sealed all of the windows to provide a controlled, artificially-lighted, air-conditioned environment with fans blowing twenty-four hours a day. He turned the Rubinstein picture gallery into a ballroom with a huge adjoining kitchen even though these rooms were never used in all of Revson's years here. He died of cancer in 1975 and the apartment was sold to the twin sister of the **Shah of Iran** for $1.4 million.

3/Lillian Hellman and Artur Rubinstein

630 Park Avenue at 66th Street (southwest corner).

This was **Lillian Hellman's** last home in New York. She moved into a tenth-floor co-op apartment in this building in 1970. She also had a home at Martha's Vineyard.

Her apartment on Park Avenue had a large living room and two bedrooms, one of which she made into a workroom. She decorated the place with many family mementos and photographs, including a large one in her living room of her former companion, **Dashiell Hammett** who had died in 1961.

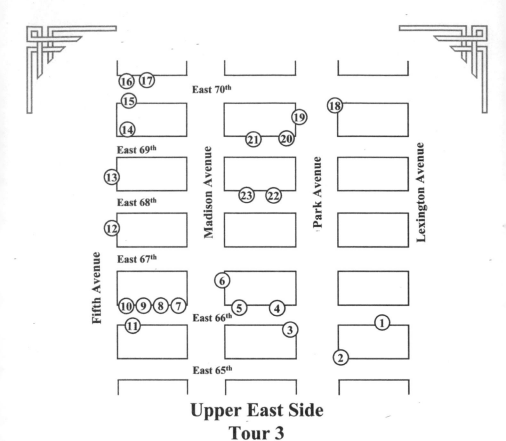

Upper East Side
Tour 3

1. Isak Dinesen
2. Helena Rubinstein and Charles Revson
3. Lillian Hellman and Artur Rubinstrin
4. Andy Warhol
5. Boris Karloff
6. Walter Lippmann
7. Anthony Perkins
8. Dashiell Hammett
9. Charles Scribner
10. Ulysses S. Grant
11. Baruch, Hearst, Lindbergh

12. Charles Yerkes
13. Gertrude Vanderbilt Whitney
14. E.H. Harriman
15. Joan Crawford
16. Henry Clay Frick
17. Anastasia
18. Elizabeth Taylor
19. Dave Garroway
20. Joseph Conrad
21. JFK and Marilyn Monroe
22. Dorothy Kilgallen
23. Roy Cohn

She wrote two best-selling books while she resided at this address— *Pentimento* in 1973 and *Scoundrel Time* in 1976. On January 24, 1980, she was watching television in her apartment here when she heard writer **Mary McCarthy** call her a liar on the **Dick Cavett Show**. Hellman immediately sued McCarthy for defamation of character; it was a lawsuit that dragged on until Hellman died in 1984 at the age of seventy-eight.

Pianist **Artur Rubinstein** also lived in this building from 1956 until 1972 when he moved to France. He lived to the age of ninety-five and died in Switzerland in 1982.

4/Andy Warhol

57 East 66th Street between Madison and Park Avenue.

Andy Warhol bought this Georgian-style house in 1974 for $310,000 in a depressed real estate market.It would be his last Manhattan residence. His previous places were always too small for his endless accumulation of materials but this house didn't have that problem: with its twenty-seven rooms, it was big enough to hold a huge amount of Warhol's fine art, furnishings, jewelry, and every-day objects. It was all uncataloged and much of it was tucked into shopping bags and boxes and stacked in rooms so full that the doors could not be closed.

Warhol lived on 66th Street until his death in 1987. He entered the hospital on February 21st for gall bladder surgery and died the next day of a heart attack. Note the Warhol plaque near the front door.

5/Boris Karloff

45 East 66th Street at Madison Avenue (northeast corner).

When the British actor came to New York in 1940 to perform on Broadway in the play *Arsenic and Old Lace*, he made this large Gothic-style apartment building his temporary home. **Karloff** lived here with his wife, **Dorothy Stine** and their first child, **Sara**, born in 1938.

He had spent much of the 1930s in California, acting mostly in horror films—he became instantly famous in 1931 when he played the part of the monster in **James Whale's** *Frankenstein*. In New York, *Arsenic* became a great hit and Karloff appeared in it for over three years. It ran for 1,444 performances.

6/Walter Lippmann

785 Madison Avenue between 66th and 67th Street.

At the end of World War I, political columnist **Walter Lippmann** had been living in France where he served on **President Woodrow Wilson's** commission charged with making recommendations for the eventual peace settlement after World War I. It was in this capacity that Lippmann helped to draft and publicize Wilson's famous Fourteen Points.

In 1919, he returned to America with his wife, **Faye Albertson,** and took an apartment in this building. He returned to his old job as a writer for *The New Republic* until 1923 and then landed the position of editorial writer for the liberal *New York World*. Lippmann and his wife lived here on Madison Avenue until late

1923 when he moved to Greenwich Village.

7/Anthony Perkins
21 East 66th Street between Fifth and Madison Avenue.

In 1936, **Osgood** and **Janet Perkins** and their four-year-old son **Tony** moved into an apartment in this eleven-story brick building.They had previously lived at 137 East 28th Street (see Section Three, Tour 2, Number 9).

Osgood Perkins was one of Broadway's and Hollywood's most well-known actors and he was absent from the Perkins household much of the time, leaving the mother and young son alone together. "I became abnormally close to my mother," Tony confessed years later, "and whenever my father came home, I was jealous. I loved him but I also wanted him to be dead so I could have her all to myself."

He was describing an infant's fantasy that was strangely echoed in his most famous film role years later when he played the disturbed killer **Norman Bates** who had an abnormal attachment to his mother in **Alfred Hitchcock's** *Psycho.*

Perkins's real life father, Osgood, died when Tony was only five years old in 1937.

8/Dashiell Hammett
15 East 66th Street between Fifth and Madison Avenue.

After his discharge from the U.S. Army in 1945, the detective writer took an apartment in this building. He was fifty-one years old.

Hammett divided his time between here and **Lillian Hellman's** farm in Westchester, New York. By then, he had a serious alcoholic problem and had given up writing entirely. Yet his income remained high due to the three weekly radio serials based on his fictional characters; he collected a total of $1300 a week from them.

He continued to lend his support to left-wing political causes and he began to teach a course in mystery writing at the **Jefferson School of Social Science.**

Hammett moved to 28 West 10th Street in Greenwich Village in the winter of 1947.

9/Charles Scribner
9 East 66th Street between Fifth and Madison Avenue.

Charles Scribner's Sons, one of America's greatest publishing houses, was run by five family members (four of them named Charles) continuously from the firm's beginning in 1846 until 1986. In the company's golden age, it was guided by **Charles Scribner II,** son of the founder, who presided from 1879 to 1930.

He lived in this beautiful house for many years. Under his leadership, Scribner's published a host of great writers, notably **John Galsworthy, Rudyard Kipling, William Faulkner, F. Scott Fitzgerald,** and **Ernest Hemingway.**

Charles Scribner died in his house here in 1930. The building is now the **Permanent Mission of Poland to the United Nations.**

10/Ulysses S. Grant
3 East 66th Street near Fifth Avenue.

Civil War hero and eighteenth president **U.S. Grant** had been out of the White House for four years by 1881 when he moved with his wife, **Julia**, into a four-story house on this site.

Ex-presidents received no pension in those days and Grant was able to purchase the house only because wealthy friends had raised a gift of $350,000. The place was so crammed with Grant's memorabilia that it looked like a museum.

By 1884, Grant had become virtually destitute after the failure of the brokerage firm in which he had invested; one of the company's partners had secretly milked the firm of all its assets. In order to recover financial security, Grant agreed to write his war memoirs for publication and as he began to work on them, he was diagnosed with terminal cancer of the throat.

"Grant sat at a large square table in the front room on the second floor," wrote his biographer **William McFeeley**, "and worked with wonderful steadiness mornings and afternoons. Pain and doctors interrupted him, and so did a swirl of children and grandchildren, but nothing diverted him from his work." He was often visited here by **Mark Twain,** who became his chief literary advisor and later his publisher. Grant completed the memoirs only days before he died; the end came at Mount McGregor, a resort in upstate New York where he passed away on July 23, 1885.

The proceeds from his book allowed his wife to live comfortably for another seventeen years until her own death in 1902.

11/Baruch, Hearst, Lindbergh
4 East 66th Street near Fifth Avenue.

Beginning in 1946, **Bernard Baruch**, the multi-millionaire financier and advisor to many U.S. presidents, lived in a huge eighteen-room apartment in this 1920 building designed by **James E.R. Carpenter**. It was his home until his death which came in his apartment here on June 20, 1965 at age ninety-four After his death, the residence sold for the then-astounding price of $200,000.

Number 4 was also the last New York home of **Mrs. William Randolph Hearst.** She moved here from the mammoth Clarendon apartment house on Riverside Drive in 1938 when her newspaper tycoon husband was forced to sell it during his financial difficulties. By that time Mr. Hearst was living openly with his mistress, **Marion Davies,** and his wife lived here alone. Mrs. Hearst continued to be active in charity work until the end of her life. She died in her apartment on August 4, 1974 at the age of ninety-two.

This address was also an early home of **Anne Morrow**, daughter of businessman and diplomat **Dwight Morrow.** The family moved to an eleventh-floor apartment here after Morrow went to work for **J.P. Morgan and Company** in 1913. Anne was a teenager at the time. She married famed aviator **Charles Lindbergh** in 1929 and the couple was still in mourning when they came to live in the Morrow apartment in 1932 after the kidnapping and death of their first child, **Charles, Jr.** Anne was pregnant again by then and, in light of the public hysteria surrounding the Lindberghs during that time, it was decided to have Anne deliver the baby in the privacy of her parents' home. Their second son, **Jon,** was born here in August 1932.

12/Charles Yerkes
864 Fifth Avenue between 67th and 68th Street.

Charles Yerkes was the ultra-rich public transportation mogul of Chicago who developed that city's street railway system while bilking the taxpayers out of millions of dollars. By the 1890s when Chicago would no longer tolerate his financial and political corruption, he moved to New York with his large collection of paintings and $15 million in cash and built a huge mansion on this site.

The place was opulent to the extreme—luxurious, overdecorated rooms in several styles, great galleries hung with valuable art, historic fireplaces, columns, and stairways everywhere.

Yerkes divorced his first wife with their six children and brought his beautiful second wife, **Mara,** here with him. He was ready to divorce her, too, when he developed cancer and died in 1905. His estranged wife continued to live in the mansion, in a lifestyle that rapidly diminished her remaining fortune. She auctioned off much of her assets; the art collection went for over twenty million dollars and the house for over a million. It was later demolished by the next-

door resident; he used the space for a garden that was adjacent to his own fifty room mansion.

Gertrude Vanderbilt Whitney

13/Gertrude Vanderbilt Whitney
871 Fifth Avenue between 68th and 69th Street.

Gertrude Vanderbilt Whitney, remembered today as one of New York's greatest art patrons and at one time as the richest woman in America, lived in a palatial, mansard-roofed mansion on this site. The house had originally been a wedding gift to her and her husband, **Harry Payne Whitney**, in 1896 from her father-in-law **William Whitney.** He hired architect **Stanford White** to remodel it for the newlyweds at a cost of $2 million.

Gertrude was the aunt of young **Gloria Vanderbilt**; in a celebrated 1934 court battle that made headlines all over the country, she won custody of the ten-year-old child from **Gloria Morgan Vanderbilt**, the child's mother.

Gertrude died in 1942 and most of the huge collection of her paintings, sculpture, tapestries, and furniture were dispersed to museums and private collections around the world. The mansion was demolished and replaced by this modern nineteen-story building.

14/E.H.and Averell Harriman

1 East 69th Street at Fifth Avenue (northeast corner) (or 880 Fifth Avenue).

E.H. Harriman, one of the country's legendary business leaders and the man known for developing the **Illinois Central and Union Pacific** railroads, lived in a brownstone on this site up to the time of his death in 1909. He died at age sixty-one at his upstate New York home called **Arden**.

His widow, Mary, was his sole beneficiary and became one of the world's richest women with a fortune worth between $70 and $100 million. She soon became one of New York's greatest philanthropists. Mary continued to live here on East 69th Street until 1915 when her son **Averell**, destined to be a New York governor and advisor to U.S. presidents, was given the house as his mother's wedding gift.

15/Joan Crawford

2 East 70th Street at Fifth Avenue (southeast corner).

Movie actress **Joan Crawford** lived in a huge penthouse apartment in this building with her last husband, Pepsi-Cola chairman **Alfred Steele**, from 1957 to 1959. Steele purchased two apartments totaling eighteen rooms and then merged them into one large residence at a cost nearly one million dollars.

Crawford had a fetish for cleanliness and it extended even to her flowers and plants which were plastic so that they could be regularly washed in soapy water. Visitors were not allowed to wear shoes beyond the entrance hall because the actress didn't want her pure white rugs soiled.

Steele died here in 1959 and Crawford was selected to fill his vacancy on the Pepsi board of directors. When she discovered that her husband had died broke, she also returned to the movies, taking a part in the film **The Best of Everything.**

16/Henry Clay Frick

1 East 70th Street at Fifth Avenue (northeast corner).

Frick, the millionaire steel magnate and partner of **Andrew Carnegie** was sixty-five-years old when he moved to New York from Pittsburgh in 1914 to live in this three-story limestone mansion.

Frick had become a business rival of Carnegie by then and he vowed to make Carnegie's house on 91st Street "look like a miner's shack." Frick's house cost $5 million and he lived here with his wife, **Adelaide**, their daughter, **Helen**, and as many as twenty-seven servants.

Frick had gained national attention in 1892 when he was badly wounded but survived an assassination attempt on his life by anarchist **Alexander Berkman** after Frick had ruthlessly crushed a steelworkers strike at Homestead, Pennsylvania. He built this mansion on Fifth Avenue not only as his residence but also to house his large collection of European art.

When he died in 1919, his estate was valued at $92 million. After his wife's death in 1935, the house was converted into the public museum, the **Frick Collection.**

17/Anastasia

9 East 70th Street between Fifth and Madison Avenue.

Anna Anderson, the twenty-eight year old woman who claimed to be **Anastasia Romanov**, one of the daughters of **Czar Nicholas** of Russia, came to the United States in 1928. Many people believed that she had somehow survived the wholesale assassination of the entire royal family by the Bolsheviks in 1919.

In this country, Anna was under the care and patronage of **Annie Burr Jennings**, wealthy daughter of a director of the Standard Oil Trust and she stayed here at the Jennings house on 9 East 70th Street (where the garden court of the Frick Museum now stands). She had hired an attorney to fight for her claims to the Romanov inheritance in Europe and during the year that she lived in this house, waiting for the legal struggle to end, she passed the time by attending an

endless number of parties, teas, and dinner dances in New York society. She soon grew tired and bored with this lifestyle, seeking solitude in her room with her parakeets, and attempting to write her memoirs. Meanwhile, the Jenn-ings family became more and more disenchanted with her. Anna suffered a nervous breakdown in 1930 and was institu-tionalized at Katonah, New York. She was allowed to return to Europe in 1931. She died in Vir-ginia in 1984 at the age of eighty-two. DNA tests later proved that she was the daughter of a Polish peasant, not a Russian czar.

18/Elizabeth Taylor

715 Park Avenue at 70th Street (southeast corner).

The actress lived in this seventeen-story red brick building with her third husband, film producer **Mike Todd**, in 1957 and 1958. They were married in Mexico in 1957, the year that he produced the popular movie *Around the World in Eighty Days.* On March 21, 1958, while Taylor was filming *Cat on a Hot Tin Roof* in Los Angeles, Todd left her to fly to New York. He was killed when his plane crashed over New Mexico. Taylor's third child, **Liza Todd**, was born in 1958 while she lived at this Park Avenue address.

19/Dave Garroway

710 Park Avenue between 69th and 70th Street.

Dave Garroway, the pioneer of live morning television, lived in this apartment building during the years that he was the original host of NBC's **Today Show** from 1952 until 1961.

20/Joseph Conrad
39 East 69th Street at Park Avenue (northwest corner).

Joseph Conrad, age sixty-five, was at the end of his illustrious writing career in the spring of 1923 when he traveled from his home in England to New York as a guest of publisher **Frank Doubleday**. He was treated like visiting royalty during his stay. The highlight of the trip was Conrad's May 10th lecture and reading to a gathering of two hundred people at a mansion that stood on this site at Park Avenue and 69th Street. It was the home of the wealthy railroad magnate **Arthur Curtiss James.** This was one of the few times that Conrad had ever spoken in public and he was extremely nervous; still, he managed to spend over an hour talking and reading from his novel *Victory*, to the delight of his audience.

Conrad returned to England on June 2. He died fourteen months later.

21/John F. Kennedy and Marilyn Monroe
33 East 69th Street between Madison and Park Avenue.

33 East 69th Street was, for many years, the home of **Arthur Krim** and his wife, **Mathilde**. Krim, as the chairman of **United Artists Studios** from 1951 to 1978 and then of **Orion Pictures** from 1978 to 1992, had been the producer of more than a thousand motion pictures. He was also highly active in Democratic Party affairs as a fundraiser and advisor to **Presidents Kennedy, Johnson,** and **Carter.**

His town house here on 69th Street was the scene of numerous celebrity events. One of the more memorable was a birthday party that took place on the night of May 19, 1962; it was given by Krim in honor of his friend, **President John F.Kennedy** and it was attended by the likes of **Arthur Schlesinger, Jr., Adlai Stevenson, Bobby Kennedy,** and **Marilyn Monroe.**

Earlier that evening, Monroe had drawn the attention of New Yorkers when she appeared at the birthday salute given Kennedy at **Madison Square Garden** and sang "Happy Birthday" to him in a $12,000 beaded gown. At around 1 A.M. the next morning, after Krim's party, Kennedy and Monroe, who were conducting an affair, were escorted by Secret Service agents to the basement of this apartment house and through a series of tunnels that led to the **Carlyle Hotel** on 76th Street where JFK maintained a penthouse.

22/Dorothy Kilgallen
45 East 68th Street between Madison and Park Avenue.

This four-story brick building was the last home of the famous gossip columnist and panelist on the popular CBS game show of the 50s, *What's My Line?* **Kilgallen** died here on the night of November 8, 1965 in her sleep of an apparent drug overdose although there were some who insisted that she was murdered.

She had made a career of covering

famous criminal trials and she had recently attended the trial of **Lee Harvey Oswald's** killer, **Jack Ruby.** Conspiracy theorists claimed that Kilgallen had been preparing a major scoop that would expose the Warren Commission's report as a fraud and that she was therefore "silenced" by the real forces behind the Kennedy assassination.

23/Roy Cohn
39 East 68th Street between Madison and Park Avenue.

Lawyer **Roy Cohn**, who gained notoriety in the early 1950s as counsel for **Senator Joseph McCarthy** during his communist witchhunt, lived and kept offices in this white stone house for many years. During a legal career that spanned almost four decades, Cohn became a political power broker, a friend of the rich and fashionable, and the attorney of numerous controversial clients. His townhouse on 68th Street was the scene of many lavish parties attended by his friends and clients.

By 1986, when he was dying of AIDS-related liver cancer and had been disbarred from practicing law in New York, he still received guests here in his increasingly run-down house. Cohn "held forth...in his bedroom," said his biographer **Nicholas Von Hoffman**, "bulging with stuffed animals, in this enormous turn-of-the-century townhouse, the plaster cracking, the paint all but gone from the walls, leaks squirting, and drafts finding their way through the ill-attended cracks."

Cohn died in August 1986 at the age of fifty-nine.

TOUR 4

1/Robert Chesebrough
24 East 71st Street at Madison Avenue (southwest corner).

Industrialist **Robert Chesebrough**, the man who invented **Vaseline** petroleum jelly, lived in this five-story Italian Renaissance house. He built it in 1911. Chesebrough stayed here for several years and then sold the place to **Harry Guggenheim,** the philanthropist who founded the *Newsday* newspaper. After 1929, retail establishments opened on the lower floors.

2/Alan Jay Lerner
42 East 71st Street between Madison and Park Avenue.

Lyricist **Alan Jay Lerner**, who with **Frederick Loewe** wrote the music for such memorable Broadway shows as *Brigadoon* and *My Fair Lady,* bought this five-story red brick house in 1960. By that time, the team's new production, *Camelot*, had become another hit. Lerner moved in with his fourth wife, patent attorney **Michelline Muselli**.

The sixteen-room 20-foot-wide house is one of seven on 70th and 71st Streets between Madison and Park built in 1929 by the Rheinstein Construction Company. Each was built 60 feet deep on a 100-foot lot, with a garden in the rear. Lerner's only son, **Michael,** was born while he lived here. By 1964, Lerner and Muselli were feuding and when she filed for divorce, she obtained a court order barring him from the house.

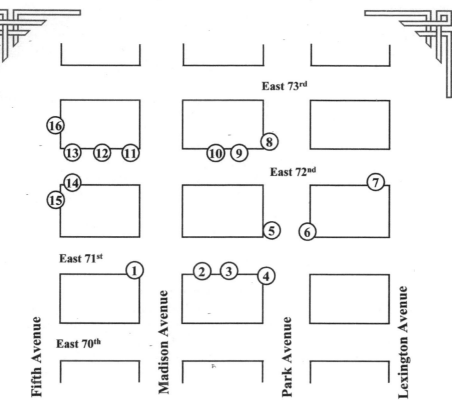

Upper East Side
Tour 4

1. Robert Chesebrough

2. Alan Jay Lerner

3. David Sarnoff

4. Richard Rodgers and
   Edna Ferber

5. John D. Rockefeller, Jr. and
   Jacqueline Kennedy Onassis

6. Sophie Tucker

7. George Gershwin and
   Jimmy Walker

8. Tyrone Power

9. Gloria Vanderbilt

10. Teilhard de Chardin

11. Charles Tiffany

12. Benjamin Guggenheim

13. Joseph Pulitzer

14. Henry Luce

15. Pola Negri

16. Arnold Rothstein

But on May 14, 1964 the forty-five-year-old songwriter managed to get in by entering the house next door at 40 East 71st Street, climbing to the roof, and crossing over to his own roof. He gained entrance from there and suprised his wife as she was tending their five-year-old son. When he refused to leave, four policemen and six lawyers rushed to the scene and he was ejected from the premises. The house was later restored to him when the final divorce settlement was made. Lerner was married four more times before his death in 1986.

3/David Sarnoff
44 East 71st Street between Madison and Park Avenue.

This was the residence of the radio and televison broadcasting pioneer who rose from a $5.50-a-week office boy to become chairman of RCA Corporation and later NBC. **David Sarnoff** lived in this six-story, thirty-room, thirty-four-foot-wide townhouse with his wife, **Lizette**.

In 1969 at age seventy-eight, Sarnoff developed a mastoid infection that spread to his nervous system and finally destroyed his ability to speak, see, hear, and even swallow. The following year, his wife had him moved to the solarium on the top floor of the house; the room was turned into a private infirmary with nurses on duty twenty-four hours a day. For a time, Lizette had a telegraph key installed by his bed so that he could communicate with operators at RCA. It was a return to the days of his youth because Sarnoff had started his career as a telegraph oper-

ator. Sarnoff died here on East 77th Street on December 11, 1971 at the age of eighty.

4/Richard Rodgers and Edna Ferber
70 East 71st Street at Park Avenue (southwest corner)

Richard Rodgers, the composer of countless Broadway musical scores and popular songs lived in this large co-op building (also known as 730 Park -Avenue) with his wife, **Dorothy**, and his two daughters, from 1945 to 1971. It was the period when he collaborated with **Oscar Hammerstein II** to produce a string of musicals that made Broadway history, starting with *Carousel* in 1945 and following with *South Pacific, The King and I, Flower Drum Song,* and *The Sound of Music.* After Hammerstein died in 1960, Rodgers continued to work on his own or with new partners.

The Rodgers apartment here was a spacious duplex staffed by three servants. Dorothy was an interior decorator and the apartment that she designed had a living room big enough to accommodate two grand pianos along with Louis XV chairs and Regency-period furniture. The carpeting, walls, curtains and woodwork were decorated in olive green.

In 1971, Rodgers and his wife moved to the **Hotel Pierre** where they lived for the rest of his life.

Novelist and playwright **Edna Ferber** took a large apartment in this building in 1950. She was sixty-five years old by then and had been a best-selling author for years. Previously, she had lived in a large country house in Connecticut called **Treasure Hill,** which had been her home since the mid-1930s. Ferber completed her popular novel *Giant* while she lived here. In 1959, an older book, *Saratoga Trunk,* was turned into a Broadway musical.

Ferber lived at 730 Park for eighteen years. She died in her apartment on April 16, 1968, after a long battle with cancer. Her age was eighty-three.

5/John D. Rockefeller, Jr. and Jacqueline Kennedy Onassis
740 Park Avenue at 71st Street (northwest corner).

The son of the founder of Standard Oil Company, **John D. Rockefeller,** Jr., was sixty-two years old in 1936 when he moved to a spacious penthouse apartment in this building with his wife, **Abigail.** By that time, Rockefeller had distinguished himself by directing huge amounts of the vast family fortune to philanthropic causes. Also by then, the youngest of his six children, **David,** had graduated from college and John D. felt it was time to leave the family house on 10 West 54th Street, where all six had been raised.

Rockefeller was devastated by Abigail's death in 1948. He was remarried in 1951 to **Martha Baird Allen** who was twenty years his junior. The couple continued to make this 740 Park Avenue address their New York City home until Rockefeller's death in 1960.

Jacqueline Kennedy Onassis lived in an eleven-room duplex apartment here as a child. Her father, **John "Black Jack" Bouvier** and mother, **Janet Norton Lee**, were married in 1928 and Jackie was born in July of the following year. The family resided here until 1938 when, after John and Janet decided to separate, young Jackie and her sister **Lee** moved into an apartment with their mother at 1 Gracie Square (see this section, Tour 11, Number 11).

740 Park Avenue was also the home of financier **Saul Steinberg,** who occupied the old John D. Rockefeller Jr.'s duplex after 1960. His thirty-four room residence sold for $35 million in 2000.

6/Sophie Tucker
737 Park Avenue at 71st Street (northeast corner).

Sophie Tucker, known as "The Last of the Red Hot Mamas," was a great star in burlesque, vaudeville, nightclubs, and English music hall during the first half of the twentieth century. This apartment building was her last home. She died here on February 9, 1966 of a lung ailment at the age of seventy-nine.

7/George Gershwin and Jimmy Walker
132 East 72nd Street near Lexington Avenue.

George Gershwin lived in this fifteen-story weathered brick building from 1933 until 1936. This was the composer's last New York home; it was a huge fourteen-room duplex apartment complete with an art studio, gymnasium, and perhaps the largest private bar in New York. The place was furnished with three Steinway pianos. Gershwin had a direct telephone line connected to his lyricist brother **Ira's** house, which was across the street at 125 East 72nd Street, so that the two could be in instant contact. While he lived here, Gershwin began work on *Porgy and Bess*. He and Ira also completed another musical comedy *Let 'Em Eat Cake*. George Gershwin moved to California in 1936.

Ex-New York mayor **Jimmy Walker** and his second wife, show-girl **Betty Compton**, lived in this same building from 1935 until their divorce in 1941.They had moved here after spending three years in France (see this section, Tour 1, Number 17).

8/Tyrone Power

760 Park Avenue at 72nd Street (northwest corner).

Actor **Tyrone Power** was forty years old when he rented a small, two-bedroom penthouse in this building in 1954. During this period, he appeared on Broadway in a play called T*he Dark is Light Enough,* co-starring with **Katharine Cornell.**

9/Gloria Vanderbilt

49 East 72nd Street between Madison and Park Avenue.

Socialite and famous international beauty **Gloria Morgan Vanderbilt**, the widow of millionaire **Reginald Vanderbilt**, rented a townhouse on this site from 1932 to 1936 (the modern apartments here today are numbered 45 East 72nd). She lived here with her young daughter, **Gloria**, during the court battle in 1934 with her sister-in-law **Gertrude Vander-**

bilt Whitney over the custody of the ten-and-a-half-year-old child. It was the most sensational custody trial in U.S. history.

Mrs. Whitney, who accused her sister-in-law of being an unfit mother, won the case in November 1934 and little Gloria went to live with her at her 871 Fifth Avenue mansion (see this section, Tour 3, Number 13). The girl visited her mother here on 72nd Street on weekends until 1936 when, low on funds, the elder Gloria was forced to move away to cheaper surroundings. She died in California in 1965.

10/Teilhard de Chardin

39 East 72nd Street between Madison and Park Avenue.

Pierre Teilhard de Chardin was a Jesuit priest and a paleontologist. In his third role as a philosopher, his attempts to fuse Catholic doctrine with the theory of evolution had caused a great deal of controversy in the Roman Catholic Church.

In 1955, at age seventy-three and in poor health, Teilhard was living in New York at the **Hotel Fourteen** at 14 East 60th Street (see this section, Tour 1, Number 1). On Easter Sunday in 1955, he was visiting his friend **Rhoda de Terra** in her apartment in this building when he collapsed and died of a cerebral hemorrhage.

11/Charles L. Tiffany

19 East 72nd Street at Madison Avenue (northwest corner).

One of the earliest large mansions of the Upper East Side once stood on this site. Built in 1882, it was the gigantic Romanesque-style home of **Charles L. Tiffany**, the founder of the famous jewelry store. The house was one of the early designs of architect **Stanford White** of the firm McKim, Mead and White, done in collaboration with the jeweler's son, **Louis Comfort Tiffany.**

Constructed at a cost of over $500,000, it was designed as a triple house; the lower floors housed the owner, the third floor was built for his daughter, while the floors at the top, furnished in a very eclectic style, were set aside for the Tiffany son, whose artistic **Tiffany Studios** were responsible for the famous Tiffany lamps of bronze and stained glass. The Tiffany mansion was demolished in 1936, not long after the death of **Louis Comfort Tiffany**, who had remained in residence to the end of his life.

12/Benjamin Guggenheim
15 East 72nd Street near Fifth Avenue.

Benjamin Guggenheim was the sixth of seven sons of mining baron **Meyer Guggenheim.** From 1898 to 1911, he lived in this four-story house with his wife, **Florette,** and his three daughters.

Ben was a notorious playboy and spent much of his time in Europe, away from his family. On the night of April 14, 1912, he was on board the *Titanic* with his mistress, returning to New York to celebrate his daughter **Hazel's** ninth birthday. As the doomed ship when down, Guggenheim and his valet discarded their life jackets, dressed in their evening clothes, and went up on deck. Declaring that they were going down with the ship "like gentlemen," they helped people into the lifeboats, shouting "women and children first!" Guggenheim told a steward to relay this message: "Tell my wife in New York I did my best in doing my duty."

Guggenheim was only forty-seven when he died and it was soon discovered that he had squandered an estimated $8 million on bad investments, leaving his three children with a meager $450,000 each, and prompting his daughter **Peggy** to say that she "felt like a poor relative and suffered great humiliation thinking how inferior I was to the rest of the family."

13/Joseph Pulitzer
9 East 72nd Street near Fifth Avenue.

The famed newspaper publisher leased this Beaux Arts-style house called the **Sloane Mansion** from 1900 to 1904. The building was designed by Carrere and Stone and built in 1894. **Pulitzer** moved here after his previous home at 10 East 55th Street burned down. He was only fifty-three years old but his newspaper, *The New York World,* had made him wealthy and he had retired from its day-to-day management. During his stay on 72nd Street, Pulitzer used $2 million to establish a school of journalism at Columbia University and, in 1904, he set aside $16,500 for the establishment of the **Pulitzer Prize.**

In that same year Pulitzer moved one block north to his new home (see this section, Tour 5, Number 3). The Sloane Mansion housed the bilingual school called the **Lycee Francais de New York** from 1964 until 2001 when the building was sold again to private residents.

14/Henry Luce
4 East 72nd Street at Fifth Avenue.

In 1932, **Henry Luce**, whose *Time* magazine had become one of journalism's great success stories, rented a large apartment in this building with his first wife, **Lila,** and their two sons, aged nine and five.

He was living at this address in December 1934 when he attended a party at the Waldorf-Astoria Hotel, where he encountered the beautiful **Clare Boothe**, the young managing editor of *Vanity Fair.* Luce had been smitten during his first meeting with Boothe and now he seemingly decided on the spot to end his marriage of eleven years. Luce and Lila were eventually divorced and he married Boothe in November 1935.

After Luce moved out of his apartment here on 72nd Street, he purchased a fifteen-room triplex at River House at 435 East 52nd Street (see Section Two, Tour 5, Number 1).

15/Pola Negri
907 Fifth Avenue at 72nd Street (southeast corner).

The beautiful silent screen star lived in this building in the 1950s. **Pola Negri** was born in Poland and began her acting career in European films before coming to America in 1922. She never made a successful transition to talking movies and her film career was over by the 1940s.

Probably her greatest claim to fame was as the self-proclaimed last lover of **Rudolph Valentino;** when he died in 1926, her stylized grief was recorded by news photographers and cameramen all over the world. Neighbors here at 907 Fifth Avenue reported that a large portrait of Valentino hung in a prominent place in her foyer.

Negri moved to Texas at the end of the 1950s and died there in 1987.

16/Arnold Rothstein
912 Fifth Avenue between 72nd and 73rd Street.

Notorious gambler and underworld kingpin **Arnold Rothstein**, often accused of being the man who fixed the **1919 World Series**, lived in an eight-room apartment in this building with his wife, **Carolyn**, during the last four years of his life.

Early in 1928, he moved away after arguing with his wife about his affairs with other women; he took temporary quarters at the Fairfield Apartments on 20 West 72nd Street.

On November 4, 1928, Rothstein was shot in a room at the **Park Central Hotel** during an argument about gambling debts. He was rushed to the hospital but died soon afterward. His killer was never officially identified. Rothstein was only forty-six years old.

TOUR 5

1/Luise Rainer
28 East 73rd Street at Madison Avenue (southwest corner).

Austrian-born actress **Luise Rainer** lived in an apartment in this building in the early 1940s. She was working on Broadway at that time, appearing in a play called *A Kiss for Cinderella.*

During the previous decade, Rainer had been one of Hollywood's most prominent performers, winning Oscars two years in a row for *The Great Ziegfeld* in 1936 and *The Good Earth* in 1937, after which her film career sputtered. Her marriage to playwright **Clifford Odets** ended while she lived here on 73rd Street. Rainer married publisher **Robert Knittel** in 1945 and they moved into a townhouse on Sutton Place.

2/Gloria Swanson
920 Fifth Avenue at 73rd Street (southeast corner).

Film star **Gloria Swanson** took a large apartment in this building in 1938. It was on the ground floor and boasted a small back-yard patio; it was her principal residence for the rest of her life.

By the late 1930s, Swanson's movie career had faded— she became a successful business woman—but she made a spectacular comeback in 1950 when director **Billy Wilder** chose her to play the part of silent film star Norma Desmond in his movie *Sunset Boulevard.* Swanson won the Academy Award for Best Actress. She died while living at this

Gloria Swanson

address in 1983 at the age of eighty-four.

Joseph Pulitzer

3/Joseph Pulitzer
11 East 73rd Street between Fifth and Madison Avenue.

Joseph Pulitzer commissioned **Stanford White** to design this mansion after his previous house at 10

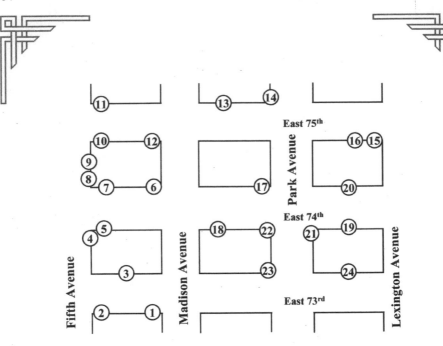

Upper East Side
Tour 5

1. Luise Rainer
2. Gloria Swanson
3. Joseph Pulitzer
4. Mary Tyler Moore
5. Marc Chagall
6. Dorothy Parker
7. Richard Croker
8. Woody Allen
9. Charles E. Mitchell
10. Thomas Watson
11. Ellin Mackay Berlin
12. Lillian Hellman

13. George Balanchine
14. Arthur Kobler
15. Lunt and Fontanne
16. Tandy and Cronyn
17. Eleanor Roosevelt
18. Harry Guggenheim
19. Jerome Kern
20. Jacqueline Kennedy Onassis
21. Edna Ferber
22. Woody Allen
23. Dag Hammarskjold and
    Gary Cooper
24. Charles Dana Gibson

East 55th Street burned down in 1900. The cost was $644,000 and Pulitzer and his family settled here in 1904. He had decided that he would never again occupy a house that could burn and he ordered White to make it fireproof.

Pulitzer had also grown acutely sensitive to noise and the builders labored to make his bedroom apartment soundproof. But the faint sound of a pump in the basement still managed to drive him frantic and he declared the house "a wretched failure." The architects continued to tinker with the design to please the owner's wishes until they were finally able to declare the house absolutely impervious to sound.

This was Pulitzer's last home. He died while living here on October 29, 1911 at the age of sixty-four. The building was later converted to apartments, some of which are quite distinctive.

4) Mary Tyler Moore

927 Fifth Avenue at 74th Street (southeast corner).

This twelve-story neo-Italian Renaissance limestone building, built in 1917, was the recent home of actress **Mary Tyler Moore** and her husband, **Dr. Robert Levine.** They owned a cooperative apartment here on the eighth floor until the summer of 2005.

While she lived here, Moore became embroiled in a headline-making controversy over the presence on the face of the building of a red-tailed hawk—dubbed **Pale Male** by the passionate bird watchers who gathered in Central Park each day to

Pulitzer at 11 East 73rd Street

observe his activities. In 1993, the hawk and a succession of his mates had built a nest on the top of the cornice molding that frames the top center window of the building.

In December 2004, the board of 927 Fifth ordered the removal of the raptor's nest, causing an uproar among animal rights groups and leading to protests which took place day after day in front of the building. The board's decision caused dissention among the owners in the building and Moore, who was vocal in her criticism of the decision, cheered the protesters.

Eventually the board reversed its decision, Pale Male and his mate, **Lola,** were allowed to rebuild their nest, and the actress decided to move away. Her three-bedroom apartment was sold for a reported $18 million in June 2005.

5/Marc Chagall
4 East 74th Street near Fifth Avenue.

Painter **Marc Chagall**, with his wife, **Bella**, rented an apartment in this six-story Beaux-Arts townhouse in September 1941 soon after they had arrived in New York from Nazi-occupied France. They decorated the walls of their place with Chagall's paintings to create the illusion of being back in Paris.

After Bella's death in 1944, Chagall's daughter persuaded him to move into her large apartment at 75 Riverside Drive. In 1998, this East 74th Street townhouse was put on sale for $13.5 million.

The Volney

6/Dorothy Parker
23 East 74th Street between Fifth and Madison Avenue

The **Volney** was a residence hotel popular with literary and theater people. **Dorothy Parker** moved here in 1952 and made it her home for most of the last fifteen years of her life. Her two-room furnished apartment cost $275 a month. It was the perfect living place for her dog, **Misty**, because the Volney had more than forty other dogs in residence.

In 1964, her friend **Sara Murphy** moved to the Volney after the death of her husband, **Gerald.** Sara and Dorothy, both increasingly frail, kept an eye on each other. During her last three years, Parker moved to a smaller, less expensive, apartment on the eighth floor. By then her health had deteriorated and she weighed only eighty pounds.

Before she died, Parker made a will leaving her entire estate of $20,000 to **Dr. Martin Luther King** and his cause. She was found dead of a heart attack in her rooms on June 7, 1967. She was survived by her dog.

In 1962, gangster **Meyer Lansky**, recovering from heart trouble and recently released from the hospital, lived in Suite 8E at the Volney with his wife, **Teddy.**

Lansky was one of America's most powerful crime bosses and the FBI was interested in his current activities. They arranged to bug his room so that they could monitor his conversations, but they found out nothing more important than that his favorite foods were matzos, sardines, Jell-O, Irish lamb stew, and ham.

7/Richard Croker
5 East 74th Street near Fifth Avenue.

Croker was one of the most powerful political bosses in New York's history. He controlled the corrupt **Tammany Hall** machine from 1886 until 1901 when a reform mayor, **Seth Low**, was elected and forced him out. In 1890, Croker, then firmly entrenched in power, moved from Harlem to this five-story house. He paid $200,000 for it. After his ouster in 1901, Croker moved back to Ireland, the country of his birth, and spent the rest of his life there on a large estate. He died in 1922.

8/Woody Allen
930 Fifth Avenue at 74th Street (northeast corner).

Woody Allen lived in the duplex penthouse of this building from 1970 until 1999. His eight-room apartment with double terraces afforded a spectacular view of Central Park.

At about the time that he moved here, he began to write, direct, and act in many of the movies that made him famous; scenes from a few were filmed here. After his marriage to **Mia Farrow's** daughter, **Soon-Yi,** Allen sold the penthouse for a reported $14 million and moved with her to a $17 million townhouse at 48 East 92nd Street (see this section, Tour 14, Number 13).

9/Charles E. Mitchell
934 Fifth Avenue between 74th and 75th Street.

This large neo-Renaissance building was the home of banker **Charles Mitchell.** His name is no longer well-known to the public but in the early days of the Great Depression, he was in the spotlight after Federal investigators exposed a number of his questionable financial operations.

Mitchell was the president of **National City Bank** and during the 1920s he converted his institution into the first modern retail banking operation, allowing individual consumers to take out personal loans. National City was the largest agency in the world for the distribution of securities and Mitchell both encouraged and participated in the excessive speculation that led to the stock market crash of 1929. In 1933, a Senate committee uncovered a number of occurrences of financial abuse and fraud in which Mitchell was involved and he was forced to resign from his position at the bank.

10/Thomas Watson
4 East 75th Street near Fifth Avenue.

Thomas J. Watson, the chairman and driving force behind the **IBM Corporation**, purchased this French Renaissance-style house in 1939. He lived here until his death.

Watson started as a successful salesman for National Cash Register Company at the turn of the last century and when he was fired in 1913, he took over a small business machine company that eventually grew into the giant IBM firm.

After World War II, his company got into the computer business and by the 1960s, it was producing seventy percent of all the computers in the world. Watson died of a heart attack in June 1956 at the age of eighty-two.

11/Ellin Mackay Berlin
3 East 75th Street at Fifth Avenue.

Novelist and short-story writer **Ellin Mackay** was better known as the wife of songwriter **Irving Berlin**. They were married for sixty-two years. She lived in this elegant limestone mansion as a young girl; it was owned by her father **Clarence Mackay**, a multimillionaire telegraph magnate.

He was a strict Roman Catholic and opposed the marriage of his daughter to Berlin, an Orthodox Jew. In 1925, after Ellin met Berlin, father and daughter quarreled and Ellin moved out of the mansion here; she took an apartment just up the street at 36 East 75th Street.

On January 4, 1926 she and Berlin were married in a civil ceremony without the knowledge of Ellin's father, who promptly excluded her from his will and refused to speak to his daughter or her new husband for the next five years. Clarence Mackay never really warmed to his new son-in-law even though, during the Depression, Mackay's financial empire collapsed and Berlin came to his rescue with a gift of one million dollars.

Ellin Mackay Berlin died in 1988 at the age of eighty-five. Irving Berlin died fourteen months later. He was 101 years old.

12/Lillian Hellman
14 East 75th Street between Fifth and Madison Avenue.

In 1935, **Lillian Hellman** took a duplex apartment in this building. The place is across the street from the **Whitney Museum of Art.** Hellman had recently become wealthy due to the success of her play *The Children's Hour* and to the money she was making writing screenplays for Hollywood.

She furnished her apartment here with prints of the works of Picasso and acquired a large apricot poodle named Jumbo. She also threw elaborate parties; **George Gershwin** showed up at one to play the grand piano that Hellman had purchased. Hellman was living here when she wrote her second play *Days to Come*. It closed in 1936 after six performances. It was also during this period that she secretly joined the Communist Party.

13/George Balanchine
41 East 75th Street between Madison and Park Avenue.

In 1948—the year that choreographer **George Balanchine** was made artistic director of the **New York City Ballet Company**—he moved into a walkup, one-bedroom apartment on the top floor of this brownstone (now numbered 43). He lived here with his fourth wife, ballerina **Maria Tallchief**, the daughter of an Osage Indian.

The apartment was furnished modestly; most of the space was taken up by two grand pianos that Balanchine and Tallchief both played for pleasure. He also used them to arrange his choreographic pieces.

The couple separated in 1951 and, after the marriage was annulled, Balanchine married ballerina **Tanaquil LeClerq** in 1952. They stayed in this building, but moved to an apartment on the first floor. Under Balanchine's direction, LeClerq became a star with the **New York City Ballet,** until she came down with polio in 1954. The couple separated in 1967.

14/Arthur J. Kobler

820 Park Avenue at 75th Street (northwest corner).

Arthur Kobler was one of **William Randoph Hearst's** top executives. In 1917, he was appointed head of advertising for the weekly supplement of the *New York Journal American* and proceeded to increase its circulation by over twenty million.Commissions brought Kobler's salary to over $450,000 a year and later he became publisher of Hearst's *New York Daily Mirror.*

He built this fourteen-story building in 1926, living on the top three floors himself, and renting the five duplexes below. He filled his place with his own collection of art treasures and antiques, including tapestries once owned by Henry VIII of England and furniture from the Strozzi Palace in Florence. Kobler's neighbors in the building included New York Governor and Senator **Herbert Lehman,** who lived on the tenth and eleventh floors, and investment banker **Herbert S. Martin** on the eighth and ninth floors.

Martin jumped to his death here in 1930, not long after the stock market crash. Kobler leased his own triplex to automobile manufacturer **Walter Chrysler** in 1937. After 1941, the huge residences here were gradually subdivided into smaller units. The building is a co-op today.

15/Alfred Lunt and Lynn Fontanne

130 East 75th Street at Lexington Avenue (southwest corner).

Lunt and Fontanne, the husband-and-wife stars of New York theater, leased a luxury seven-room apartment in this building in 1936. They moved in during production of **Robert Sherwood's** play *Idiot's Delight* which became a great success, running for 300 performances and winning a Pulitzer Prize.

The Lunt-Fontanne apartment was decorated in the Swedish style with baroque floral designs on many of the walls.Fontanne purchased a large bed, six feet by five feet, which she proudly described as "the best in America and why not?"

The couple made East 75th Street their New York home until 1949; their main residence was located in Genesee Depot, Wisconsin.While they lived here, the two were often on the road; they took part in a nationwide acting tour of sixty cities between 1938 and 1940 and spent the years 1943-45 in Europe performing for British audiences and Allied troops.

16/Jessica Tandy and Hume Cronyn

120 East 75th Street between Park and Lexington Avenue.

This nine-story apartment building was the New York home in the 1960s and 70s of the husband-and-wife acting team of **Jessica Tandy** and **Hume Cronyn.** The couple were married in 1942 in Hollywood but made their first stage appearance together in 1951 in the Broadway play *The Fourposter.* They were living here when they starred in **Edward Albee's** play *A Delicate Balance* in 1966.

In 1978, Tandy won a Tony Award and Cronyn won a Tony nomination for their collaboration in the play *The Gin Game,* which became their trademark performance.

17/Eleanor Roosevelt
55 East 74th Street near Park Avenue.

This beautiful five-story house was the final New York residence of **Eleanor Roosevelt.** She was seventy-five years old when she purchased it in 1958 with her close friend, **Dr. David Gurewitsch** and his wife, **Edna.**

Mrs.Roosevelt had numerous friends and the place was always full. She entertained people from all walks of life. **President John F. Kennedy** came here for breakfast and she once invited Russian premier **Khrushchev** for tea.

The former First Lady hosted an annual party on New Year's Eve that started after midnight; the front door was left open and the guests were always served champagne.

In 1960, Mrs. Roosevelt was diagnosed with a severe form of anemia that was later determined to be bone-marrow tuberculosis.Even during this period of illness, she remained active in UN and Democratic Party affairs and worked on her last book *Tomorrow is Now.*

She died at her home here on November 7, 1962.

18/Harry Guggenheim
34 East 74th Street between Madison and Park Avenue.

Harry F. Guggenheim, financier, philanthropist, horseman, and publisher of *Newsday,* the largest suburban daily newspaper in the country, lived in this narrow five-level townhouse.

Harry was the son of **Daniel Guggenheim**, who ran the family's mining empire for many years. Besides the newspaper which he founded with his wife, **Alicia Patterson**, in 1941, Harry Guggenheim was probably best known for his philanthropic support of a wide variety of activities designed to stimulate development of the aviation industry and to educate the public on the importance of aviation. His early promotion of the science of rocketry led to the development of **Saturn V**, the rocket that sent Apollo XI to the moon.

19/Jerome Kern
128 East 74th Street between Park and Lexington Avenue.

Songwriter **Jerome Kern** was five years old in 1890 when he moved with his family into this four-story house. He was the youngest of nine boys, only three of whom survived into adulthood.

Kern's mother, **Fanny**, was an excellent pianist and Jerome was studying the instrument under her care by the time they moved here. He spent endless hours at the piano and quickly learned to play most tunes he heard by ear.In 1895, Kern's family moved to Newark, New Jersey after his father purchased a merchandising business.

20/Jacqueline Kennedy Onassis
125 East 74th Street between Park and Lexington Avenue.

Jacqueline Kennedy Onassis's father **John ("Black Jack") Bouvier** and her mother, **Janet Lee Bouvier**, were divorced in 1940 when Jackie was eleven years old. Her father, age forty-nine, moved into a four-room bachelor apartment in this building while Jackie lived with her mother and her sister, **Lee**, at their new home at 1 Gracie Square (see this section, Tour 11, Number 11).

John Bouvier, a Yale-educated socialite, worked as a stockbroker but he was now experiencing a period of decline—his business was failing and he had a growing drinking problem.

Every Sunday, Bouvier, driving his Mercury, would pick up his young daughter, Jackie, at her mother's apartment. They would take walks or go horse-riding in Central Park, lunch at Schraft's, see the races at Belmont Park. They often spent time here at his apartment.

In 1942, Janet Lee married **Hugh Auchincloss** and Jackie moved with her mother and sister into her new stepfather's home in McLean, Virginia. But Jackie continued to maintain a close relationship with her father until his death in 1957. Whenever she visited New York, he cancelled all of his other social engagements to spend time exclusively with her.

21/Edna Ferber
791 Park Avenue at 74th Street (southeast corner).

In the late 1920s and early 1930s, **Edna Ferber** was one of America's most successful novelists and playwrights. By then she was living in a large apartment in this building. Her mother, **Julia**, a constant companion throughout Ferber's life, was here with her. The penthouse apartment had a huge outdoor terrace, big enough to play tennis on, and a lush garden complete with peach trees.

Ferber co-wrote three plays with **George S. Kaufman** during this period: *The Royal Family* in 1927, *Dinner at Eight* in 1932, and *Stage Door* in 1936. She also wrote a novel called *Cimarron* in 1930.

22/Woody Allen
784 Park Avenue at 74th Street (southwest corner).

In 1963, **Woody Allen** leased an apartment in this building and moved in with his actress girlfriend, **Louise Lasser.** He had recently separated from his first wife. Allen was just beginning to establish himself as a popular stand-up comedian in clubs around New York and other cities. His fame increased when he began to appear on the late-night television shows hosted by **Johnny Carson** and **Steve Allen.**

In 1965, he made *What's New, Pussycat?,* his first feature film as an actor and writer. Woody Allen and Louise Lasser were married in 1966 while they were residents here on Park Avenue.

23/Dag Hammarskjold and Gary Cooper

778 Park Avenue at 73rd Street (northwest corner).

This eighteen-story apartment building which opened in 1930 at the beginning of the Great Depression was designed by **Rosario Candela,** probably New York's greatest luxury apartment house architect. (He also designed the apartment building across the street at 770 Park Avenue which opened in the same year.)

Dag Hammarskjold, the Swedish diplomat who served as Secretary General of the United Nations from 1953 to 1961, occupied a large apartment here on 778 Park.Hammarskjold's place was simply furnished; he decorated the walls with romantic landscape paintings from Sweden and hung a simple drawing by Matisse over his writing desk.

In the midst of his hectic UN schedule, Hammarskjold found time to explore the surrounding neighborhood, attending movies and plays, listening to musical performances, and shopping for himself.

He was only fifty-six years old when he died in a plane crash during a peace-keeping mission to Africa in 1961.He was posthumously awarded the Nobel Peace Prize.

Actor **Gary Cooper** married socialite and former actress **Veronica Balfe** in the apartment of her stepfather Wall Street tycoon **Paul Shields** here in December 1933. Cooper was thirty-two years old and already an established star; Balfe was twenty. The marriage lasted until his death in 1961.

Thomas Watson, IBM pioneer, also lived in this building in the 1930s.

24/Charles Dana Gibson

127 East 73rd Street between Park and Lexington Avenue.

This townhouse, designed by **Stanford White** in the neo-Federal style and completed in 1904, was the home of illustrator **Charles Dana Gibson,** who was famous at the beginning of the twentieth century for his pen-and-ink sketches of the *"Gibson Girls."* He lived here with his wife, **Irene Langhorne**, whom he married in 1895. After Gibson died in 1944, Irene sold the house and it was later occupied by the **American Scandinavian Foundation.** It has been recently purchased by a private owner again and undergone extension renovation.

TOUR 6

1/Grace Kelly and Benny Goodman

200 East 66th Street at Third Avenue (southeast corner).

This nineteen-story luxury apartment building called **Manhattan House** opened in 1950. It was owned by the **New York Life Insurance Company**, which took steps to protect the building's light and preserve its pristine status by purchasing many of the lower-lying buildings surrounding it.

Actress **Grace Kelly** moved here shortly after it opened and stayed here until 1954. Her apartment was on the ninth floor with a terrace facing south. She shared it with **Sally Parrish**, an actress who would be a bridesmaid at her wedding. During this period, Kelly starred in such movies as *High Noon, Rear Window,* and *The Country Girl,* for which she won an Academy Award. A biographer said that her apartment was unpretentious and often cluttered. Her only pet was a parakeet named **Henry,** but Kelly was seldom lonely —friends dropped by at all hours of the day and night.

Clarinetist **Benny Goodman**, one of the world's greatest jazz artists, lived at Manhattan House for a number of years. He died of a heart attack here on June 13, 1986 at the age of seventy-seven.

Manhattan House was also the New York home of comic actress **Imogene Coca**, co-star of television's *Your Show of Shows* with **Sid Caesar.** Coca lived here until the late 1990s.

2/Malachi Martin
217 East 66th Street between Third and Second Avenue.

The Irish-born former Jesuit priest and Vatican scholar who went on to write thrillers about the Roman Catholic Church lived in Apartment 2A of this white brick building. **Malachi Martin** dropped out of the Jesuit order in 1965 and moved to New York to write full time after brief stints as a cab driver and dishwasher.

One of his best-known books was *Hostage to the Devil* (published in 1976, shortly after the release of the movie *The Exorcist*) in which Martin described the real-life account of the possession and exorcism of five Americans.

Martin died in July 1999 at the age of seventy-eight while he was living here. The cause of death was a head injury resulting from a fall.

3/Sara and Gerald Murphy
131 East 66th Street at Lexington Avenue (northeast corner).

The **Murphys**—who were hosts to many of the key writers and artists of the 1920s and 30s at their villa on the French Riviera and were themselves the models for **Dick** and **Nicole Diver** in **F. Scott Fitzgerald's** *Tender is the Night*—lived in this large apartment house from 1940 to 1949.

The neo-Renaissance building, erected in 1906, was originally meant to house artists and it combined large, double-height studios with single-height dwelling spaces.

The Murphys' residency here was a period of emotional recovery for them—their two young sons had died tragically only a few years earlier.

In their huge living room, they continued to play the role of amiable hosts, entertaining the likes of **John Dos Passos, Archibald MacLeish, Fernand Leger, Edmund Wilson,** and **Lillian Hellman.**

In 1949, the couple moved to a house at Sneden's Landing, above Manhattan on the west bank of the Hudson River.

4/Barbra Streisand
1157 Third Avenue between 67th and 68th Street.

Streisand, age nineteen, rented a tiny, cold-water flat on the third floor of this five-story building in 1961. The rent was $67.20 a month.

She had just landed her first big role on Broadway as *Miss Marmel-*

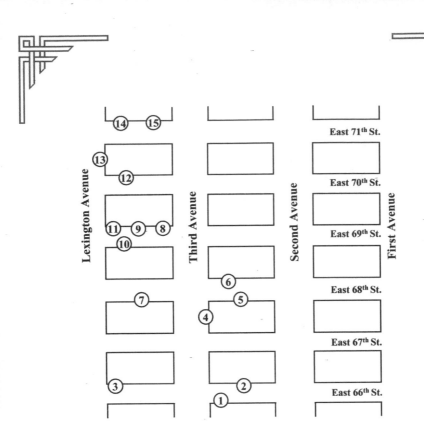

Upper East Side
Tour 6

1. Grace Kelly and Benny Goodman
2. Malachi Martin
3. Gerald and Sara Murphy
4. Barbra Streisand
5. Rita Hayworth
6. Sammy Cahn
7. Joan Crawford
8. Rube Goldberg

9. Mark Rothko
10. Lucille Ball
11. Edward Steichen
12. Frank Loesser
13. Lunt and Fontanne
14. Robert Sherwood
15. "Breakfast at Tiffany's"

stein in **David Merrick's** *I Can Get It For You Wholesale.*

Streisand's apartment was on top of a seafood restaurant named **Oscar's Salt of the Sea**; the smell of cooked fish drifted upstairs to her place. The only window looked out onto a black brick wall. The bathtub was in the kitchen and when she wasn't using it, she covered it with a board and piled her dishes on top.

Before long, her boyfriend, actor **Elliott Gould**, moved in here with her; they were married in 1963. Streisand became a huge star when she took the Broadway role as **Fanny Brice** in *Funny Girl* in 1964.

5/Bartley C. Crum and Rita Hayworth

236 East 68th Street between Third and Second Avenue.

Bartley Crum was a San Francisco attorney who earned headlines in 1947 when he defended two of the screenwriters who were members of the *"Hollywood Ten,"* accused of being communists, before the House Un-American Activities Committee.

For a decade beginning in 1951, Crum lived in this narrow four-level house with the French windows. Probably his most famous client was the glamorous actress **Rita Hayworth,** who sued her playboy millionaire husband, **Prince Aly Kahn**, for divorce and child custody in 1951.

Crum's daughter, **Patricia Bosworth**, remembers Hayworth coming to their house here on 68th Street at odd hours, always alone, to confer with her attorney father. When she visited for the first time, Bosworth was disappointed in the way Hayworth looked: "no makeup, hair brown, not died red; dressed in a man's baggy shirt, slacks, and bobby socks."

The actress would enter the house and hurry to the bar in the back study where she would sit with her attorney, often for hours. In 1953, Crum won a divorce and custody settlement for Hayworth in which Khan agreed to establish a one million dollar trust fund for their three-year-old daughter, **Yasmin.**

Crum committed suicide in 1959 at age fifty-nine.

6/Sammy Cahn

215 East 68th Street near Third Avenue.

The songwriter who wrote the words to many of **Frank Sinatra's** signature songs lived in an apartment in this building during his last years. **Sammy Cahn** teamed first with composer **Jule Styne** and later **Jimmy Van Heusen** on such hits as *All The Way, Call Me Irresponsible, Three Coins in the Fountain,* and *My Kind of Town.* He won four Academy Awards. Cahn died of heart failure in 1993.

This building was also the New York home of playwright **Arthur Miller** in the 1980s and early 90s. His main residence was in Connecticut.

Stephen Vincent Benet, the Pulitzer Prize-winning poet, occupied a house on this site earlier in the last century. He died there on March 13, 1943 at the age of forty-four.

7/Joan Crawford
158 East 68th Street between Lexington and Third Avenue.

Here on the spot now occupied by the **Jack I. Poses Park** of Hunter College, was the site of movie actress **Joan Crawford's** last home. It was where she died of a heart attack, in her apartment, on May 10, 1977.

During the final years of her life, she became the first woman to serve on the board of directors of the **Pepsi Cola Company** and worked as the corporation's major public relations spokesperson and official hostess.

Mark Rothko

8/Rube Goldberg
169 East 69th Street at Third Avenue (northwest corner).

This building was the New York home of **Rube Goldberg**, the cartoonist. His most enduring creation was the character **Professor Lucifer Gorgonzola Butts,** who invented various complicated (and hilarious) contraptions designed to accomplish the simplest of ends.

Goldberg's comic strips and editorial cartoons ran in the *New York Sun* and *New York Journal-American* for over fifty years and were syndicated worldwide. He won a Pulitzer Prize in 1948.

Goldberg died of cancer in his home here on December 7, 1970. He was eighty-seven years old.

9/ Mark Rothko
157 East 69th Street between Lexington and Third Avenue.

Mark Rothko made this converted carriage house with the black trim his last New York studio. The painter lived and worked here alone during the last fourteen months of his life; he moved in after separating from his wife, **Mell**, in late 1968.

While he was here, he worked on a cycle of paintings commissioned by the **de Menil** family for a chapel in Houston, Texas.

Rothko's studio in the former riding rink at the back of the building had thirty-foot yellow brick walls and a large skylight. He regulated the studio's light by covering the skylight with a huge canvas parachute which he could manipulate with pulleys and ropes.

Rothko lived in the two front rooms of the building. It was in this house that he was found dead of suicide on February 25, 1970, lying in a pool of blood, his arms slashed at the elbow.

10/Lucille Ball
150 East 69th Street between Lexington and Third Avenue.

Lucille Ball moved to New York from Los Angeles in 1960, soon after her divorce from **Desi Arnaz**, and rented two apartments on the top floor of this luxury high-rise called the **Imperial House**

The actress knocked down the walls separating the two flats to create a sunny sixty-by-thirty foot living room with views of both the East and Hudson Rivers. She filled the place with French Provincial and contemporary furniture and five vanloads of personal items, shipped from her former home in Beverly Hills.

Ball had come to New York to star in the Broadway musical *Wildcat;* it opened to mixed reviews and closed after a short run. It was during this period that she met her second husband, comedian **Gary Morton.**

11/Edward Steichen
143 East 69th Street at Lexington Avenue (northeast corner).

Photographer **Edward Steichen** maintained his studio here from 1934 to 1938. During his years at this site, he concentrated on fashion photography and portraits of celebrities. His work appeared regularly in *Vogue* and *Vanity Fair* magazines.

Steichen's solution to the problem of parking in Manhattan streets was recorded by one amazed witness who one day watched the photographer drive up to the building here—like many of the buildings on this block it was a one-time carriage house—open a huge door that doubled as a reception-room wall, and steer his roadster over the tile floor past his secretary's desk and into his large studio.

In 1928, Steichen and his wife, **Dana**, purchased a farm near West Redding, Connecticut, which became their main home away from his New York studio.

12/Frank Loesser
161 East 70th Street between Lexington and Third Avenue.

Song lyricist and composer **Frank Loesser** lived in this elegant three-story red brick house during the last years of his life. His second wife, actress **Jo Sullivan**, lived here with him.

Loesser wrote songs for a number of movies and for such hit plays as *Where's Charley?* and *How to Succeed in Business Without Really Trying,* but he is best known for his masterpiece, *Guys and Dolls,* which opened on Broadway in 1950 and played more than a thousand performances.

Loesser died of lung cancer in March 1969. He was only fifty-nine years old.

13/Alfred Lunt and Lynn Fontanne
969 Lexington Avenue between 70th and 71st Street.

Soon after their wedding in May 1922, **Lunt and Fontanne** started married life in New York in a four-room apartment on the second floor of this building. They were just beginning to gain notice in the Broadway theater for their exceptional performances. The couple was living here in 1924 when they opened in the play called *The Guardsman,* which made them immediately famous. They received rave notices and the play ran for 248 performances.

Lunt and Fontanne lived in this apartment until 1925. After that they occupied a series of hotel suites for ten years until they settled into a more permanent place in 1936 at 130 East 75th Street (see this section, Tour 5, Number 15).

14/Robert Sherwood

153 East 71st Street at Lexington Avenue (northeast corner).

Playwright and screenwriter **Robert Sherwood** moved to this four-level house with the walk-down entrance in 1922 after he married his first wife, **Mary Brandon.** He was twenty-six years old and supported himself as an editor and movie critic for *Life* magazine.

Sherwood began writing his first plays while he lived here, beginning with *The Road to Rome* in 1927. Before his career was over, he won three Pulitzer Prizes for drama, one for nonfiction (his book *Roosevelt and Hopkins*) and an Academy Award in 1946 for his screenplay of *The Best Years of Our Lives.*

Sherwood lived on East 71st Street until 1930 when he separated from Mary Brandon.

15/Breakfast at Tiffanys

171 East 71st Street between Lexington and Third Avenue.

Truman Capote's popular 1958 novella *Breakfast at Tiffanys*—which tells the story of the charming and talented misfit **Holly Golightly** who comes to New York from Tulip, Texas—doesn't specifically state where her apartment was. The reader is only told that she lives in a brownstone near Third Avenue in the East 70s during the early years of World War II. But when director **Blake Edwards** made the movie version of *Breakfast* in 1961, starring **Audrey Hepburn** as **Holly,** he placed her apartment in this real-life townhouse at 171 East 71st Street, where the exteriors were filmed.

TOUR 7

1/Ethel Merman

20 East 76th Street between Fifth and Madison Avenue.

This residential hotel called the **Surrey** was the last home of the great musical comedy star. **Ethel Merman** entertained Broadway audiences for over fifty years, starring in one hit after another. Her career took off in 1930 when she brought down the house singing *I Got Rhythm* in the **George Gershwin** musical *Girl Crazy* at the Alvin Theater.

Her last major appearance in New York was in 1982 at a Carnegie Hall benefit concert. Merman underwent surgery to remove a brain tumor in 1983 and she died alone in her apartment here on February 15, 1984. She was seventy-six.

2/Irwin Piscator

17 East 76th Street between Fifth and Madison Avenue.

Irwin Piscator was the foremost experimental stage director of Berlin in the 1920s—he was as prominent a symbol of that city's avant-garde as Bertolt Brecht was. Piscator was a Marxist and fled Nazi Germany for New York in 1939, eventually settling in this four-story house.

During his twelve-year stay in America, he ran the **Dramatic Workshop** at the **New School** and taught such young actors as **Marlon Brando, Harry Belafonte, Tony Curtis, Shelly Winters,** and **Rod Steiger.** His uses of stage technology, his experiments with mime, and his adaption of the documentary and

Franklin & Eleanor Roosevelt

propaganda as dramatic tools became part of the modern theater of the twentieth century.

Piscator abruptly left the United States for Europe in 1951 after being subpoenaed to appear before the House Un-American Activities Committee.

3/Franklin and Eleanor Roosevelt

6 and 8 East 76th Street near Fifth Avenue.

The wedding of **Franklin** and **Eleanor Roosevelt** took place in these adjoining houses on March 17, 1905. Number 6 was the home of Eleanor's great aunt, **Mrs. Edward H. Ludlow** and the connected house at Number 8 belonged to Eleanor's cousin, **Susan Parish**.

Eleanor's uncle was **President Theodore Roosevelt**—fresh from his

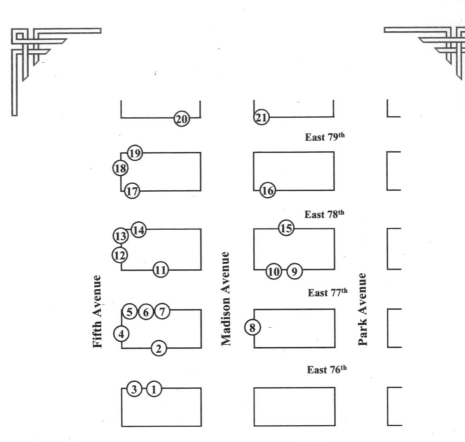

Upper East Side
Tour 7

1. Ethel Merman
2. Erwin Piscator
3. Franklin and Eleanor Roosevelt
4. Winston Churchill
5. Leo Castelli
6. Gloria Vanderbilt
7. Woody Allen
8. The Carlyle
9. Victor Herbert
10. "Three Days of the Condor" house
11. George Balanchine
12. Henry Luce
13. Lee Bouvier Radziwill
14. Woody Allen
15. Ozzie and Harriet
16. Cass Gilbert
17. Doris Duke
18. John Hay Whitney
19. Harry Sinclair
20. John O'Hara
21. Emily Post

inauguration two weeks earlier, he came to New York to give the bride away. Many of the guests had difficulty reaching the house on time that day because of a large parade on Fifth Avenue that blocked the streets.

The actual wedding ceremony took place in the Ludlow house where an altar had been arranged in front of a fireplace. At the reception following, most of the guests were more interested in seeing and hearing the President and soon the young couple was left standing alone. That night they took the train to Hyde Park where they began their honeymoon.

4/Winston Churchill
Fifth Avenue between 76th and 77th Streets.

On the evening of December 12, 1931, an accident took place on the street here that almost changed the course of world history.

Winston Churchill, age fifty-seven, was visiting New York as part of a U.S. lecture tour and on that night he was in a taxi on Fifth Avenue, trying to find the home of **Bernard Baruch,** where he had been invited for dinner.

Churchill emerged from the cab on the Central Park side of Fifth Avenue and, turning to cross in the middle of the street, looked the wrong way. He was hit by a car going thirty miles per hour driven by an unemployed mechanic named **Mario Constasino**.

Churchill, though conscious, was severely injured, suffering a scalp cut and two cracked ribs. He was taken to Lenox Hill hospital where he recovered after a few days. Constasino came to the hospital to

apologize and the two became friendly. Churchill gave the mechanic a copy of his latest book *The Unknown War.*

5/Leo Castelli
4 East 77th Street at Fifth Avenue.

Art dealer **Leo Castelli,** who moved to New York from Paris in 1941, lived for many years in this five-story, white stone house with his wife, **Ileana Schapira,** and his daughter, **Nina.**

In 1957, at age fifty, he opened his own art gallery in his fourth-floor apartment here and it soon became a center of the New York world of modern art in the 1960s and beyond. In the beginning, he used the walls of his living room to display his artists while turning his daughter's bedroom into an office. He gave **Jasper Johns, Frank Stella,** and **Roy Lichtenstein** their first one-man shows and brought attention to **Andy Warhol, Robert Rauschenberg, Richard Serra**, and others.

In 1971, Castelli moved his headquarters to 420 West Broadway in Soho, signaling the emergence of that neighborhood as Manhattan's new art center.

6/Gloria Vanderbilt
12 East 77th Street between Fifth and Madison Avenue.

This five-story brownstone was the home of **Reginald Claypoole Vanderbilt,** the playboy son of millionaire **Cornelius Vanderbilt II.** Reggie seemed to spend most of his waking hours drinking and gambling and by the time he proposed to his second wife, **Gloria Morgan**, he had blown most of his personal fortune.

They were married in 1923 and a year later their daughter, also named **Gloria**, was born. Reggie died of a hemorrhage related to alcoholism in 1925 and his wife soon discovered that her husband had died penniless, leaving the child with a $2.5 million trust fund and her with nothing but the ownership of this mansion on East 77th Street.

In 1934, Gloria Morgan lost custody of little Gloria to the young girl's aunt, **Gertrude Vanderbilt Whitney**, in a celebrated court battle.

7/Woody Allen
14 East 77th Street between Fifth and Madison Avenue.

This brownstone contained the studio apartment that **Woody Allen** lived in after his separation from his first wife, **Harlene**, in 1962. He moved here with his new girlfriend, actress **Louise Lasser**, who later became his second wife.

Allen was still doing stand-up comedy in those days at clubs like the **Blue Angel** and the **Americana Hotel's Royal Box** and he was establishing a reputation as the hottest comic in the country.

8/The Carlyle
Madison Avenue between 76th and 77 Street (east side).

The thirty-eight story **Carlyle** is one of New York's most famous and elegant residences. Built in the Art Deco style, it consists of a hotel with 190 guest rooms and suites for transients whose entrance is on Madison

Avenue, and an apartment tower above, with its entrance on the north side of the building at 50 East 77th Street.

The Carlyle gained national attention for the first time when **President Harry Truman** began to stay here on his New York visits and could be seen taking leisurely strolls in the neighborhood. His daughter **Margaret Truman** and her husband, *New York Times* editor **Clifton Daniel**, had a permanent home in the Carlyle.

President **John F. Kennedy** had a duplex apartment (Number 34A) in the Carlyle Apartments on the north side and made it his base whenever he stopped in New York. The hotel management catered to his every whim and had total respect for his privacy. Kennedy's friend, **Marilyn Monroe**, visited him here frequently after her breakup with **Arthur Miller**.

Even when the press was on watch downstairs, Secret Service men would accompany Kennedy on his private escape route, a series of tunnels that connected the Caryle with a number of nearby buildings (see this section, Tour 3, Number 21).

Composer **Richard Rodgers** and his wife, **Dorothy**, lived in a nine-room apartment in the Carlyle from 1931 until 1945. They moved here soon after the birth of their daughter **Mary**. While he lived here, Rodgers and his lyricist partner **Lorenz Hart** teamed up to write the music for such shows as *Jumbo, The Boys From Syracuse, By Jupiter,* and *Pal Joey.* After Rodgers and Hart split up, Rodgers worked here in collaboration with **Oscar Hammerstein II** on the score for the ground-breaking show *Oklahoma!* which opened in 1943.

Daughter Mary remembered her father composing at his piano in their apartment during those years: "The sound was the pleasantest thing in my childhood," she said. "Daddy wrote at home with the door open— he didn't care who heard as long as someone wasn't going by singing or disturbing him in some way or other."

Ring Lardner

Writer **Ring Lardner** lived at the Carlyle briefly in the 1930s, not long before his death. Playwright **Robert Sherwood** and businessman **Henry Ford II** were also former residents.

9/Victor Herbert
57 East 77th Street between Madison and Park Avenue.

Victor Herbert was America's first significant composer for the popular musical theater and was known for

writing such operettas as *Babes in Toyland* and *Naughty Marietta*.

By 1924, his popularity was in decline. One day in May of that year, he came to this building to visit his doctor; he had become ill after having lunch with friends at the **Lambs Club**. When Herbert discovered that the physician was not in his office, he decided to take a walk around the block and return later. Instead, he collapsed on the stairs and died instantly of a heart attack. He was sixty-four years old.

This building, erected in 1877 when most of this block was developed, has undergone recent renovations to its façade.

10/"Three Days of the Condor" House
55 East 77th Street between Madison and Park Avenue.

Fans of the 1975 film thriller *Three Days of the Condor* may recognize this Beaux-Arts style town house. It was used as the location of the **"American Literary Historical Society"**—really a front organization for a CIA operation where the character played by **Robert Redford** is employed.

Early in the movie, while Redford is out getting lunch, six of his colleagues are assassinated in the building by a renegade branch of the CIA. He returns to find their bodies scattered on two floors of the house.

In the 1930s, in real life, this building was the residence of the German consul-general to the U.S. who represented the Nazi government. In 2004, 55 East 77th Street was completely renovated by its current owners.

11/George Balanchine

11 East 77th Street near Fifth Avenue.

In 1938, the choreographer and artistic director of the **New York City Ballet** moved into this beautiful narrow brownstone with the walk-down entrance. He had recently married his second wife, dancer **Vera Zorina.**

George Balanchine lived here until his third marriage to **Maria Tall-chief,** also a ballerina. Soon after their wedding in 1946, the couple began a long performance tour of Europe and had to give up their apartment here on 77th Street. During his residence in this house, he staged the dances for such Broadway musicals as *Cabin in the Sky, Babes in Arms,* and *Where's Charley?*

12/Henry Luce and Clare Boothe Luce

960 Fifth Avenue between 77th and 78th Street.

This luxury apartment house, built in 1929 by famed architect **Rosario Candela,** was the last New York home of *Time* magazine publisher **Henry Luce.** He moved here in the 1960s with his wife, **Clare Boothe.** By 1967, his health had deteriorated but he continued to maintain a vigorous schedule. He could often be seen taking long walks in Central Park across the street from his home. Luce died at his western home in Phoenix, Arizona on March 1, 1967 at the age of sixty-eight.

960 Fifth Avenue was also the residence of **Claus Von Bulow,** who was convicted of the attempted murder of his wealthy wife in 1982 and then found innocent in a later trial.

13/Lee Bouvier Radziwill

969 Fifth Avenue at 78th Street (southeast corner).

Lee Bouvier, sister of **Jacqueline Kennedy Onassis,** married Polish aristocrat, **Stanislaus Radziwill** in 1959 and, soon after, they moved into an eleven-room duplex in this sixteen-story cooperative building.

In May 1965, Lee threw a party here for her sister who was slowly coming out of seclusion following the assassination of her husband **John Kennedy** in 1963. "It was a teeny, tiny dance for less than a thousand," said Bouvier of the event. The guests included **Mike Nichols, Leonard Bernstein, Robert Kennedy, John Kenneth Galbraith, Pierre Salinger,** and **Franklin Delano Roosevelt Jr.**

Lee and her husband lived in the building together until their divorce in 1974; she gained possession of the apartment in the settlement and continued to live here until 1979 when money problems forced her to sell the place and move to smaller quarters at 875 Park Avenue (see this section, Tour 9, Number 2).

14/Woody Allen

4 East 78th Street at Fifth Avenue.

Woody Allen was a young comedy writer in 1959 when he rented an apartment in this five-story brownstone with his first wife, **Harlene Rosen.** She was a student at Hunter College near here and he was busy peddling his jokes to various television artists. Allen was living here when he was hired to write for some of **Sid Caesar's** comedy shows and joined the legendary team of writers that included **Mel Brooks, Carl Reiner, Neil Simon,** and **Larry Gelbart.**

Allen lived in this house until 1961 when he met actress **Louise Lasser** and separated from his wife. He moved a block away to 14 East 77th Street (see number 7 above).

15/Ozzie and Harriet

50 East 78th Street between Madison and Park Avenue.

Ozzie Nelson, then the leader of a popular band, married singer **Harriet Hilliard** in 1935 in New Jersey. They lived in an apartment in this building for two years, starting in 1936.

Their oldest son, **David,** was born while they resided at this address. The Nelsons moved to Los Angeles in 1941 and soon began a family radio show. By the early 1950s, they had switched to television and their show, *Ozzie and Harriet,* which featured David and their youngest son **Ricky,** became one of America's most popular programs.

16/Cass Gilbert

45 East 78th Street near Madison Avenue.

Architect **Cass Gilbert** came to New York from St. Paul, Minnesota in 1900, not long after he had completed the design of the new **Minnesota State Capitol Building.** After living briefly on Central Park West, he moved to this four-story red brick house where he resided until 1913 with his wife, four children, and four servants.

During those years, he designed two of his most notable buildings:the **U.S. Customs House** facing Bowling Green at the foot of Broadway, and the **Woolworth Building** at 233 Broadway. In 1913, Gilbert moved to 42 East 64th Street (see this section, Tour 1, Number 19).

17/Doris Duke

1 East 78th Street at Fifth Avenue (northeast corner).

James B. Duke, millionaire founder of the **American Tobacco Company,** built this fifty-four room, three-story limestone mansion in 1912 at a cost of one million dollars. The architect for the building was **Horace Trumbauer.** Duke's only child, **Doris,** was born in that same year and when her father died in 1925, she inherited $50 million, mostly in trust funds, mak-

James B. Duke

ing her perhaps the richest teenager in the world. She lived here with her mother and fourteen servants and sometimes laughingly referred to the house as "the rock pile."

At age twenty-one, Doris received a third of her trust and then, against her mother's wishes, she married a man sixteen years older than she. It was the first of two marriages—both ended in divorce. After her separation from her second husband, playboy **Porfirio Rubirosa**, in 1948, she remained single for the rest of her life.

When she died in 1993 at the age of eighty in Beverly Hills, she had only servants at her bedside. Doris Duke's mother continued to live in the mansion here on 78th Street until 1957, when she donated it to the **Fine Arts Institute of New York University.**

18/John Hay Whitney
972 Fifth Avenue between 78th and 79th Street.

This mansion, built for **Payne Whitney** in 1909 by architect **Stanford White**, was the New York home of millionaire socialite **John Hay Whitney**, financier, philanthropist, sportsman, and ambassador, and the grandson of **John Hay,** who was **Abraham Lincoln's** private secretary.

Whitney was also the last owner and publisher of the *New York Herald Tribune*, one of the city's greatest newspapers. He purchased it in 1958 and controlled it until 1966, when it ran into insurmountable financial troubles and had to close down. It was one of Whitney's few public failures.

Two of his most notable investments were in show business: he financed the play *Life with Father,* which set records on Broadway for longevity and he was responsible for bringing to the screen *Gone With the Wind* in collaboration with David Selznick. One scene in the movie was shot on the staircase here at Whitney's house on Fifth Avenue.

Whitney was a major promoter of **Dwight Eisenhower** for president in 1952 and he served as Ike's ambassador to Great Britain.

He died in 1982. His house is now the **Cultural Service of the Embassy of France.**

19/Harry Sinclair
2 East 79th Street near Fifth Avenue.

Harry Sinclair was one of the richest and most powerful corporate entrepreneurs of the last century; in 1916 he created the **Sinclair Oil Company,** which became one of the giants of the petroleum industry. Sinclair lived here at 2 East 79th Street from 1920 to 1930.

It was during that period that he became a major figure in the **Teapot Dome** scandal of the Harding administration in which he was accused by Federal authorities of bribing U.S. Secretary of the Interior **Albert Fall** to receive favored treatment in the leasing of government oil properties. Although Sinclair was never found guilty of the original charges, he served seven months in prison for contempt of Congress and contempt of court.

Sinclair sold his house here to a descendant of **Peter Stuyvesant** in 1930; the new owner, **Augustus Van**

Horne Stuyvesant, Jr., a bachelor and recluse, lived here alone with a butler and footman until 1953. The building became the home of the **Ukranian Institute** in 1955.

20/John O'Hara

27 East 79th Street between Fifth and Madison Avenue.

Author **John O'Hara,** with his wife, **Belle,** took an apartment in this building in 1944. The flat, on the ground floor, had a dark interior but Belle cheered it up with posters, bright cushions, and modern furniture.

O'Hara, who had just turned forty, had finally achieved celebrity status when a series of his *New Yorker* short stories were turned into a successful Broadway play called *Pal Joey.*

But since the beginning of the war, he had difficulty writing and produced only a few stories while he lived here. In his frustration, he began to drink heavily.

The O'Haras moved uptown to a place on East 86th Street in 1946 (see this section, Tour 13, Number 12).

21/Emily Post

39 East 79th Street at Madison Avenue (northeast corner).

The "First Lady of Etiquette" lived in this red brick apartment building for thirty-five years.

Emily Post, who wrote the bible on good manners—the first edition was published in 1922—decided in 1925 to build her own co-op building after finding all of the apartments in New York inadequate to her needs for superior light, space, and design.

She organized a circle of friends (including **Mrs. Stanford White** and **Mrs. James Roosevelt**) who jointly erected the building here and ran it as one of the dozen or so tenant-sponsored cooperatives in New York's history.

Post, who was the daughter of architect **Bruce Price**, may have helped her architect **Kenneth Murchison** to design it.

Post had been a forty-eight-year-old novelist in the early 1920s when she was recruited to write her book *Etiquette.* It became an instant best-seller and its popularity has continued to this day.

Post spent her days in her apartment writing her syndicated newspaper column, answering letters (up to 6,000 a week), and revising her book.

During the 1930s, she was one of the first women in broadcasting—her weekly radio show reached millions of people.

She died of pneumonia in her bedroom here on September 25, 1960 at the age of eighty-six. Post's apartment with its two-story living room went on the market in 1989 for $2.9 million.

Upper East Side
Tour 8

1. Thomas Dewey
2. John Steinbeck
3. Elia Kazan
4. Helen Hanff
5. Ethel Barrymore
6. Diane Arbus
7. Frank Sinatra
8. George Plimpton
9. Richard Avedon
10. Joe Namath
11. Andy Warhol
12. Lotte Lenya
13. James Farrell
14. Elia Kazan
15. Henry Fonda and Yul Brynner
16. Ogden Nash

Hudson River

York Avenue

First Avenue

Second Avenue

Third Avenue

Lexington Avenue

East 76th

East 75th

East 74th

East 73rd

East 72nd

TOUR 8

1/Thomas Dewey
141 East 72nd Street at Lexington Avenue (northeast corner).

Thomas Dewey, who served as governor of New York for three terms, and ran twice unsuccessfully for U.S. President, lived in this fifteen-story building from 1955 until his death in 1971. Dewey moved to 141 East 72nd Street with his wife, **Frances Hutt,** shortly after serving his last term as governor. He first lost to **Franklin Roosevelt** in the national election of 1944. In 1948, he was the overwhelming favorite to beat **Harry Truman** but lost in the greatest upset in presidential election history.

After leaving politics, Dewey became senior member of a law firm with offices on lower Broadway and began a lucrative new career as a private attorney. His wife died in July 1970, just eight months before Dewey himself passed away at the age of sixty-eight at a resort in Bal Harbor, Florida.

2/John Steinbeck
206 East 72nd Street between Second and Third Avenue.

John Steinbeck lived in a brownstone on this site where the **Wellesley** now stands from 1951 until his death in 1968. He wrote his 1952 novel *East of Eden* while he lived here; his friend and neighbor **Elia Kazan** (see number 3 below) turned it into a movie starring **James Dean** in 1955. In the 1960s, Steinbeck could often be seen by neigh-bors walking his dog, **Charley,** along 72nd Street to Central Park. The author traveled around the country with his pet—one trip inspired his 1966 book *Travels With Charley.*

Steinbeck also wrote *Winter of Our Discontent* while living on this block and, in 1962, he won the Nobel Prize.

Steinbeck acknowledged the difficulty of living in New York City with its many flaws but, he said, "there is one thing about it—once you have lived in New York and it has become your home, no place else is good enough."

3/Elia Kazan
212 East 72nd Street between Second and Third Avenue.

Elia Kazan, one of the few people to gain fame as a director of both stage and screen, lived in this four-level town house from 1955 until the early 1960s with his first wife, **Molly.** The place was close to his friend **John Steinbeck's** house at 206 East 72nd Street (number 2 above).

Kazan moved here soon after he had won the Academy Award for his film *On the Waterfront* with **Marlon Brando.** It was three years after he had testified and "named names" before the House Un-American Activities Committee.

While he lived in this neighborhood, Kazan directed *Cat on a Hot Tin Roof* and *Dark at the Top of the Stairs* for the stage and *Baby Doll, A Face in the Crowd,* and *Splendor in the Grass* for the movies.

4/Helene Hanff

305 East 72nd Street at Second Avenue (northeast corner).

Writer **Helene Hanff** is remembered as the author of the popular 1970 memoir *84, Charing Cross Road*, a record of a twenty-year correspondence with a London bookseller she never met.

Hanff lived in a studio apartment in this seventeen-story building. She began ordering books by mail from **Marks & Company** in 1949 and soon was exchanging friendly letters with the store's chief buyer, **Frank Doel.** When the correspondence was published, the book brought Hanff, an unheralded writer, undreamed-of attention. It was made into a hit play performed both in Britain and America. It became a film in 1987. One wall of Hanff's apartment here was filled from floor to ceiling with her beloved books ordered from Marks & Company.

But Hanff's book never gave her total financial security. In her last years, she eeked out a living on royalties and Social Security checks. When she became ill, a $5,000 grant from the Authors League Fund helped pay her hospital bills.

She died in New York in April 1997 at the age of eighty. In her memory, this building was named **Charing Cross House** (see plaque at the building's front).

5/Ethel Barrymore

320 East 72nd Street between First and Second Avenue.

The actress was sixty-one years old in 1940 when she began performing

Ethel Barrymore

in one of her most successful roles on the stage in *The Corn is Green*. During this period, **Barrymore** lived in an apartment in this large brown brick building.

She gave 475 performances on Broadway in the play before touring nationwide with it for more than two years. Barrymore retired from stage acting in 1946 after fifty-one years and moved to Hollywood to make movies.

6/Diane Arbus

319 East 72nd Street between First and Second Avenue.

Photographer **Diane Arbus** lived in a triplex on this site with her husband, **Allen,** from 1954 to 1958. It was the same apartment that sculptor **Paul Manship** had once occupied and the Arbuses used it as both their studio and residence.

Their living room was two stories high with white walls and very little furniture.One end was crammed with photographic equipment. During this period, the couple worked together as fashion photographers, doing covers and advertising layout for the magazines *Glamour, Vogue,* and *Seventeen.*

But by 1957, Diane had grown tired of doing fashion work and she began working independently, taking photos by herself as she walked the streets near their apartment.(The house at Number 319 was taken down not long after the Arbuses left, along with four adjoining ones, and replaced with the modern apartment house numbered 315 East 72nd Street.)

7/Frank Sinatra
540 East 72nd Street at the East River.

Frank Sinatra had a penthouse apartment in this white brick building on the East River in the 1950s and 60s. The place, tucked away in a cul-de-sac, is called the **Edgewater** and it's since been renumbered—it's now 530 East 72nd Street.

Singer **Eddie Fisher** had the penthouse next door to Sinatra. Sinatra's valet **George Jacobs** remembered the place for its good views and even better privacy. In the high-rise next door, said Jacobs, lived dozens of fancy call girls. Because of the dead-end location, limos could easily double-park while celebrities and politicians went inside to be serviced. Sinatra made this his New York home until he moved to a suite in the **Waldorf Astoria Towers** (see

Section Two, Tour 7, Number 14).

8/George Plimpton
541 East 72nd Street at the East River.

541 East 72nd Street was the home of writer **George Plimpton** for over forty years. The place was known as the liveliest literary salon in New York—home of what someone once called the *"Paris Review* Crowd." In collaboration with his friends **Harold Humes** and **Peter Mathiessen,** Plimpton launched the famous literary magazine in 1953 during a visit to Paris. As the first editor-in-chief, Plimpton guided its development as a journal dedicated to publishing talented and unknown writers. The magazine also began running long interviews with notable authors—the most famous was the one Plimpton conducted himself with **Ernest Hemingway** in 1959.

When he returned to the United States, Plimpton's bachelor apartment here on 72nd Street became a mecca for literary New York.He hosted hundreds of parties for thousands of guests, sometimes at a rate of one a week. On any night, one would find the likes of **Irwin Shaw, Norman Mailer, Philip Roth, Lillian Hellman, James Jones, William Styron, Truman Capote**, and, occasionally, Plimpton's friend, **Jackie Kennedy.**

While he lived here, Plimpton wrote his popular books about his personal involvement with professional athletes and teams: *Out of My League* in 1961, *Paper Lion* in 1966, and *The Bogey Man in 1968.* He died in his apartment on September 26,

2003 at the age of seventy-six.

9/Richard Avedon
407 East 75th Street between First and York Avenue.

Fashion and portrait photographer **Richard Avedon** lived and worked in this narrow four-story red brick townhouse for the last thirty-five years of his life. He lived on the top floor and in the studio below created some of the world's most famous photographs.

Beginning his career at *Harper's Bazaar* magazine in 1946, Avedon revolutionized fashion photography; later his portraits of the major newsmakers of the twentieth century gave him a high reputation in the art world as well. Although he traveled extensively, he spent much of his time here on 75th Street in his studio, where he could control the lighting and reactions of his famous subjects. Avedon died while on assignment in Texas in October 2004. He was eighty-one.

10/Joe Namath
370 East 76th Street near First Avenue.

Joe Namath, the star quarterback of the New York Jets, lived in this high-rise apartment building called **Newport East** beginning in 1966. He shared it with a friend and a teammate; the rent was $500 a month. Their exotically-furnished penthouse pad featured a large terrace with a view, a rooftop swimming pool, a bathroom with eighteen-carat-gold fixtures, and a llama-skin rug that was six inches deep.

Sammy Davis, Jr. was a neighbor in the building. It was in 1969 that Namath and the Jets shocked the sports world when they won Super Bowl III by beating the heavily-favored Baltimore Colts 16-7.

11/Andy Warhol
216 East 75th Street between Second and Third Avenue.

Andy Warhol rented an apartment here in the fall of 1952. It was a dirty cold-water basement flat under the tracks of the now-demolished Third Avenue elevated train.

Before long, Warhol's mother, **Julia**, moved in with him, sharing a bedroom in which they slept on mattresses on the floor. The kitchen table was the artist's work space. The apartment was infested with mice and, soon, the Warhols acquired a large collection of cats.

Warhol had recently experienced his first solo exhibition entitled *Fifteen Drawings Based on the Writings of Truman Capote* at the **Hugo Gallery** in the summer of 1952. The Warhols lived here until 1953.

12/Lotte Lenya
300 East 74th Street at Second Avenue (southeast corner).

Lotte Lenya, the legendary German singer and actress, moved to the apartment of her friend **Margo Harris** in this thirty-five-story high-rise in October 1981 after she was released from the hospital, dying of cancer.

Here, on the thirty-third floor, Harris installed a hospital bed for

Lenya in a small second bedroom that she normally used as her sculpture studio. At one point, Lenya's friend, Metropolitan Opera star **Teresa Stratas**, arrived and stayed for several weeks, sleeping on the floor next to the actress's bed. Lenya lingered for a month before passing away on November 27, 1981.She was eighty-three years old.

13/James T. Farrell
345 East 73rd Street between Second and First Avenue.

This large apartment building was the last home of **James T. Farrell**, whose three *Studs Lonigan* novels made him a dominant figure among realistic novelists of the Depression era. The Lonigan trilogy, published between 1932 and 1935, was a chronicle of Irish-American working class life on Chicago's South Side. Millions of copies of the books were sold and Farrell became world-famous.

His later work received little critical or commercial success but he continued to be productive in his final years. He moved to an apartment in this thirteen-story building in 1978 with his companion, **Cleo Paturis**. Farrell died in his bed here in the early morning of August 22, 1979. He was seventy-five years old.

14/Elia Kazan
167 East 74th Street between Lexington and Third Avenue.

Kazan, the director of stage and film, lived in this four-story brownstone house with his first wife, **Molly**, and their four children from

1945 until 1955. Elia Kazan's years here were perhaps the time of his highest achievement. He directed two of the greatest productions in Broadway's history—**Tennessee Williams's** *A Streetcar Named Desire* and **Arthur Miller's** *Death of a Salesman*. In Hollywood, he made the film version of *Streetcar* along with the movie *Viva Zapata!*, both starring **Marlon Brando**.

Kazan was also living here in 1952 when he testified before the House Un-American Activities Committee and "named names" of his former colleagues in the Communist Party.

15/Henry Fonda and Yul Brynner
151 East 74th Street between Lexington and Third Avenue.

Henry Fonda purchased this attractive four-story brick townhouse in 1950 when he married his second wife, **Susan Blanchard**. They lived here in the following decade with Fonda's children, thirteen-year-old **Jane** and ten-year-old **Peter**, both born to Fonda's first wife, **Frances Seymour Brokaw**.

After Fonda moved out, he rented this house to actor **Yul Brynner,** who lived here for many years. In the 1930s and 40s, baking millionaire **Raoul Fleischmann** lived in this house. Fleischmann is better known as the man who collaborated in 1925 with **Harold Ross** to create *The New Yorker* magazine.

16/Ogden Nash
149 East 73rd Street at Lexington Avenue (northeast corner).

Poet **Ogden Nash**, master of light

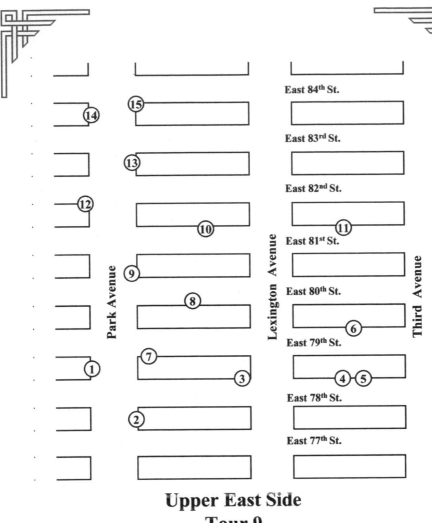

East 84th St.

East 83rd St.

East 82nd St.

East 81st St.

East 80th St.

East 79th St.

East 78th St.

East 77th St.

Park Avenue

Lexington Avenue

Third Avenue

Upper East Side
Tour 9

1. J.C. Penney and Edith Wharton
2. Fred Astaire
3. Irving Berlin
4. Brendan Gill
5. Minnie Marx
6. Groucho Marx
7. Leonard Bernstein
8. Raymond Massey

9. Katharine Hepburn
10. Jerome Robbins
11. Nathanael West
12. Joan and Constance Bennett
13. Madeline Kahn
14. Teilhard de Chardin
15. Marlene Dietrich

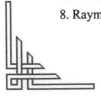

verse, lived in an apartment in this eleven-story tan brick building with his parents beginning in the late 1920s.

After he graduated from Harvard in 1921, he took a job with a publisher on Long Island and began sending his whimsical poems to editors and publishers around New York. He was living here while he courted his future wife, **Frances Leonard.** They were married in 1931—the same year that Nash rose to prominence with the appearance of his first book of verse *Hard Lines*.

When another book *Happy Days* was published in 1933 along with the offer of a long-term contract to write for *Saturday Evening Post*, Nash decided to become a full-time writer and the family—now with two young daughters—moved from New York to Baltimore where he was able to operate with far fewer expenses.

TOUR 9

1/J.C. Penney and Edith Wharton
888 Park Avenue at 78th Street (northwest corner).

James Cash Penney, founder of the chain of retail stores that bear his name, lived in this apartment house. It was built in 1926 to replace four Victorian row houses which had stood on this block since 1884. The houses were similar to the one still standing here at 890 Park. Penney lived to be ninety-five years old and died in 1971.

One of the demolished row houses mentioned above (numbered 884 Park) was the home of writer **Edith Wharton**, who lived there with her

Edith Wharton

husband, **Edward**, from 1885 to 1906. It was at that address that she wrote her first important novel, *The Greater Inclination*, in 1899. Her next novel, *The House of Mirth*, was published in 1905 and soon became the best selling book in New York. Wharton's friend, **Henry James**, came to her house here on New Year's, 1905, and stayed a number of weeks during one of the snowiest Manhattan winters in memory. The Whartons left 884 Park in 1906 to live in France.

2/Fred Astaire
875 Park Avenue between 77th and 78th Street.

Fred Astaire lived in this twelve-story brick building in the late 1920s and early 1930s. Still a bachelor, the dancer shared the penthouse apartment with his mother and his sister, dancing partner **Adele**. Although he

Irving Berlin

owned a $22,000 Rolls-Royce, he took a taxi to and from the theater every night, always with the same driver.

While they lived here, Fred and Adele starred in a Ziegfeld production called *Smiles* in 1930 (it was a flop) and then in *The Band Wagon*— a huge hit written by the **Gershwin** brothers. After this last show closed, Adele decided to drop out of show business and marry. Fred began a solo career by starring in **Cole Porter's** *Gay Divorce*. It would be his last Broadway show and, in it, he sang his trademark song *Night and Day*.

In 1930, Astaire was asked to help choreograph dance numbers for the new **George Gershwin** show *Girl Crazy*. One of the performers was the young **Ginger Rogers** and, during the run of the show, they occasionally dated. Soon after, they both moved

to Hollywood to begin movie careers and were reunited in the 1933 film *Flying Down to Rio* as dancing partners. It was the first of ten movies in which they would co-star.

From 1979 to 1983, 875 Park Avenue was also the home of **Lee Bouvier Radziwill,** sister of **Jacqueline Kennedy Onassis**.

3/Irving Berlin
129 East 78th Street near Lexington Avenue.

The songwriter lived in this attractive brown house in the mid-1940s. While he was here, **Berlin** wrote the revue *This is the Army* which featured one of his best-known songs, *Oh! How I Hate to Get Up in the Morning*. In 1943, he took the popular show to Europe where it played before both civilian and military audiences. Over two million people saw it somewhere in the world during its three-year run and it raised nearly $10 million for the Army. The show was later made into a movie.

After the war, Berlin returned to New York and wrote one of his greatest musicals *Annie Get your Gun*, starring **Ethel Merman,** which opened in 1946. In that same year, Berlin moved with his wife from this 78th Street apartment to 17 Beekman Place (see Section Two, Tour 5, Number 14).

4/Brendan Gill
157 East 78th Street between Lexington and Third Avenue.

This red brick townhouse was the home of versatile writer **Brendan Gill** from 1942 until the 1960s. He lived here with his wife, **Anne Barnard**, and their seven children. The house had six bedrooms and four bathrooms and when the Gills moved in, three of their children had been born.

Gill, who had started writing for *The New Yorker* in 1936, worked under the first four editors of the magazine and his literary range encompassed all forms—fiction, poetry, reporting, biography and social history as well as film, theater, and architecture criticism.

His home was the scene of many a party given for *New Yorker* colleagues; in his memoir about the magazine, Gill recalls a late-night lark as guests **Philip Hamburger** and cartoonist **Charles Addams** joined Gill on a tricycle race at top speed around the dining room table. The Gills moved to Bronxville, New York in the 1960s.

5/Minnie Marx

169 East 78th Street between Lexington and Third Avenue.

On September 13, 1929, the **Marx Brothers** family held their last reunion in this eight-story building.It took place in the apartment of **Herbert** (Zeppo), the youngest of the five boys, and all seven family members were present including the other four brothers, **Groucho, Chico, Harpo,** and **Gummo,** and the Marx parents, **Sam and Minnie.**

The comedy team had taken time off from their rehearsals for their upcoming Broadway show *Animal Crackers* to be here that night. After partaking in a merry, conversation-filled dinner prepared by Sam, they topped off the evening with a round-robin ping-pong match.

As the parents headed home, driving across the Queensboro Bridge, Minnie suffered a stroke and was quickly returned to Zeppo's apartment. She died here an hour later, in Zeppo's arms. Minnie, the driving force behind the Marx Brothers' act, who pushed the boys into show business and nurtured their success in the early years, was sixty-five years old.

A few weeks later, after *Animal Crackers* had opened to acclaim, the stock market collapsed and most of the brothers' assets were wiped out. But their popularity assured them of continuing lucrative work and they survived the crisis, eventually becoming one of the most popular attractions in 1930s motion pictures.

Note: There has been some dispute about the birthplace of **Groucho Marx**. One of his biographers, **Hector Arce**, says that birth records show Groucho's birth at 239 East 114th Street. However, in interviews later in his life, Groucho gave his birthplace as "East 78th Street between Lexington and Third," where his brother was living on the night of their mother's death.

6/Groucho Marx

161 East 79th Street between Lexington and Third Avenue.

Groucho, with his first wife, **Ruth**, and young son, **Arthur**, rented an apartment in this twelve-story brick building in 1921. Groucho and his three brothers were still traveling the country in vaudeville and he had, by then, developed all the trademarks for which he would become famous

—the cigar, the grease-paint mustache, the funny walk.

In 1922, the Marx Brothers' stage act hit a low point and no one would hire them. Then, Chico made a deal for the team with producer **Joseph Gaites** to perform in a revue called *I'll Say She Is,* which opened in New York in 1923 to rave reviews. The show became a huge success and launched the Brothers' legendary career on Broadway. Later they became even more successful in the movies. Groucho lived here on 79th Street until 1924 when the family moved to an apartment on Riverside Drive.

7/Leonard Bernstein
895 Park Avenue at 79th Street (southeast corner).

Leonard Bernstein, with his wife, **Felicia**, and their two children, moved to a fifteen-room duplex at the top of this apartment building in 1961. His position as the head of the **New York Philharmonic** had made him one of the most famous men in town by then and this residence reflected his status.

The lower floor had the family bedrooms and servants' living quarters. The penthouse floor, where they entertained, had a library, large dining room, and a reception room equipped with two grand pianos and a harpsicord. It was here that the Bernsteins hosted their infamous fund-raising party for the **Black Panthers** in 1970, setting off a media furor and attracting the intense interest of the FBI. **Tom Wolfe** immortalized the event in his essay *Radical Chic*. Leonard Bernstein lived here at 895 Park for thirteen years, until 1974 when he moved across Central Park to the **Dakota** on West 72nd Street.

8/Raymond Massey
132 East 80th Street between Park and Lexington Avenue.

The well-known stage, screen, and television actor lived in this four-level red brick town house from the late 1930s until the 1950s. **Raymond Massey's** portrayal of **Abraham Lincoln** in **Robert Sherwood's** play *Abe Lincoln in Illinois* had made him famous after it opened on Broadway in 1939.

During his career, he appeared in more than sixty films and then gained new popularity in his role as **"Dr. Gillespie"** in the long-running television series *Dr. Kildare.*

Massey had rich neighbors when he lived on this block. Millionaire **Vincent Astor** built the house next door at 130 East 80th in 1927. He inherited his fortune of $87 million in 1912 when his father, **Colonel John Jacob Astor**, died on the *Titanic*. The house at 124 East 80th was owned by **Clarence Dillon**, who gained control of the Dodge automobile company in 1925 and then arranged its merger with Chrysler, making Chrysler-Dodge one of the Big Three car makers.

9/Katharine Hepburn
925 Park Avenue at 80th Street (northeast corner).

After her graduation from Bryn Mawr College in 1928, **Hepburn** came to New York to pursue an acting career. In that year, for a number of months, she lived in an apartment in this building. It was the family residence of a college friend named **Megs Merrill**.

While Hepburn stayed here, she got her first role in a play called *The Big Pond* but was fired after one performance. She also started a serious relationship with a college friend named **Ludlow Ogden Smith**. After the two were married in December 1928, she moved with him to an apartment at 146 East 39th Street (see Section Three, Tour 1, Number 4).

10/Jerome Robbins
117 East 81st Street between Park and Lexington Avenue.

Jerome Robbins, one of the world's greatest choreographers, occupied this four-story townhouse during the last three decades of his life. He worked in both the world of ballet and the Broadway musical, crossing over from his work with the **New York City Ballet** to create the dances for such popular musicals as *The King and I, West Side Story,* and *Fiddler on the Roof.*

Robbins bought this place on 81st Street at a bargain price in 1965 and spent months renovating it before he moved in, installing both a dance studio and a photographic darkroom. After his death, the house sold for approximately three million dollars. Robbins passed away here on July 29, 1998 after suffering a stroke four days earlier. He was seventy-nine years old.

11/Nathanael West
151 East 81st Street between Lexington and Third Avenue.

The author of the novels *Miss Lonelyhearts* and *The Day of the Locust* was born in this seven-story apartment house called **The Guilford** on October 17, 1903. **West**, whose real name was **Nathan Weinstein**, was the son of **Max Weinstein**, a builder of luxury homes in Manhattan. Nathanael West lived here for the first five years of his life until the family moved to the Upper West Side.

12/Joan and Constance Bennett
950 Park Avenue at 82nd Street (southwest corner).

The **Bennett** family, all actors, lived in an apartment in this building in the 1920s. **Richard Bennett** was one of America's greatest stage performers in the early twentieth century. His wife was actress **Adrienne Morrison** and their three daughters, **Constance, Joan,** and **Barbara**, all followed their parents into show business.

By 1922, at age eighteen, Constance had already made three silent films; she went to Hollywood to become one of its most popular stars of the 1930s. Joan, five years younger, ran away with the son of a millionaire at age sixteen and was a mother at seventeen. She began making movies in 1929 and her career lasted into the 1970s. Barbara Bennett, the youngest of the thespian clan, had a brief career as an actress but never matched the fame of her older sisters.

Silent screen actress **Louise Brooks** was a young dancer in New York in the early 1920s when she befriended Barbara. In her memoirs, Brooks remembered her visits to the colorful Bennett household in this Park Avenue building, where she soon became an unofficial member of the family.

13/Madeline Kahn
975 Park Avenue between 82nd and 83rd Street.

This building was the home of actress/comedian **Madeline Kahn.** Perhaps her most remembered role was as Wild West saloon singer **Lili von Shtupp** in the 1974 **Mel Brooks** film *Blazing Saddles.* Her portrayal of a Germanic femme fatale was a burlesque of **Marlene Dietrich** and the performance earned her an Academy Award nomination.

Ironically, Dietrich lived in Manhattan only one block away from Kahn (see number 15 below). Kahn died of ovarian cancer in December 1999 at age fifty-seven.

14/Teilhard de Chardin
980 Park Avenue between 83rd and 84th Street.

The controversial Jesuit philosopher whose attempts to fuse evolutionary theory with Christian doctrine brought him criticism from his Roman Catholic Church lived in the rectory of this **St. Ignatius Loyola Church** from 1951 to 1954.

Teilhard was forced to vacate the premises when the church made plans to remodel the rectory; he moved to the **Hotel Fourteen** on 14 East 60th Street, his last New York address. He died in April 1955 at the home of a friend (see this section, Tour 1, Number 1).

15/Marlene Dietrich
993 Park Avenue at 84th Street (southeast corner).

Actress **Marlene Dietrich** purchased a four-room penthouse (No. 12E) in this building in 1959. The actress used the place as a pied-a-terre. Her living room held a grand piano and a personal art collection that included works by Chagall, Cezanne, and Picasso. In the corner stood a French Provincial writing desk—a gift from **Ernest Hemingway**—decorated with personal notes from such famous friends as **Orson Welles, Noel Coward,** and **Edward R. Murrow.**

Dietrich also possessed a large collection of ashtrays which she had lifted from the best hotels in the world. According to her daughter, all of the mirrors in the apartment were smoked because, as she aged, the actress never wanted to see her accurate reflection during the course of the day.

Dietrich abandoned this apartment in 1978 and made her main home in Paris. Following her death in 1992, the place remained untouched until her heirs sold it in 1997 for close to the asking price of $625,000. After extensive renovations, it was put on sale again in 2002 for $1.895 million.

TOUR 10

1/Grace Kelly
988 Fifth Avenue at 80th Street (southeast corner).

In 1954, **Grace Kelly** acquired an elegant, high-ceilinged apartment in this thirteen-story building designed by architect **James Carpenter**, across from the **Metropolitan Museum of Art**. She moved here soon after she had won the Academy Award as best actress for *The Country Girl*. Kelly hired a decorator who specialized in the French antique style and furnished the place with faded silk rugs, polished Louis XV pieces, and old-looking curtains to give it the appearance of haze and duskiness.

Kelly didn't live in the place for long; she met **Prince Rainier** of Monaco in December 1955 and married him four months later. This was her last New York apartment.

2/Arthur Hays Sulzberger
5 East 80th Street near Fifth Avenue.

Sulzberger was the publisher of the *New York Times* for more than twenty-five years, becoming the newspaper's chief in 1935, after the death of his father-in-law **Adolph Ochs**, who had been the owner since 1896.

Sulzberger moved into this four-story townhouse with his wife, **Iphigene**, and four children in 1928. The residence, which had been previously owned by a member of the Rothschild family, was purchased by **Adolph Ochs** as a gift (for $80,000) to his daughter and his new son-in-law. Sulzberger remained the *Times*

publisher until 1961 when he turned the position over to his son, **Arthur Ochs Sulzberger.**

3/Frank Woolworth and Barbara Hutton
990 Fifth Avenue at 80th Street (northeast corner).

The mansion of dime-store millionaire **Frank Woolworth** once stood on this site He lived in the four-story, thirty-six-room house from 1901 until his death in 1919. Woolworth also purchased four old houses on the south side of East 80th Street between Fifth and Madison, just across the street from his house, demolished them, and built four residences—one was used to house Woolworth's servants and he gave the other three to his daughters as wedding gifts. The home at 2 East 80th Street was given to his daughter, **Edna**, who married **Franklyn Hutton** in 1907. Their child, **Barbara Hutton**, born in 1912, was raised in this house during the first five years of her life.

When Frank Woolworth moved to 990 Fifth Avenue, his business empire was just beginning to grow; by 1912, he had 596 stores and his company was the world's largest merchandising operation. A year later, his **Woolworth Building** at 233 Broadway opened; it was the tallest building in the world and he paid for it out of his own pocket.

Woolworth's young granddaughter, **Barbara**, lived with him in his Fifth Avenue mansion for a time after her mother committed suicide by taking strychnine in her suite at the **Plaza Hotel** in 1917. When Barbara came

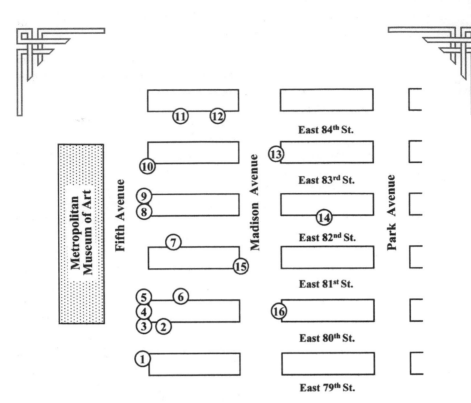

Upper East Side
Tour 10

1. Grace Kelly	9. Stella Adler
2. Arthur Hays Sulzberger	10. Barbara Hutton
3. Frank Woolworth and Barbara Hutton	11. August Belmont
	12. Ogden Mills Reid
4. George M. Cohan	13. Alfred Stieglitz
5. Charlie Parker	14. Lillian Hellman
6. W. Averell Harriman	15. Frank Campbell Funeral Home
7. Louise Bryant	16. Wanda Gag
8. Wendell Willkie	

into her inheritance at age twenty-one, her estimated worth—at the beginning of the Depression—was in excess of fifty million dollars.

The Woolworth residence here was sold by the family in the early 20s and later demolished to make room for the elegant limestone apartment house designed by **Rosario Candela** that stands on this corner today. In 1964, **Patricia Lawford Kennedy**, after separating from her husband, actor **Peter Lawford**, purchased an apartment here for $250,000.Her place featured five master bedrooms, a library, a huge dining room, and three servant's rooms.

4/George M. Cohan
993 Fifth Avenue between 80th and 81st Street.

The legendary song-and-dance man of Broadway lived in an apartment in this building during the final years of his life. **George M. Cohan**, who is remembered for such songs as *Over There, I'm a Yankee Doodle Dandy,* and *Give My Regards to Broadway*, moved here in the 1930s.

He had undergone intestinal surgery in 1941 and his weakened condition had prevented him from performing his daily routine as an air raid warden. But he could often still be seen walking the paths of Central Park, talking with people and feeding the pigeons. Cohan died of cancer in his bedroom here on November 5, 1942. He was sixty-four.

5/Charlie "Bird" Parker
995 Fifth Avenue at 81st Street (southeast corner).

George M. Cohan

The elegant **Stanhope Hotel**, designed by architect **Rosario Candela** and standing across from the **Metropolitan Museum of Art**, will always be identified with one of America's greatest musicians: jazz saxophonist **Charlie Parker**. He died here on the night of March 12, 1955.

Parker had stopped at the Stanhope three days earlier to visit his friend, **Baroness Pannonica de Koenigswarter,** who had a permanent suite at the hotel. She was a wealthy supporter of music and musicians who drove herself to jazz clubs in a silver Rolls Royce.Her apartment in the Stanhope had become a crash pad for many jazz musicians. Parker was clearly ill when he arrived that March night, vomiting blood, and when he refused to be hospitalized, the Baroness agreed to take care of him. Parker was watching television on the couch when he collapsed and died. The official cause was pneumonia, complicated by cirrhosis of the liver. He was only thirty-four years old.

Princess Grace and **Prince Rainier** of Monaco usually made the Stanhope their home when they visited New York in the 1950s and 60s.

The Stanhope closed in 2005 to be converted into condominiums.

6/W. Averell Harriman
16 East 81st Street between Fifth and Madison Avenue.

Averell Harriman was serving as Secretary of Commerce in **President Truman's** cabinet in 1948 when he purchased this three-level townhouse in anticipation of his return to private life. He had been serving in the federal government since the beginning of World War II. Harriman, a Democrat, continued to act as Truman's advisor until **Dwight Eisenhower** became president in 1953 and, during that time, this house functioned as his New York headquarters, presided over by his wife, **Marie**.

He was living here on 81st Street when he won the state's governorship in 1954 and was still here in 1958 when he lost the same office to **Nelson Rockefeller.**

Marie died in 1970 and Harriman married his third wife, **Pamela Churchill**, the following year. But by then, he found this house gloomy and too full of memories and he sold it in 1972.

7/Louise Bryant
12 East 82nd Street between Fifth and Madison Avenue.

Louise Bryant, the former wife and partner of radical journalist **John Reed** occupied this attractive red brick house for a year, beginning in the fall of 1927. She lived here with her second husband, wealthy diplomat **William Bullitt,** whom she married in 1923, three years after Reed died of typhus in Russia.

Bryant and Bullitt split their time between France and the U.S. after the birth of their daughter, **Anne**, in 1924, making this place on 82nd Street their New York headquarters. But the marriage didn't last and after the couple separated, Louise's life took a downward spiral.She ultimately settled in France and died alone, almost penniless, in a seedy Paris hotel in 1936.

8/Wendell Willkie
1010 Fifth Avenue at 82nd Street (northeast corner).

Wendell Willkie lived in an apartment here for the last fifteen years of his life. The building is directly across from the **Metropolitan Museum of Art** and was designed and built by **Fred F. French.**

This was Willke's home in 1940 when he won the Republican Party nomination for president and lost a close election to incumbent **Franklin Delano Roosevelt.** He continued to be influential in Republican Party affairs; his book *One World,* published in 1943, sold over a million copies.

In September 1944, he entered a

New York hospital with a stomach disorder. A month later, shortly before he was to be discharged, he died of a heart attack. Willke was only fifty-two years old.

In the days after his death, as his wife mourned, thousands of telegrams and letters of sympathy, as well as phone calls, flowed into the Willke home here.

9/Stella Adler
1016 Fifth Avenue at 83rd Street (southeast corner).

Acting teacher **Stella Adler**, who for over a half-century taught an impressive list of America's greatest performers — including **Marlon Brando, Robert DeNiro, Ellen Burstyn, and Warren Beatty** — made this building her home for many years, up to her death.

She had a spacious apartment decorated in the Italian Renaissance style, furnished with antique sofas and chairs and classic paintings in ornate frames.

Adler was born near the turn of the last century into a celebrated acting family rooted in the Yiddish theater; her father was the legendary actor, **Jacob Adler**. Stella joined the **Group Theater** in the 1930s and then studied drama in Russia with the great teacher **Stanislavsky**, bringing back to the United States her interpretation of his "Method" technique of acting which eventually revolutionized American theater.

Adler was teaching right up to the time of her death, at age ninety-two, in 1992.

10/Barbara Hutton
1020 Fifth Avenue at 83rd Street (northeast corner).

In 1926, **Barbara Hutton,** known as one of the "poor little rich girls," was fourteen years old. In that year, her father, **Franklyn**, placed 50,000 shares of the girl's Woolworth Company stock for sale on the market— dimestore millionaire **Frank Woolworth** had been Barbara's grandfather. The transaction netted the young heiress ten million dollars and her father used the windfall to purchase two adjoining duplex apartments in this fourteen-story luxury building.

It was decided that Barbara would occupy her own expansive place while Franklyn and his wife (Barbara's stepmother) would take the other. Barbara's duplex cost $90,000 to purchase and $250,000 to renovate. She continued to own it into the 1930s.

The top triplex at 1020 Fifth was once owned by the **Kress** family who also made their fortune in discount retailing. **Samuel Kress** owned the largest collection of Italian Renaissance paintings ever assembled by an American and kept the items in his apartment here. Later they were donated to more than twenty American museums.

11/August Belmont
9 East 84th Street between Fifth and Madison Avenue.

This was the one-time home of **August Belmont, Jr.**, a prominent New York financier in the late nineteen and early twentieth century.

Belmont gained fame for being the creator of the **Belmont Park** racing track on Long Island but he is chiefly remembered today as the financial organizer of New York's subway system.

His corporation, the **Interborough Rapid Transit Company**, began building the first underground lines in 1900 and on October 27, 1904, the city's first subway train left its station at City Hall and ran up to 145th Street, twenty-six minutes later. The new system received immediate public support and was soon carrying 600,000 passengers daily.

9 East 84th Street now houses the **United Nations Mission of Bulgaria**.

12/Ogden Mills Reid

15 East 84th Street between Fifth and Madison Avenue.

For over thirty years, beginning in 1912, **Ogden Mills Reid** was the president of one of New York's greatest newspapers, *The Herald Tribune*. He lived in this elegant, five-story townhouse with his wife, **Helen Rogers**, from 1927 until his death in 1946.

Rogers took over the ownership of the paper after Reid passed away. Reid was the son of **Whitelaw Reid**, who gained control of the *Tribune* after founder **Horace Greeley's** death in 1872. The Reid family owned the newspaper until **John Hay Whitney** purchased it in 1958. But by that time, it was no longer a profitable venture and its last issue was printed on April 24, 1966.

Before the Reids lived in this 84th Street house, it was occupied by oil investor **Edward L. Doheny** who was indicted for bribery and conspiracy in the **Teapot Dome** scandal in 1924. The mansion is now the headquarters of the **American Jewish Congress**; the building is called the **Stephen Wise Congress House**.

13/Alfred Stieglitz

1111 Madison Avenue at 83rd Street (northeast corner).

The famed photographer was thirty-four years old in August 1898 when he moved into a twelve-room apartment here with his first wife, **Emmeline**. The building was the first luxury apartment house in the neighborhood to be constructed east of Fifth Avenue.

The couple's daughter, **Kitty**, was born here soon after they settled in. **Stieglitz** received a small annual stipend from his wealthy father but he was able to continue his artistic endeavors only because the rent was paid by his wife's annuities from her brother's business. Stieglitz started the influential journal *Camera Work* in 1902 and opened his famous **"291" Gallery** in 1905. He lived here on Madison Avenue with Emmeline until 1918—the year that he fell in love with the young artist **Georgia O'Keeffe**.

This building is now the **Permanent Mission of the Czech Republic to the United Nations**.

14/Lillian Hellman

63 East 82nd Street between Madison and Park Avenue.

Lillian Hellman owned this beautiful four-story yellow brick townhouse from 1944 to 1970. She paid $33,000 for it and decorated it in eighteenth century English style.

Hellman's longtime companion, **Dashiell Hammett**, lived here with her at two different times: in 1948, she helped him to recover from illnesses caused by his chronic alcoholism; in 1958, once again in poor health, he came back to live here and remained in her care, financial and otherwise, for the last three years of his life. He died in the hospital on January 10, 1961.

While Hellman lived in this house, she made her controversial appearance before the House Un-American Activities Committee in 1952 when she refused to "name names" and pleaded the Fifth Amendment, stating that "I cannot and will not cut my conscience to fit this year's fashions."

Hellman was subsequently blacklisted in Hollywood but worked sporadically in the theater.She wrote her 1960 play *Toys in the Attic* while she lived here on 82nd Street. In 1970, she moved to 630 Park Avenue (see this section, Tour 3, Number 3).

15/Frank Campbell Funeral Home
1076 Madison Avenue at 81st Street (northwest corner).

The **Campbell Funeral Home** has been the final rest stop for many famous New Yorkers for over a century. It first gained national attention in 1926 (when its location was on the Upper West Side) as the place for the funeral of silent screen legend **Rudolph Valentino** which drew the attention of thousands of mourners. At this Madison Avenue site, where it moved in 1937, Campbell's has buried many a star, including **Montgomery Clift, Joan Crawford, Tommy Dorsey, John Garfield, James Cagney,** and **Judy Holliday.**

Probably its most famous service was the one for **Judy Garland** when she died in 1969. An estimated 22,000 fans filed past her casket and comedian **Alan King** reportedly quipped that this was the first time that Garland had ever been on time for a performance. Television host **Dick Cavett** remembers meeting a depressed **Groucho Marx** for the first time outside of Campbell's in June 1961 after the funeral of **George S. Kaufman.** The two walked together down Fifth Avenue to Groucho's lodgings at the **Plaza Hotel**—beginning a friendship that lasted until Groucho's death in 1977.

16/Wanda Gag
1061 Madison Avenue between 80th and 81st Street.

Artist and writer **Wanda Gag** lived in an apartment in this five-story brownstone from December 1928 to the summer of 1931. She lived here with her companion, Earle Humphreys. Gag, born and raised in Minnesota, preferred country living to the city and spent only the winter months of the year in this Madison flat. Her most famous work, the best-selling children's book, *Millions of Cats,* which she both wrote and illustrated, was published not long before she moved here.

In 1931, she felt financially secure enough to purchase a farm for $3,000 near Milford, New Jersey. She left New York at that time.

Upper East Side
Tour 11

1. W.H. Auden and Christopher Isherwood
2. Bert Lahr
3. Cary Grant
4. James Farrell
5. James Cagney
6. Wanda Gag
7. Helen Hayes and Ring Lardner
8. Walter Cronkite
9. Ernie Kovacs
10. Robert Moses
11. Jacqueline Kennedy Onassis
12. Sherman Billingsley

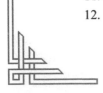

TOUR 11

1/W.H. Auden and Christopher Isherwood

237 East 81st Street between Third and Second Avenue.

British poet **W.H. Auden** moved to the U.S. with his friend, writer **Christopher Isherwood,** in early 1939. In April of that year, they rented a cheap apartment in this four-story brownstone tenement building. In those days, Yorkville was a heavily German neighborhood and Isherwood noted the number of Nazi restaurants, bookshops, and movie theaters.

Their flat had a large living room and two bedrooms. Auden appropriated a small room for his study which was soon ankle-deep in crumpled manuscripts and letters. Isherwood claimed that the building was haunted; footsteps could be heard in the apartment during all hours of the day but when anyone checked their origin, nobody was there.

Isherwood soon moved to California and lived there for the rest of his life. Auden stayed here on 81st Street until the middle of 1939 when he left on a cross-country tour. When he returned to New York in the fall, he moved to Brooklyn.

2/Bert Lahr

1570 First Avenue between 81st and 82nd Street.

Comic actor **Bert Lahr,** who will always be remembered for his role as the **Cowardly Lion** in the 1939 film, *The Wizard of Oz,* was born in a five-story tenement on this site on August 13, 1895. His real name was **Irving Lahrheim** and the family's three-room flat was a walk-up on the fourth floor. Lahr's father, born in Germany, worked thirteen hours a day, six days a week, at an upholstery shop on 88th and Columbus on the Upper West Side. He made twelve dollars a week.

The young Lahr developed an early enthusiasm for the theater even if it was beyond his budget. But "when he could afford a ticket," said his son and biographer **John Lahr,** "nothing offered greater pleasure. He walked to 107th Street and Third Avenue regularly to see the traveling melodramas." Often he would hitch a ride on his cousin's horse-drawn express cart to Broadway to see a vaudeville show and then meet the cart on its return trip uptown.

3/Cary Grant

325 East 80th Street between First and Second Avenue.

The young **Cary Grant** made his first appearance on Broadway in 1927 in the operetta *Golden Dawn.* He was only twenty-three and still went by his real name, **Archie Leach.**

Grant had a minor role in the production and also understudied the leading man. During that period, the actor moved into an apartment in this building. The show closed in six months but it was the break that he needed, eventually leading to small roles in other shows. The actor lived here on 80th Street until 1930.

In early 1932, he finally left New York for California to try his hand in motion pictures. He landed his first

James Cagney

role in a Paramount film called *This Is the Night.*

4/James Farrell
308 East 79th Street between Second and First Avenue.

Writer **James Farrell**, the creator of the *Studs Lonigan* trilogy in the 1930s, lived for a decade in this seventeen-story apartment building with his companion **Cleo Paturis,** beginning in 1969. Farrell, who was twenty-three-years older than his partner, walked her to the bus stop on Second Avenue each morning—she worked for a midtown publisher—and then returned to the apartment where he would spend his entire day writing, often skipping lunch. Farrell wrote three novels while he lived here. In the winter of 1978, the couple moved

six blocks south to a more luxurious apartment at 345 East 73rd Street (see this section, Tour 8, Number 13).

5/James Cagney
420 East 78th Street between York and First Avenue.

James Cagney lived in an apartment in this four-story building with his parents and four siblings, beginning in 1917. He was eighteen years old. He attended Columbia College briefly in 1918 but when his father died, Cagney was forced to quit to help support the family.

After working at various odd jobs, he broke into show business in 1919 as a chorus girl, in full drag, in a show called *Every Sailor.*

A year later, he met his future wife, **Frances Willard Vernon,** a dancer, while he performed in a Broadway musical called *Pitter Patter.* They were married in 1922; it was a union that would last for over sixty years. After experiencing financial difficulties, the young couple moved in with Cagney's family here on 78th Street for a time. He eventually obtained better roles on Broadway and finally made his debut in the movies in 1930 in S*inner's Holiday.*

6/Wanda Gag
527 East 78th Street at Cherokee Place (east of York Avenue).

Artist **Wanda Gag** lived in Apartment 21 of this building, across the street from John Jay Park, from 1920 until 1928. At first, she shared it with fellow artists **Lucille Lundquist** and **Violet Karland,** but she had a larger circle of friends who came and went freely.

To save money, the group regularly cooked meals together. Gag used the flat as her studio; in her journal, she said, "I like this place. We are on the East River and have a wonderful big view. I am fortunate to have the biggest and lightest room in the house because I am the one who works at home in the daytime."

Gag had her first one-person exhibit at the **New York Public Library** in February 1923. In 1928, not long before she moved away from here, her children's book *Millions of Cats* —destined to become a classic of its genre—was published.

Zelda Fitzgerald

7/Helen Hayes and Ring Lardner

25 East End Avenue at 80th Street (northeast corner).

Actress **Helen Hayes** and her husband, writer **Charles MacArthur,** lived in this fifteen-story apartment building called the **Yorkgate** in the 1930s. Their next-door neighbor was actress **Bea Lillie.**

Hayes and MacArthur entertained frequently and their guests were many of the famous writers, artists, and actors living in New York in those days.One night, **Laurence Olivier** and **Vivien Leigh** arrived dripping wet and hammering at their door; they had been sailing up the Hudson River on **John Hay Whitney's** yacht and when a storm began, they came to their friends' apartment for shelter.

Another night, **F. Scott Fitzgerald,** a friend of MacArthur's, showed up unannounced and stayed for three days. **Zelda** had recently been committed to a mental hospital and Scott needed consoling.

In September 1931, **Ring Lardner** and his wife, **Ellis,** took an apartment here at the Yorkgate. By this time, the writer's drinking had badly affected his health and he had just been released from the hospital. The Lardners were only able to remain at this address for six months before he was forced to return for treatment. Ring Lardner died in September 1933 at the age of forty-eight.

8/Walter Cronkite

45 East End Avenue at 81st Street (northeast corner).

Broadcaster and journalist **Walter Cronkite** lived in this large apartment building in the 1950s and 60s as he was becoming the most popular news anchor on national network television. In 1952, he was covering the Korean War for a local station in Washington D.C. when he was hired by CBS to anchor the network's first televised coverage of the presidential conventions. It wasn't long before he became a familiar face in America's living rooms.

Cronkite hosted a number of news and documentary programs in the 50s, including *You Are There*, until he became the anchorman for the *CBS Evening News*, a job he held from 1962 until 1981.

9/Ernie Kovacs

55 East End Avenue at 82nd Street (southeast corner).

Ernie Kovacs, one of television's most original comedy writers and performers, lived in a five-room apartment in this fifteen-story building overlooking the East River. He came here with his new wife, singer **Edie Adams,** after they were married in 1954; his two daughters from a previous marriage joined them soon after.

At the time, Kovacs was the host of a morning radio show at WABC. He had already made his name in television in a series of popular comedy shows for both CBS and NBC, full of the sight gags and off-the-wall humor that were his trademarks. By 1955, NBC had hired him again to host yet another *Ernie Kovacs Comedy Hour.* He won three Emmy Awards during the 1956-57 season.

10/Robert Moses

1 Gracie Terrace (at 82nd Street between East End Avenue and the East River. Entrance at 75 East End Avenue.

New York's master planner and builder lived in a large apartment at 1 Gracie Terrace with his wife, **Mary,** and two daughters from 1939 until his death forty-two years later. **Robert Moses,** working mainly behind the scenes, was one of the most powerful public figures in the history of New York State. Although he was never elected to any public office, he occupied a number of key state and city posts that allowed him to play a major role in molding the state's physical and political environment.

During over fifty years of public service, Moses developed public works costing over $27 billion, including bridges, highways, playgrounds, parks, and public buildings. In the process of doing this, he developed a political machine that functioned as a fourth branch of government, defying and controlling governors and mayors alike.

Moses worked long hours, six days a week, and even when he did relax on Sundays, he still kept a yellow pad on his lap for making notes. He was a familiar figure in this East Side neighborhood, often spotted at night walking his dog. Moses was finally stripped of his power by **Governor Nelson Rockefeller** in 1968. He died in 1981 at the age of ninety-two.

11/Jacqueline Kennedy Onassis

1 Gracie Square (84th Street between East End Avenue and the East River).

This short block, called **Gracie Square,** is the southern border of Carl Schurz Park. Number 1 Gracie Square, designed by famed architect **Rosario Candela** (in collaboration with William Lawrence Bottomley), was a childhood home of **Jacqueline Kennedy Onassis.**

She moved to this address in 1938 at age nine after her mother, **Janet Norton Lee Bouvier,** separated from (and later divorced) Jacqueline's father, **John Bouvier.** Jacqueline's sister, **Lee,** also lived here.

Every Sunday, John Bouvier would come here to pick up his daughters and take them out for a day on the town (see this section, Tour 5, Number 20). Mother and daughters lived at Gracie Square until Janet's second marriage to lawyer and investment banker **Hugh Auchincloss** in 1942. The three then moved to the Auchincloss home in Washington, D.C.

Robert Moses lived at 7 Gracie Square with his wife, Mary and two daughters, from 1930 until 1939. It was the period when he was becoming one of the most powerful government officials in the state's history. In 1939, Moses moved two blocks south to 1 Gracie Terrace (see number 10 above). Actress **Cornelia Otis Skinner** also lived at 7 Gracie Square in the 1940s.

The architectural jewel of Gracie Square is **Number 10,** with its fully-covered block-long driveway protected by an attendant in a sentry box behind locked gates. The building had a private club in its lower level and a private yacht mooring on the East River in the days before the FDR Drive was built.

Number 10 was the one-time home of **John Barrymore's** ex-wife, **Michael Strange** and her daughter, **Diana Barrymore.** Soprano **Lily Pons** and her husband, musician **Andre Kostelanetz**, resided here from 1938 to the early 1940s. **Gloria Vanderbilt** and conductor **Leopold Stokowski** lived here during their marriage from 1945 to 1955. During her marriage to her next husband, movie director **Sidney Lumet,** Number 10 became the scene of some of New York's most memorable parties of the 1950s, attended by the likes of **Marilyn Monroe, Lena Horne, Truman Capote, Stephen Sondheim, Judy Holliday,** and **Isak Dinesen.**

Vanderbilt eventually moved away but returned three decades later to make it her home for a second time. Ten Gracie Square was the last home of **Madame Chiang Kai-shek.** The wife of the leader of Nationalist China lived here after she moved to New York from Taiwan in 1975 following the death of her husband. She lived out her final years protected by a pack of black-suited bodyguards who cleared the lobby of the apartment building every time she entered or left. Madame Chiang died on October 23, 2003 at the age of 105.

12/Sherman Billingsley

500 East 83rd Street at York Avenue (southeast corner).

The flamboyant owner of the **Stork Club**, once America's most famous night club, lived in this large white apartment building. **Sherman Billingsley**, born in Oklahoma, came to New York as a young man in the early 20s and opened a drug store that sold bootleg liquor. He parlayed his profits into his famous club which he opened in 1929 as a speakeasy at 132 West 58th Street.

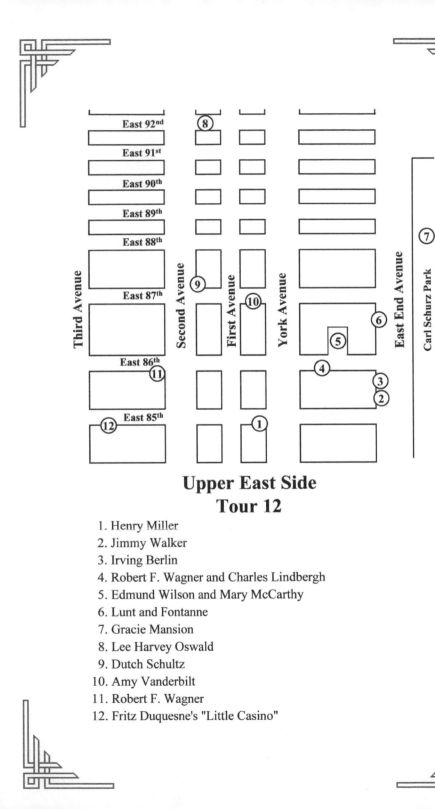

Upper East Side
Tour 12

1. Henry Miller
2. Jimmy Walker
3. Irving Berlin
4. Robert F. Wagner and Charles Lindbergh
5. Edmund Wilson and Mary McCarthy
6. Lunt and Fontanne
7. Gracie Mansion
8. Lee Harvey Oswald
9. Dutch Schultz
10. Amy Vanderbilt
11. Robert F. Wagner
12. Fritz Duquesne's "Little Casino"

After Prohibition, he moved it to its most well-known location at 3 East 53rd Street and it was there that its glory years began. Anyone who was famous or infamous in New York eventually went there—to drink, to dance, to be entertained—and Billingsley soon became a wealthy man. But by the 1960s, he encountered troubles with the labor unions which allegedly sabotaged his business and even, he claimed, threatened his life. "At night when I went home," he wrote in his memoirs, "I would have all lights out in the house, would have to feel my way...to my bedroom with keys in one hand and pistol in the other."

The Stork Club closed in 1965 and Billingsley died in his apartment here of a heart attack, exactly one year later, in 1966. He was sixty-six years old.

TOUR 12

1/Henry Miller

450 East 85th Street at York Avenue (southwest corner).

The novelist who wrote **Tropic of Cancer** and **Tropic of Capricorn** was born on the top floor of this red brick building on December 26, 1891. **Henry Miller's** grandparents had emigrated from Germany and settled here in Yorkville many years earlier. Miller's father was a tailor. The family moved to Brooklyn while Henry was still an infant but, as a young boy, he came back to this neighborhood for a couple of weeks each summer to stay with his cousin, **Henry Bauman,** who lived in a house on this block.

Henry Miller residence

2/Jimmy Walker

120 East End Avenue at 85th Street (facing Carl Schurz Park).

This beautiful limestone apartment house, built by **Vincent Astor** in 1931, was the last home of the former mayor of New York, **Jimmy Walker.** He moved here in 1945 with his two adopted children, his sister, and his two nephews.It was four years after his second wife, **Betty Compson,** had divorced him.

The flamboyant Walker had been forced to resign from office in disgrace in 1932 after the Seabury investigation found that he had committed numerous wrongdoings during his tenure. Now, while he lived here on East End Avenue, he had returned to the Catholic faith, confessing his sins, and again receiving the sacraments. He also returned to public life, addressing rallies to aid the war effort and attending the Friday night boxing matches. Walker was living in

Jimmy Walker

this building when he died on November 18, 1946 of a brain clot.

Choreographer **George Balanchine** lived in this building in the early 1940s with his wife, dancer **Vera Zorina.**

Actors **Jessica Tandy** and **Hume Cronyn** also made this place their home for many years, beginning in the 1950s.The couple performed together for the first time in the play *The Fourposter* in 1951 and went on to co-star in ten plays on Broadway during their fifty-two-year marriage.

Vincent Astor, this building's one-time owner, originally took the entire seventeenth floor for his residence.

3/Irving Berlin
130 East End Avenue at 86th Street (facing Carl Schurz Park).

Irving Berlin moved into Apartment 16 of this large building in 1933 with his wife, writer **Ellin Mackay**, and his children. In that year, his new musical revue *As Thousands Cheer*

was Broadway's biggest box-office hit and signaled his return to popularity after a brief slump in his career.

The Berlin apartment here had a formal appearance with its many antiques and floor-to-ceiling bookshelves.The family lived here until 1942 and during that period, Berlin wrote such standards as *Easter Parade, Heat Wave, Cheek to Cheek,* and *I've Got My Love To Keep Me Warm.*

Aviator hero **Eddie Rickenbacker** also lived in this building during the 1940s and 50s.

4/Robert F. Wagner and Charles Lindbergh
530 East 86th Street between York and East End Avenue.

Robert Wagner, who served as New York's U.S. senator for over twenty-five years, lived in this Yorkville apartment house across from Henderson Place from 1939

Irving Berlin

until his death in 1953. The building served as his New York home when he wasn't working in Washington. Wagner, a widower for many years, shared the residence with his son, **Robert F. Wagner, Jr.**, who later became the mayor of New York City.

The senior Wagner was one of American history's greatest senators, sponsoring landmark social welfare and labor legislation.During the time that he lived in this building, he introduced his last major bill in the Senate:The Public Housing Act of 1949. He also successfully pressured Presidents Roosevelt and Truman to support the creation of a Jewish state in Palestine.

Charles Lindbergh and his wife, **Anne Morrow Lindbergh**, rented a riverview apartment here from January to July 1934. They came with their seventeen-month-old son, **Jon.** The Lindberghs were looking for a safe place to raise their child after their first son had been kidnapped from their home in Hopewell, New Jersey in February 1932.

Anne located a nursery school around the corner to which she walked Jon and the dogs every morning.She finished writing her first book *North to the Orient* while she lived here.But the restless couple quickly grew disenchanted with life in New York City and moved to the Morrow family estate in Englewood, New Jersey.

5/Edmund Wilson and Mary McCarthy

86th Street between York and East End Avenue (north side).

This neighborhood was formerly

Henderson Place

part of the country estate of **John Jacob Astor**.In 1882, **John Henderson**, who had made a fortune in furs and fur hats, built thirty-two houses on this spot, creating a small enclave called **Henderson Place.** Today, only twenty-four of these three-story red brick Queen Anne-style houses remain.

The construction of modern apartments on both sides has spoiled the original atmosphere but it's still a wonderful New York locale.Probably Henderson Place's most famous residents were literary critic **Edmund Wilson** and his wife, novelist **Mary McCarthy**, who lived at 14 Henderson Place with their young son in 1944. Their tempestuous relationship would soon lead to a bitter separation and divorce and, when Wilson lived here alone in the near-empty house that winter, the place had been stripped bare by McCarthy, right down to the toilet paper.

Poet **Archibald MacLeish** rented the house at 10 Henderson Place in 1930-31 during a period when he was a staff writer for *Fortune* magazine.

6/Alfred Lunt and Lynn Fontanne
150 East End Avenue between 86th and 87th Avenue.

Actors **Lunt** and **Fontanne** were performing on Broadway in the play *I Know My Love* in 1949 when they purchased this four-story red brick house across the street from Carl Schurz Park.

They had the place entirely remodeled, adding eighteenth century French and Italian furniture.Overhead was a roof garden, with potted plants, deck chairs, and canopies, where in warm weather the couple ate many of their meals. The magazine *Ladies Home Journal* furnished their kitchen for them in exchange for photographs and an interview.

Lunt and Fontanne lived here until their retirement from the Broadway theater in September 1972, when they sold the house for $125,000 and moved permanently to their rural home in Genesee Depot, Wisconsin.

7/Gracie Mansion
Carl Schurz Park near 88th Street.

Carl Schurz Park, which runs along the East River between Gracie Square at 84th Street and its northern border at 90th Street, is the site of

Mayor Fiorello LaGuardia

Gracie Mansion. This Federal-style country house, located opposite 88th Street, has been the official residence of New York mayors since 1942.

The sixteen-room wooden structure was built in 1799 by wealthy merchant **Archibald Gracie** on the foundation of **Jacob Walton's** house of about 1770 and close to the site where a Revolutionary War fort had been erected in 1776.Among the famous guests entertained by Gracie here were **John Quincy Adams, Alexander Hamilton, Washington Irving, James Fenimore Cooper,** and **John Jacob Astor.**

After serving as home successively to the **Gracie, Foulkes,** and **Wheaton** families, the house was purchased by the city in 1887 along with the land that became the surrounding park. For years the mansion served the Parks Department and then in 1927 it became the first home of the **Museum of the City of New York.**

Still later, municipal officials decided that the city should maintain an official residence for **Mayor Fiorello LaGuardia** and his successors. Up to that point, LaGuardia, like all former mayors, had lived and paid for a place of his own choosing. In 1942, he moved to Gracie Mansion from his tenement apartment on 1274 Fifth Avenue in East Harlem.

One of the rooms was converted into a private radio studio and La-Guardia used it for his regular Sunday afternoon broadcasts called *Talks to the People* on **WNYC**.

8/Lee Harvey Oswald
325 East 92nd Street between First and Second Avenue.

In 1964, the Warren Commission decided that **Lee Harvey Oswald** was **President John F. Kennedy's** assassin. Twelve years earlier, when Oswald was twelve years old, he moved to New York from Fort Worth, Texas with his mother, **Marguerite.** They moved into the small apartment of Lee's older brother, **John Pic**, in this five-story red brick building.

Pic, who had joined the Coast Guard and was stationed in New York, lived here with his wife and their baby son. Tension quickly developed between Marguerite and her daughter-in-law and Lee added to the strain by fighting with his mother and often striking her. One day, a few months after they had arrived, Lee pulled a knife on his brother's wife after she had asked him to turn down the volume on the television.

Lee and Marguerite were immediately asked to leave.They moved north to a one-room flat in the Bronx. Eleven years later, on November 24, 1963, Lee Harvey Oswald, after allegedly killing the president, lay dead in the basement of Dallas police headquarters, shot by night-club-owner **Jack Ruby.** Oswald remained at the center of the controversy over President Kennedy's assassination for years to come.

9/Dutch Schultz
1690 Second Avenue at 87th Street (northeast corner).

This spot, where a modern apartment building now stands, was the birthplace of one of New York's most vicious mobsters—**Arthur Flegenheimer,** alias **Dutch Schultz**. He was born here on August 6, 1902 in what was then the toughest section of Yorkville.

Like so many of the famous criminals of that period, Schultz made the most of the opportunities presented to him by the onset of Prohibition; by the mid-1920s, he controlled bootlegging and the speakeasy trade in the entire nearby Bronx, gaining that position by violently eliminating all of his competition.

His empire began to unravel in the mid-1930s as federal investigators began to harass him and rival gang leaders moved into his territory. When he announced plans to kill mob prosecutor **Thomas Dewey**, a move opposed by top New York boss **Lucky Luciano**, orders were sent out to eliminate Schultz. The end came on October 23, 1935 at the **Palace Chop House** in Newark, where he was shot down by Luciano's killers in the men's room.

10/Amy Vanderbilt
438 East 87th Street between York and First Avenue.

Amy Vanderbilt, the syndicated columnist who was a world-famous expert on etiquette, lived in this townhouse during the last years of her life. It was here on the night of December 27, 1974, that she fell to her death from a second-floor window. Her body was found lying near the front steps of the four-story building by a passer-by. She was sixty-six years old.

Vanderbilt was a descendant of a first cousin of **Commodore Cornelius Vanderbilt**, the railroad baron. Her 1952 book, *Amy Vanderbilt's Complete Book of Etiquette,* sold millions of copies; she rivaled **Emily Post** on this subject for a number of years.

11/Robert F. Wagner

244 East 86th Street at Second Avenue (southwest corner).

New York's great Democratic U.S. senator lived in this red brick apartment building in the 1920s. The building, which is called the **Manhattan** and has recently been refurbished, was erected in 1880 and is the oldest extant large luxury apartment house in Manhattan.

This address is in the neighborhood known as **Yorkville**, once a village originally centered on 86th Street and Third Avenue, which was the heart of the German-American community in Manhattan. It was a natural location for **Robert Wagner,** who was born in the Rhineland in 1877 and came to the U.S. when he was nine. After serving fourteen years in the state legislature, he became a member of the New York Supreme Court between 1918 and 1926.

During his years in Albany, Wagner still loved the big city; he hurried back to his New York apartment here on weekends to play poker with his Tammany friends, eat in the neighborhood restaurants, and attend the opera. He loved to hear the rumble of the Second Avenue elevated train outside of his home. In 1926, he was elected U.S. senator and served in Washington for twenty-three years.

12/Fritz Duquesne

206 East 85th Street between Second and Third Avenue.

In the late 1930s, this building housed a bar called the **Little Casino** which served the many German-Americans living in the neighborhood. The place was a sort of haunt for members of the American Nazi Party and those individuals sympathetic to Hitler's Germany. **Frederick Joubert "Fritz" Duquesne**, the man who led Germany's espionage effort in America, often met here with a spy named **William Sebold** to exchange secret information gathered by Nazi agents around the country. Sebold had set up a secret radio station on Long Island which he used to relay Duquesne's stolen information to the German government. But unbeknownst to Duquesne, Sebold was actually a double agent working for the FBI. He sent out false information to the Nazis to disrupt their operations, changing the facts that Duquesne fed him. Duquesne was finally arrested by the FBI in June 1941 and sentenced to eighteen years in prison. His New York residence was at 24 West 76th Street.

TOUR 13

1/Eugene O'Neill
35 East 84th Street at Madison Avenue (northeast corner).

Eugene O'Neill was fifty-seven years old in 1946 when he and his wife, **Carlotta**, moved back to New York from Sea Island, Georgia, where they had lived for the past fourteen years. They rented a six-room apartment in this building.

Between 1939 and 1942, O'Neill had written two of his greatest plays and they were both produced for the first time while he lived at this address—*The Iceman Cometh* opened on Broadway in October 1946 and *Moon for the Misbegotten* was performed in Columbus, Ohio, in February 1947.

O'Neill was now in poor health, suffering from Parkinson's Disease, and in January 1948, he fractured his shoulder in a fall at his apartment here. After a short stay in the hospital, he and Carlotta moved to Boston in April 1948.

Eugene O'Neil's Apartment

in Manhattan, he wrote a collection of short stories and four novels. In 1955, he and his wife moved to a small town on Long Island, where they lived for the rest of their lives. He died in 1975.

Diplomat and future New York governor **W. Averell Harriman** lived in Apartment 8A here during the early 1930s.

2/P.G. Wodehouse
1000 Park Avenue at 84th Street (northwest corner).

The British comic novelist lived in a duplex apartment with a rooftop garden in this building with his wife, **Ethel**, from 1948 until 1955. Wodehouse, who created **Bertie Wooster** and his butler **Jeeves**, two of literature's funniest characters, had been forced to leave England after the Second World War when he was accused of collaborating with the Germans. In the years that he lived

3/Steve Allen and Jack Kerouac
1009 Park Avenue between 84th and 85th Street.

Television personality **Steve Allen**, who once hosted America's first late-night talk show, lived in an apartment in this building in the late 1950s with his wife, **Jayne Meadows.** It was during the period when he hosted his popular Sunday night prime-time variety show on NBC that successfully competed with **Ed Sullivan's** program on CBS.

Jack Kerouac appeared on his show

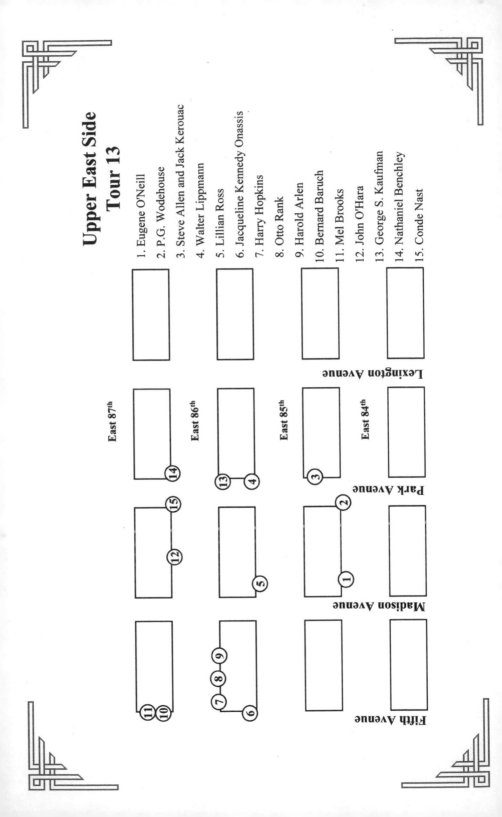

Upper East Side
Tour 13

1. Eugene O'Neill
2. P.G. Wodehouse
3. Steve Allen and Jack Kerouac
4. Walter Lippmann
5. Lillian Ross
6. Jacqueline Kennedy Onassis
7. Harry Hopkins
8. Otto Rank
9. Harold Arlen
10. Bernard Baruch
11. Mel Brooks
12. John O'Hara
13. George S. Kaufman
14. Nathaniel Benchley
15. Conde Nast

East 87th
East 86th
East 85th
East 84th

Lexington Avenue
Park Avenue
Madison Avenue
Fifth Avenue

on November 16, 1958, reading from his novel *On the Road*.

Allen had become Kerouac's friend and on another night, he invited the Beat writer to dinner at his apartment here. Allen remembered that Kerouac drank a bottle of brandy and two bottles of scotch in no time flat and continued to imbibe until, finally, in the early hours of the morning, Allen had to ask him to leave. Kerouac frantically proceeded to phone everyone he knew until he found someone who was still up. Then he left to continue his binge elsewhere.

4/Walter Lippmann

1021 Park Avenue at 85th Street (northeast corner).

Walter Lippmann moved into a seventeen-room duplex here in 1966 with his wife, **Helen**. Lippmann had started his career as a journalist in New York but had been living in Washington, D.C. since 1938 where he had written a syndicated political column for the *New York Herald Tribune* and the *Washington Post*. The journalist was now seventy-seven years old and, although retired, continued to write a weekly column for *Newsweek*.

The Lippmanns moved to the Lowell Apartments on 63rd Street in 1970 (see this section, Tour 1, Number 22).

5/Lillian Ross

35 East 85th Street at Madison Avenue (northeast corner).

Lillian Ross began writing articles for *The New Yorker* in the late 1940s. Her long profile of *Ernest Heming-*

Jack Kerouac

way in May 1950 brought her instant fame in Manhattan's journalistic circles. She continued to write for the magazine over the next fifty years, most of the time under the editorship of **William Shawn.**

In her 1998 memoir, Ross reported that she carried on a love affair with Shawn that lasted over forty years until his death in 1992. Beginning in 1958, she lived in an apartment in this large modern brick building and spent much of her time here with Shawn who divided his domestic life between Ross's place and the home that he shared with his wife on East 96th Street (see this section, Tour 15, Number 13). In 1966, Ross adopted a baby boy whom she raised in this apartment with Shawn's assistance.

6/Jacqueline Kennedy Onassis

1040 Fifth Avenue at 85th Street (northeast corner).

This large limestone building was the New York home of America's most famous First Lady. **Jacqueline Kennedy Onassis** moved from Washington D.C. into a fourteenth-floor cooperative apartment here in September 1964, ten months after her husband was assassinated. Her fifteen-room home—with its five bedrooms and five baths—was previously owned by President Kennedy's defense secretary **Robert McNamara.** She purchased it for $200,000.

The building was designed by **Rosario Candela**, the leading apartment architect of the 1920s. Mrs. Kennedy could often be spotted fast-walking around the Central Park Reservoir for exercise with a Secret Service agent following at a discreet distance. Soon after she moved here, she spent $125,000 to refurbish and redecorate the place. She filled it with antique French and English furnishings and covered the walls with her collection of animal drawings and Indian miniature paintings. In her living room stood the Louis XVI bureau on which **President Kennedy** signed the Nuclear Test Ban Treaty in 1963.

It was in her apartment here on the evening of May 19, 1994 that Mrs. Kennedy died of cancer, surrounded by her family and a few friends. She was sixty-four years old.

Outside, television lights lit up the night and hundreds of people crowded at a respectable distance outside the building. In January 1995, her apartment was sold for $9.5 million.

7/Harry Hopkins
1046 Fifth Avenue near 86th Street.

Hopkins was the chief counselor to **President Franklin Delano Roose-**velt during World War II. Earlier he had served as FDR's administrator in charge of the nation's work and relief programs; as much as any man, his name was synonymous with the New Deal.

After he resigned from **Harry Truman's** staff in August 1945, Hopkins moved into a house on this site (where the apartment building numbered 1049 now stands) with his wife, **Louise**, and young daughter, **Diana.** He had recently returned from Moscow where Truman had sent him to confer with **Marshal Stalin** about postwar conditions.

In New York, he took a job as impartial chairman of the city's Coat and Suit Industry. But Hopkins was in poor health by this time and died in Memorial Hospital on January 29, 1946. He was only fifty-five years old.

8/Otto Rank
2 East 86th Street near Fifth Avenue.

Fifty years ago, this building (since then, totally rebuilt and now numbered **1049 Fifth Avenue**, although its entrance is on 86th Street, and it is more than 100 feet from Fifth Avenue) was the **Hotel Adams.**

In 1934 and 1935, it was the home of **Otto Rank**, the famed psychoanalyst and author and onetime student and colleague of **Sigmund Freud.** He resided here in Suite 905, and used one of the rooms to see his patients.

During this period, Rank fell in love with writer/diarist **Anais Nin**, who had moved to New York from France. She soon began to practice analysis herself under Rank's instruction in a room next door.Nin dubbed the Adams "The Hotel Chaotica" with good reason—while cavorting with Rank, she secretly continued to carry on her long-standing affair with writer **Henry Miller**.When Rank found out about it, he broke off with her. Rank moved to California soon after.

British novelist **P.G. Wodehouse** lived at the Hotel Adams in 1947-48. Playwright **Arthur Miller** stayed here a few months after he separated from **Marilyn Monroe** in November 1960.

Joe DiMaggio's first wife, **Dorothy Arnold**, moved to the Adams for a few months in 1945 with her three-year-old son **Joe, Jr.**, after her divorce from the *Yankee* star became final.

9/Harold Arlen
12 East 86th Street between Fifth and Madison Avenue.

In the early 1930s, song writer **Harold Arlen** lived in this apartment building, first on the main floor, then later in a tenth-floor penthouse.At that time, the place was a residential apartment-hotel called the **Hotel Croydon.** Arlen was only twenty-four when he settled here.

Before long, he teamed up with lyricist **Ted Koehler** and wrote some of the songs that made him famous, including *Get Happy, I Gotta Right to Sing the Blues, Stormy Weather,* and *It's Only a Paper Moon.*

In 1932, Arlen met showgirl **Anya Taranda** and they lived together here. They were married in 1937 and remained partners until her death in 1970.

10/Bernard Baruch
1054 Fifth Avenue between 86th and 87th Street.

The Wall Street financier and presidential advisor bought a thirty-seven-foot-wide mansion on this site in the 1920s and lived in it until 1946. Its six stories had ten baths and thirty-two rooms, including an oval dining room, a ballroom, a smoking room lined with Norwegian pine, and a large solarium. **Baruch's** wife of forty-one years, **Annie Griffen,** died while they were living here in 1938.

In 1946, Baruch moved to 4 East 66th Street where he lived for the rest of his life (see this section, Tour 3, Number 11). Number 1054 Fifth Avenue no longer exists. The mansion, along with the two houses adjoining to the south, was demolished and replaced by this newer apartment building numbered 1050.

11/Mel Brooks
1056 Fifth Avenue at 87th Street (southeast corner).

Comedy writer and movie director **Mel Brooks** lived in an apartment here in the late 1950s. During most of this time he was a writer for comedian **Sid Caesar** who starred in a series of television shows that ran on NBC from 1950 to 1958.

Brooks, along with a staff of talented writers that included **Neil and Danny Simon, Carl Reiner,** and **Larry Gelbart,** had helped create Caesar's most famous program, *Your Show of Shows,* co-starring **Imogene Coca,** from 1950 to 1954.

After Caesar went off the air, Brooks said that for eighteen months, he would wake up at 6:30 every morning and bang his head against the bathroom wall.

He eventually continued writing comedy for other performers and in 1960 began performing himself when he released the first of a series of successful recordings called the *2,000-Year-Old-Man* with his partner, **Carl Reiner.**

12/John O'Hara
55 East 86th St. between Madison and Park Avenue.

John O'Hara lived in this fifteen-story brick apartment building with his wife, **Belle**, from 1946 to 1949. He had published three novels by this time, but his last one, *Hope of Heaven* in 1938, was not a success and during the next decade O'Hara concentrated on his short-story writing for *The New Yorker*, publishing a collection in 1947.

However, he was becoming increasingly sensitive to the critical estimate that he was only a master of the short story and, in response, he completed one of his most ambitious novels, *A Rage to Live*, in 1948. O'Hara and Belle moved out of New York permanently in 1949 when they settled in Princeton, New Jersey.

13/George S. Kaufman
1035 Park Avenue at 86th Street (southeast corner).

Playwright and Broadway director **George S. Kaufman** was a sixty year-old widower in 1949 when he married his second wife, actress **Leueen MacGrath**, who was thirty-five. In 1951, the couple moved into a penthouse apartment in this building. Kaufman had recently directed *Guys and Dolls*, which opened on Broadway in 1950 to great acclaim. He followed that up by co-writing *The Solid Gold Cadillac*, which also became a hit when it opened in 1953.

After Kaufman and MacGrath were divorced in 1957, he lived alone in the penthouse. But his health was now failing and, after a series of strokes, Kaufman died in his apartment here on June 2, 1961.

This building was also the last New York home of comic actor **Bert Lahr.** He died here on December 4, 1967.

14/Nathaniel Benchley
103 East 86th Street at Park Avenue (northeast corner).

Writer **Nathaniel Benchley**—whose father, **Robert**, was one of America's greatest humorists, and whose son, **Peter**, wrote the popular novel *Jaws*—lived in this large apartment building, located across the street from the Park Avenue Methodist Church.

Benchley was prolific; he wrote nearly two dozen children's books, fifteen novels, and a string of nonfiction works. His most celebrated book was the novel *The Off-Islanders*, written in 1961, which became the movie *The Russians Are Coming, The Russians Are Coming.*

Benchley and his wife, **Marjorie Bradford**, lived in New York until 1968. They eventually settled permanently in Nantucket. Benchley died in 1981.

15/Conde Nast

1040 Park Avenue at 86th Street (northwest corner).

Conde Nast, the millionaire magazine publisher of such titles as *Vogue, Vanity Fair, and House and Garden,* lived in a duplex penthouse in this building from 1925 until his death in 1942.

His was one of the most fabulous apartments in Manhattan: the upper level was over 5,100 square feet including its terraces, with kitchen, dining room, drawing room, library, and a twenty-three by forty-three-foot salon and ballroom. Nast turned it into a center of New York nightlife, where socialites, entertainers, statesmen, and royalty attended the elaborate dances and cocktail parties that he hosted. The January 1925 housewarming party included such guests as **George Gershwin, Fred and Adele Astaire, Edna St. Vincent Millay,** and **Katharine Cornell.**

Edna St. Vincent Millay

The 1929 stock market crash injured Nast financially and left him in only marginal control of his publishing empire but he held on to his apartment and continued to entertain in the 1930s. He died here in 1942; his employees filed past his coffin which was laid out in his drawing room. After a few years, Nast's old apartment was subdivided into five separate units.

TOUR 14

1/Andy Warhol

1342 Lexington Avenue at 89th Street (northwest corner).

Andy Warhol purchased this townhouse in 1959 for $67,000. He needed a large place to accommodate his growing collections of art, furniture, and common objects of every size and shape. His mother, **Julia,** moved in with him; she lived in the basement.

This was Warhol's residence in 1961 when he hit upon a new idea—he sent his mother out to the grocery store to buy one of each of the thirty-two varieties of Campbell's Soup and began to paint each one of them on canvas, as exactly as possible, against a white background. The result created a sensation in the New York art world.

Warhol lived at this address until November 1963 when he sold the house to his business manager and moved to 231 East 47th Street (see Section Two, Tour 6, Number 21).

2/Robert F. Wagner

1327 Lexington Avenue between 88th and 89th Street.

The U.S. senator for New York lived in this huge brick apartment building from 1930 to 1939. **Wagner** was a widower at that time and this place was his Manhattan home when he was away from his

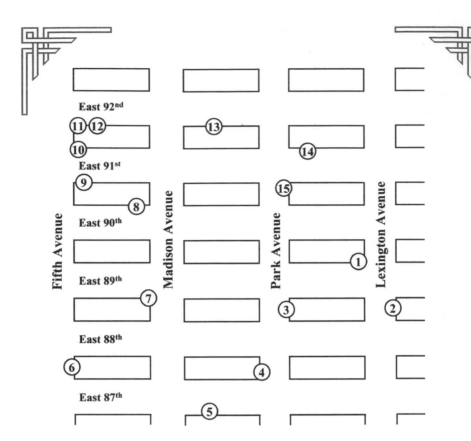

Upper East Side
Tour 14

1. Andy Warhol
2. Robert F. Wagner
3. Eugene O'Neill
4. Truman Capote
5. Dwight Macdonald
6. Oscar Hammerstein II
7. Paul Robeson
8. Sinclair Lewis

9. Andrew Carnegie
10. Otto Kahn
11. Marjorie Post and E.F. Hutton
12. John Cheever
13. Woody Allen
14. Alexander Kerensky
15. J.D. Salinger

duties in Washington D.C. While he lived here, he did probably his most productive public work, becoming the New Deal's greatest liberal senator. He was a sponsor for much of the social and economic legislation passed after 1933, including The National Industrial Recovery Act, Social Security, and various unemployment, housing, and health bills. His highest achievement was probably the National Labor Relations Act which became law in 1936.

3/Eugene O'Neill
1095 Park Avenue between 88th and 89th Street.

Playwright **Eugene O'Neill**, with his second wife, **Carlotta,** leased an eight-room duplex in this building in the fall of 1931. They had recently returned from France, where they lived for three years.

Carlotta decorated O'Neill's study to give him the utmost comfort—she created a nautical atmosphere provided by brass ship lanterns and models and pictures of old ships. While O'Neill lived here, his new play *Mourning Becomes Electra* opened on the New York stage.

But because of the distracting atmosphere of the big city, he was unable to get any serious work done and, in the summer of 1932, the couple move to a secluded home at Sea Island, Georgia.

4/Truman Capote
1060 Park Avenue at 87th Street (northwest corner).

Capote was seventeen years-old in 1942 when he left high school in Greenwich, Connecticut and joined his mother and stepfather in New York City. They took an apartment in this building. During the five years that he lived here, Capote began to pursue his calling as a writer and had his first successes. He obtained a job as copyboy at *The New Yorker* magazine; it was a position he held until the summer of 1945, when he was fired for offending poet **Robert Frost.**

In 1945 Capote saw his first short story published in *Mademoiselle* magazine. He continued to live in his parents' apartment and developed a routine: he would begin his writing at about ten at night, lying on his bed with a notebook on his knees, and working until four in the morning. He woke up at noon in time for lunch.

Capote's first novel, *Other Voices, Other Rooms*, was published in 1947. It was the year he left this apartment.

5/Dwight Macdonald
56 East 87th Street between Madison and Park Avenue.

This six-story building was for many years the home of **Dwight Macdonald,** who, in his role as writer, editor, and critic of everything from books and movies to politics and social conditions, was one of New York's most influential intellectuals.

Macdonald moved into an apartment here in 1954, at the age of forty-eight, with his newly-wedded second wife, **Gloria Lanier.** After writing for radical leftist journals like the *Partisan Review* in the 1930s and 40s, Macdonald joined *The New*

Yorker as a staff writer in 1951 and stayed there for twenty years. During that period, he was also film critic for *Esquire* magazine.

6/Oscar Hammerstein
1067 Fifth Avenue between 87th and 88th Street.

The lyricist who would later team with **Richard Rodgers** on a long string of popular Broadway musicals lived in this house next to the Guggenheim Museum, beginning in 1930. Two years before, **Oscar Hammerstein** had enjoyed his greatest early achievement when he collaborated with **Jerome Kern** to create *Show Boat* in 1928. But two years later, his career had taken a downturn and he was unable to match that earlier success. He wrote the lyrics for a show called *Free for All* in 1931. In that same year, his son James was born.

The Hammerstein family moved to Long Island in 1932. It wouldn't be until 1942 that Hammerstein would begin his work with Rodgers on the musical *Oklahoma!*—a work that would more than duplicate the success of *Show Boat*.

7/Paul Robeson
22 East 89th Street at Madison Avenue (southwest corner).

Black actor, singer, and social activist **Paul Robeson** was fifty-five years old in 1953 when he and his wife, **Essie,** sold their home in Enfield, Connecticut and moved to New York. For the next two years, they lived off and on in the apartment of his friends **Harold** and **Bert**

McGhee in this seven-story building called the **Graham House**, built in 1892. Robeson was an active supporter of the American Communist Party because he felt that it alone offered the best hope of liberating black people everywhere. Because of his leftist views, he was constantly under the surveillance of the FBI, who watched him as he came and went in the McGhee apartment here. By the end of 1954, Robeson decided that a move uptown to Harlem would offer him more privacy and security and he relocated his residence to the parsonage of a church at 155 West 136th Street.

Sinclair Lewis

8/Sinclair Lewis
21 East 90th Street at Madison Avenue (northwest corner).

Sinclair Lewis moved into an apartment in this building with his second wife, journalist **Dorothy Thompson**, in 1931. He had won the Nobel Prize for Literature a year earlier.

Their apartment had two separate sitting rooms so that Lewis and Thompson could entertain their own guests without disturbing the other. Lewis worked on his new novel *Ann Vickers* while he lived here.

In November 1931, Thompson traveled to Europe where she conducted her famous interview with **Adolph Hitler.** Lewis moved out of this flat in the summer of 1932 and joined his wife abroad. But the marriage didn't last— Lewis and Thompson separated in 1937 and were divorced in 1943.

Writer **Brendan Gill** lived in a seven-room apartment here from 1938 to 1942. The rent was $125 a month for a flat that had three baths, a wood-burning fireplace and a dozen doormen and elevator operators. Gill was hired as a staff writer for *The New Yorker* in 1936. He worked for the magazine for over sixty years.

9/Andrew Carnegie
2 East 91st Street at Fifth Avenue.

The millionaire industrialist and philanthropist built this sixty-four-room, four-story brick mansion at the turn of the last century. **Carnegie**, the founder of **U.S. Steel Corporation**, spent an estimated $2.5 million on the house, which was designed in the Scottish-Georgian style.

He began building it in 1898 when this neighborhood was considered rural and was occupied by squatters.

Anddrew Carnegie

It was ready for occupation in 1902.The place quickly became one of the best-known addresses in the country, especially to the local postal clerks who routed hundreds of letters to Carnegie daily—most of them begging for money.

Carnegie's mansion was very technically advanced for its time. It had an air-conditioning system and featured the city's first Otis passenger elevator in a private residence. Its two heating systems combined enough power to run an ocean liner; two tons of coal were needed to heat the house on a cold winter day. Carnegie installed two gymnasiums, one for himself, the other for his daughter, **Margaret**. A three-story pipe organ played wake-up music at

8 a.m. every day.

Carnegie died in 1919 but his wife, Louise continued to live here until her death in 1946. The Carnegie mansion now houses the **Cooper-Hewitt Museum** (Smithsonian's National Museum of Design).

10/Otto Kahn
1 East 91st Street at Fifth Avenue.

Otto Kahn was the German-born head of the prominent investment firm of **Kuhn Loeb & Company.** He was also one of the last century's most generous supporters of the arts. His mammoth Italianate house here on 91st Street, built in 1918, was a New York center of hospitality for artists and entertainers for many years.

Known for its luxuriousness and filled with works of art, the mansion was compared by one writer to the palaces of the Medicis. Kahn's most famous object of support was the city's **Metropolitan Opera,** which cost him almost $5 million over thirty years. But he also backed such institutions as the **Provincetown Players**, the **Theater Guild,** and the **Moscow Art Theater,** and came to the assistance of countless individuals like **George Gershwin, Paul Robeson, Isadora Duncan,** and **Hart Crane.**

Otto Kahn died suddenly of a heart attack in March 1934 while lunching with his business partners. He was sixty-seven years old. His home is now the **Convent of the Sacred Heart,** a Catholic girl's school.

11/Marjorie Merriweather Post and E.F. Hutton
1107 Fifth Avenue at 92nd Street (southeast corner).

The daughter of the founder of the **Post Cereal** empire and her famous stockbroker husband lived in this luxury apartment building until their divorce in the mid-1930s. It was built on the site of their previous mansion and had a private driveway and a separate entrance and elevator just for them and their guests.

Mr. and Mrs. Hutton's home was a mammoth three-story apartment with fifty-four rooms, including a small playroom / gymnasium, and a nearly hotel-sized kitchen. At one time, it was the largest residential apartment in New York City.

Marjorie's father, **C.W. Post,** taught her the family business and when he died in 1914, she took control. She played a critical role in the expansion of the old **Postum Company** into the modern corporate giant known as **General Foods.** With the cooperation and advice of Hutton, she developed a number of famous brands including Jell-O, Maxwell House Coffee, and Log Cabin Syrup.

Mr. and Mrs. Hutton had one daughter, actress **Dina Merrill**, who was raised in this apartment. The place has long since been subdivided.

Writer **Gore Vidal's** father, **Eugene Vidal,** lived in this building in the 1940s and 50s. In 1945, Gore Vidal, only twenty-years-old and just out of the army, moved into the back bedroom of his father's apartment here.

He took a job with a publishing company and put the finishing touches on his first novel *Williwaw.* The book was published in 1946.

12/John Cheever
8 East 92nd Street near Fifth Avenue.

John Cheever, with his wife, **Mary,** and their newborn daughter, **Susan**, rented this five-story townhouse in November 1944. It was an experiment in communal living—the Cheevers shared the place with two other couples for $200 a month, unfurnished.

Because it was wartime, it was virtually impossible to find roomy apartments for growing families— each couple had a child—and this house offered them the space that they could not afford individually. All three of the families had a bedroom, dressing room, and bath and each child had a bedroom and bath.

Cheever worked for the U.S. Army Signal Corps in Queens as a writer of scripts for a film series being made to maintain morale among the nation's servicemen. The communal experiment ultimately proved to be unsatisfactory; there were tensions among the tenants and the Cheevers were relieved to find an apartment of their own in July 1945 at 400 East 59th Street (see Section Two, Tour 4, Number 18).

Cheever, who also wrote part-time for *The New Yorker*, turned his experiences here on 92nd Street into a series of humorous stories, all published in the magazine between April 1945 and May 1946.

Townhouse of Woody Allen

13/Woody Allen
48 East 92nd Street between Park and Madison Avenue.

This twenty-two room townhouse, built in 1931, was the home of **Woody Allen**, beginning in 1999. The actor/writer/director lived here with his wife **Soon-Yi** and daughters **Bechet** and **Manzie**. Allen bought the place for $17.7 million. He sold it in 2003 for a reported $25 million.

14/Alexander Kerensky
109 East 91st Street between Park and Lexington Avenue.

Alexander Kerensky, who had ruled Russia during the first phase of the Russian Revolution until he was overthrown by **Lenin** and the Bolsheviks in 1917, emigrated to the U.S. in 1940 after living in exile in

Europe for twenty years.

From the mid-40s until 1968, he lived as the house guest of **Mrs. Kenneth Simpson** in this townhouse. He occupied the fifth and top floor. Mrs. Simpson was the widow of a New York Republican Party leader. Kerensky had befriended the Simpsons in the 1920s and he was invited to share the house when he had no other place to live.

Kerensky became a familiar figure in this neighborhood. For years, before his eyesight failed, he walked five or six miles a day; one of his favorite strolls was around the Central Park Reservoir.

He died in 1970 at the age of eighty-nine.

15/J.D. Salinger
1133 Park Avenue at 91st Street (southeast corner).

In 1932, when **J.D. Salinger** was thirteen years old, his family moved into a spacious apartment in this fifteen-story building.

The future author of *Catcher in the Rye* eventually flunked out of the **McBurrey School** in Manhattan and was sent to a military academy in Pennsylvania to complete his high school education. Soon after, while spending time in and out of college, he began to write short stories, including one in which Catcher's famous character **Holden Caulfield** first appeared.

The Three Marx Brothers: Harpo, Groucho and Gummo, circa 1912

Salinger was still living in this building with his parents in 1942 when he was drafted into the army; he returned to live here again after the war. He renewed his writing and his first stories appeared in *The New Yorker* in 1947. It was in that year that he moved away from his parents to live in Tarrytown, New York.

TOUR 15

1/The Marx Brothers
179 East 93rd St. between Lexington and Third Avenue.

In 1895, **Sam** and **Minnie Marx** moved their large family into a three-bedroom flat in this four-story building. The rent was $27 a month. In those days, this neighborhood in Yorkville was mainly Jewish, sandwiched between the Irish to the north and the Germans to the south.

Four of the five brothers had been born by then: **Chico (Leonard)** was eight, **Harpo (Adolph)** was seven, **Groucho (Julius)** was five, and **Gummo (Milton)** was three. In all, there were ten in the household, including other relatives.

Sam Marx was a tailor by trade and he worked at home; his materials took up the whole dining room and kitchen. He also did all of the cooking.

As the children grew, Minnie developed a plan to organize them into a vaudeville act. They started as singers, soon added comedy, and by 1910, the boys were full-time performers. In that year, Minnie decided that the fortunes of the family would be better served by moving to Chicago.

The Marx family didn't return to New York until 1920. By then, the boys had performed their variety stage act all over the country and they were well-known in vaudeville. Their big break came in 1923 with their Broadway show *I'll Say She Is,* which made them New York celebrities almost overnight.

2/Arthur Schwartz
139 East 94th Street at Lexington Avenue (northwest corner).

Broadway and Hollywood composer **Arthur Schwartz** lived in the twelfth-floor penthouse apartment of this building from 1948 until 1959. In a career that spanned a half-century, Schwartz collaborated on such musical standards as *Dancing in the Dark, You and the Night and the Music,* and *That's Entertainment.* His greatest achievements came with his first partner, lyricist **Howard Dietz.**

Schwartz's son **Jonathan** lived here with him.The younger Schwartz later became the popular New York disc jockey and radio personality best known for his knowledge and showcasing of the songs of **Frank Sinatra.**

3/Mark Rothko
118 East 95th St. between Park and Lexington Avenue.

Painter **Mark Rothko** moved to this red brick building with his second wife, **Mell**, and his young daughter, **Kate**, in 1960. His son, **Christopher** was born while they lived here in 1963. Rothko was at this address when he suffered an aneurysm in the

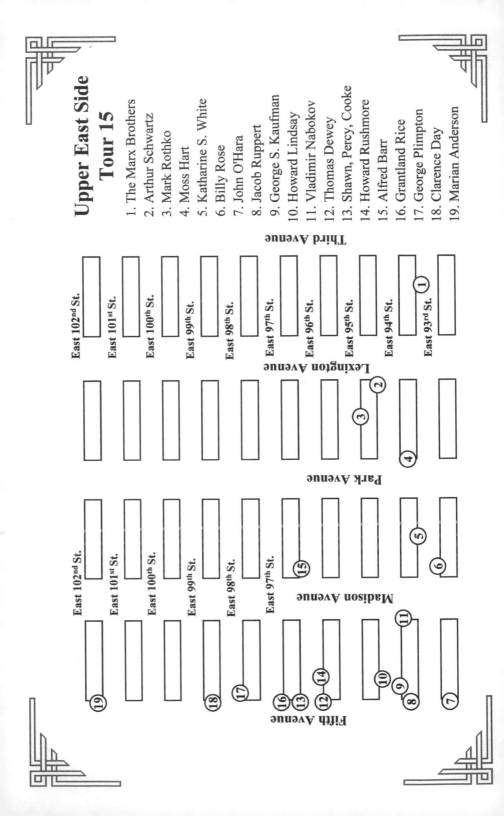

Upper East Side
Tour 15

1. The Marx Brothers
2. Arthur Schwartz
3. Mark Rothko
4. Moss Hart
5. Katharine S. White
6. Billy Rose
7. John O'Hara
8. Jacob Ruppert
9. George S. Kaufman
10. Howard Lindsay
11. Vladimir Nabokov
12. Thomas Dewey
13. Shawn, Percy, Cooke
14. Howard Rushmore
15. Alfred Barr
16. Grantland Rice
17. George Plimpton
18. Clarence Day
19. Marian Anderson

Third Avenue

East 102nd St.
East 101st St.
East 100th St.
East 99th St.
East 98th St.
East 97th St.
East 96th St.
East 95th St.
East 94th St.
East 93rd St.

Lexington Avenue

Park Avenue

East 102nd St.
East 101st St.
East 100th St.
East 99th St.
East 98th St.
East 97th St.

Madison Avenue

Fifth Avenue

spring of 1968. By then, his relationship with his wife had become strained and he began to grow distant from his family.

By late 1968, he had begun to work on a cycle of paintings for the chapel at **Rice University** in Houston. Rothko's studio was located at 157 East 69th Street and on January 1, 1969, he separated from his family and moved permanently into that studio. It would be his home for the last fourteen months of his life (see this section, Tour 6, Number 9).

4/Moss Hart
1185 Park Avenue between 93rd and 94th Street.

This was the last home of **Moss Hart**, the Broadway playwright and director. His career took off in 1930 when he collaborated with **George S. Kaufman** on the hit play *Once in a Lifetime.*

After working successfully with Kaufman during the next ten years, Hart began staging his own plays and directing the works of other playwrights. He married the actress **Kitty Carlisle** in 1946 and they took up residence in this Park Avenue apartment house with their son and daughter.

Hart was living here when he directed the popular musical *My Fair Lady,* which opened in 1956 and played for 2,717 Broadway performances. He also directed **Lerner** and **Loewe's** *Camelot* in 1960, another hit.

Hart and Carlisle left New York to live in Palm Springs, California, in 1961. He died there of a heart attack only a few weeks after the move.

5/Katharine S. White
61 East 93rd Street between Madison and Park Avenue.

Katharine S. White—her maiden name was Katharine Sergeant—lived in a six-room apartment in this red brick building with her first husband, attorney **Ernest Angell**, beginning in the early 1920s. Her first child, **Roger**, had just been born. In 1925, Katharine went to work for **Harold Ross** at the newly-formed magazine *The New Yorker* and served as one of its greatest editors until her retirement in 1961.

During that period, chiefly as fiction editor, she championed and nurtured an array of important American writers including **John O'Hara, John Cheever, Vladimir Nabokov, May Sarton,** and **John Updike,** to name just a few. In 1929, after falling in love with colleague **E.B. White**, Katharine separated from Angell and left the apartment on 93rd Street to live in Greenwich Village. Her son Roger, who later became a staff writer at his mother's magazine, continued to live here with his father. Katharine and E. B. White were married in November 1929. They were together for almost forty-eight years, until her death in 1977.

6/Billy Rose
56 East 93rd Street at Madison Avenue (southeast corner).

Theatrical producer **Billy Rose** purchased this beautiful forty-five-room mansion in 1956 from sportsman / businessman **William Goadby Loew.** The price was $430,000.

Rose, fabulously rich by then,

moved here with his third wife, **Joyce Matthews**.

They were divorced three years later but she moved back into the house soon after and they were remarried in 1961—only to be divorced again in 1963. A year later, Rose married again, this time to **Doris Warner**, daughter of movie tycoon, **Harry Warner**. It was a union that lasted only six months. Rose was living alone in this house at the time of his death. He died in 1966 at the age of sixty-six.

The Rose mansion later became the **Smithers Alcoholism Center of St. Luke's Hospital**. Writer John Cheever is among those who received treatment here. In 1999, the **Spence School** purchased the mansion.

7/John O'Hara
1115 Fifth Avenue at 93rd Street (southeast corner).

This fifteen-story luxury apartment building was designed by **James Carpenter** and opened in 1925. It is the virtual twin of its neighbor across the street at 1120 Fifth Avenue. In 1938, writer **John O'Hara** was living here in his mother-in-law's apartment with his wife, **Belle**.

One day he told his wife that he was going to Philadelphia for a few days to be alone and write. On the way to Penn Station, he decided to stop at the **Hotel Pierre** (on Fifth Avenue and 60th Street) for a quick drink. Before long he had taken a room there and went on a two-day drinking spree. After he sobered up and realized he had written nothing, the guilt set in and, now desperate, he pro-

ceeded to knock off a quick piece about a night-club master-of-ceremonies named **Joey Evans**. *The New Yorker* promptly bought his story, soon wanted more, and before long O'Hara had written fourteen more about this same character. They later became the basis for the successful Broadway play *Pal Joey*, produced in 1940, with music by **Rodgers and Hart**. The play made O'Hara an overnight celebrity.

1115 Fifth Avenue was also the home of **Arthur Hays Sulzberger,** publisher of the *New York Times* from 1935 to 1961. His eleven-room apartment was his New York residence for the last seventeen years of his life. He died in his sleep here on December 11, 1968.

8/Jacob Ruppert
1116 and 1120 Fifth Avenue at 93rd Street.

Jacob Ruppert, the millionaire owner of the *New York Yankees* for twenty-four years—a period in which they became one of the greatest baseball teams of all time—-lived in a mansion at 1116 Fifth Avenue on the southeast corner for almost three decades. (The apartment building standing there today numbered 1115 replaced it in 1925 after it was demolished—see number 7 above).

Ruppert's fortune was made in beer; his family owned the huge **Ruppert** brewery which once stood at 1693 Third Avenue, just east of here in the Yorkville neighborhood.

Ruppert purchased the *Yankees* in 1915 when they were a weak team in the American League but in 1920 he made them into an instant powerhouse when he purchased **Babe Ruth** from the *Boston Red Sox* for $125,-000. The *Yankees* went on to win ten pennants and seven World Series for him before he died.

Ruppert's large house was one of the first to be built in this part of Manhattan, which was still made up of shanties and small farms at the turn of the last century. The mansion and its large orchards in back were protected by an iron-spiked fence and two watchdogs.

The **Marx Brothers,** who lived only four blocks away when they were boys (see number 1 above), regularly braved the fence and the dogs to pilfer the fruit on Ruppert's trees.

When Ruppert had his mansion razed in 1925, he moved to this building across the street at 1120 Fifth—visually very similar to the structure that replaced his house across the street. A lifelong bachelor, he occupied a twelve-room cooperative apartment in the building and lived there until his death in 1939 at the age of seventy-one.

9/George S. Kaufman

14 East 94th Street between Fifth and Madison Avenue.

The Broadway playwright and director lived in this narrow, five-story house with the double black doors from 1932 until 1942. During the year that he moved in, his plays were doing so well that he was making more money than any other New York playwright or producer—around $7,000 a week.

While he lived on 94th Street, **Kaufman** wrote and directed four popular plays: *You Can't Take It With*

George S. Kaufman

You, George Washington Slept Here, and *The Man Who Came to Dinner* (co-written with **Moss Hart)** and *Stage Door* (co-written with **Edna Ferber**).

In 1936, Kaufman's name was linked with the actress **Mary Astor** in a sensational divorce and child custody proceeding. Astor had kept a diary detailing their three-year affair and her estranged husband released the contents of the diary to the press. Kaufman, who was subpoenaed to appear as a witness, temporarily fled to California in panic and embarrassment.

Kaufman and his wife, **Beatrice,** lived in this house until 1942, when they took a more modest residence at 410 Park Avenue.

10/Howard Lindsay
13 East 94th Street between Fifth and Madison Avenue.

By the late 1940s, playwright and actor **Howard Lindsay** and his long-time collaborator **Russel Crouse** were two of Broadway's biggest names. Their play *Life With Father*, which opened in 1939, had enjoyed the longest run in Broadway history and they had won a Pulitzer Prize in 1946 for the drama *State of the Union.*

In 1950, Lindsay moved into this five-story house on 94th Street with his wife, actress **Dorothy Stickney**. They lived here together for the next eighteen years and during that time, Lindsay and Crouse continued their success. They wrote *Call Me Madam,* with music by **Irving Berlin,** in 1950 and then *The Sound of Music,* with a score by **Rodgers** and **Hammerstein**, in 1960.

Howard Lindsay died in his home here on February 11, 1968 at the age of seventy-nine. Dorothy Stickney lived until 1998. In 2003, the house was purchased by a software entrepreneur for $11.25 million.

11/Vladimir Nabokov
1326 Madison Avenue at 94th Street (southwest corner).

Russian writer **Vladimir Nabokov** arrived in the United States from France with his wife, **Vera,** and young son, **Dmitri,** in May 1940, fleeing Paris just as the Nazis arrived. Their first home in New York was a tiny sublet apartment in this building. The Nabokovs had only about one hundred dollars to their name and Vladimir spent many hours trying, unsuccessfully, to find a job. The family spent part of the summer as guests in a farmhouse in Vermont where Nabokov was able to pursue his hobby of catching butterflies. In September, soon after returning to the city, the Nabokovs moved across Central Park to an apartment on 35 West 87th Street.

12/Thomas Dewey
1148 Fifth Avenue at 96th Street (southeast corner).

Dewey is chiefly remembered today as the man who lost two presidential elections—in 1944 to **Franklin Roosevelt** and in 1948 to underdog **Harry Truman.** But Dewey made his early reputation in the 1930s as a New York City district attorney and special prosecutor who carried on a

Home of Thomas Dewey

much-publicized campaign against organized crime.

Dewey was living in an eight-room apartment in this building with his wife and son in 1935 when he was gathering evidence to convict underworld boss **Dutch Schultz** of racketeering and murder. The enraged Schultz, in defiance of the crime syndicate's rule against killing public officials, made plans to kill Dewey. He assigned one of his henchmen to shadow Dewey each morning after he left his home here at 1148 Fifth. When **Lucky Luciano**, Manhattan's top mob boss, learned about Schultz's maverick plan, he ordered Dutch's execution. Schultz was gunned down on October 23, 1935 at a restaurant in Newark, New Jersey. Ironically, in April 1936, Luciano himself became Dewey's next victim in court; he was convicted of running a prostitution ring and given a long-term sentence.

Dewey went on to become governor of New York and received his first Republican Party nomination for president in 1944.

13/William Shawn, Walker Percy, Alastair Cooke
1150 Fifth Avenue at 96th Street (northeast corner).

William Shawn, who served as the editor of *The New Yorker* for thirty-five years, lived in a large apartment on the second floor of this building. Number 1150 Fifth Aveue was designed by **J.E.R. Carpenter** and completed in 1924.

Shawn had moved here with his wife, **Cecille,** and their three children in 1951—the year before he took over the leadership of the magazine. He succeeded legendary editor and founder **Harold Ross** who had died suddenly of cancer in 1951. Under Shawn's guidance, the magazine sustained the excellence that had made it a New York landmark institution since Ross started it in 1925.

When **The New Yorker** changed owners in 1988, Shawn was forced to resign, ending an affiliation with the publication that spanned fifty-four years. Frustrated and discouraged after that, he died of a heart attack in his bed here on December 6, 1992. He was eighty-five years old.

Novelist **Walker Percy** lived in the apartment of family friend **Huger Jervey** in this building in 1944. Percy, whose home was in Louisiana, was a young medical student at the time and occupied a room in the servant's quarters.

This building was also the New York home of British journalist **Alastair Cooke** for many years. He died here on March 30, 2004 at the age of ninety-five.

14/Howard Rushmore
6 East 96th Street near Fifth Avenue.

Across the street from the residence of *The New Yorker's* **William Shawn,** there lived an editor of quite a different magazine. The man was **Howard Rushmore**, the occupant of an apartment here at 6 East 96th Street. During the early 1950s, he was the editor and chief writer for the sleazy Hollywood expose magazine *Confidential*. Rushmore started out as a journalist for the right-wing *New*

York Journal-American, where his specialty was rooting out alleged Communists in high places. In 1953, after his credibility was finally challenged in this role, he joined the staff of *Confidential;* it was his ability to produce prurient stories about the intimate affairs of movie stars that ultimately raised the circulation of the magazine to five million at the height of its popularity.

Rushmore left the publication in 1955 and the scandal sheet began its decline soon after when a number of celebrities began lawsuits. Rushmore's career went into a tailspin during the following years and ended on a lurid note. On the night of January 3, 1958, a taxicab picked up Rushmore and his estranged wife, **Frances**, not far from his apartment here on 96th Street. In the back seat, Rushmore shot her and then turned the gun on himself. When authorities arrived, both victims were dead.

15/Alfred Barr
49 East 96th Street at Madison Avenue (northeast corner).

Alfred Barr, who in 1929 was appointed the first director of the **Museum of Modern Art,** resided for many years in this seventeen-story apartment building. For over four decades, he was largely responsible for building the museum's collections and its reputation. Barr made numerous trips to Europe in the years before World War II and brought back the many works that made up MOMA's first Van Gough, Dada, and Surrealism shows. He organized over one hundred exhibitions during his tenure and did much to create the idea of the modern art exhibition through the use of special lighting, descriptive wall captions, and scholarly, illustrated catalogues.

His apartment here on 96th Street was sparsely furnished but the walls were covered with pictures by Miro, Picasso, and Gris. Barr, who lived here with his wife, Margaret, and daughter, Victoria, often walked the forty-three blocks to the museum in the morning, making the return trip by foot at night.

16/Grantland Rice
1158 Fifth Avenue at 97th Street (southeast corner).

Grantland Rice, known as the dean of American sports writers a half-century ago, lived in this large apartment building. He came to New York from Tennessee in 1911 to work for the *Evening Mail,* where he introduced his popular column called *Sportlight*, which eventually became syndicated in hundred of newspapers around the country. It was Rice who coined the phrase "the four horsemen" to describe the legendary Notre Dame backfield of the 1920s and it was Rice who later wrote of **Coach Knute Rockne's** speech to his squad which exhorted them to "win one for the Gipper." Rice was living here on Fifth Avenue in July 1954 when he suffered a stroke and died. He was seventy-three years old.

17/George Plimpton
1165 Fifth Avenue at 98th Street (southeast corner).

This fifteen-story luxury apartment building, designed by **James E.R.**

George Plimpton's childhood home

to run his affairs from his home here. In 1903, he retired from business completely and devoted himself to writing.

Day died of a stroke in 1935—the year that his most popular book, *Life With Father*, was published. In 1939, it was adapted into a play by **Howard Lindsay** and **Russel Crouse** that nobody thought would amount to much but which became one of the most successful productions in theatrical history, running for 3,224 performances. For many years, it held the record for the longest running Broadway play.

19/Marian Anderson
1200 Fifth Avenue at 101st Street. (northeast corner)

This building was the home of contralto concert and opera singer **Marian Anderson** from 1958 to 1975. She was born in Philadelphia in 1902 and came to Manhattan in the 1920s to sing with the **New York Philharmonic** and perform at **Carnegie Hall**.

In 1936, Anderson became the first African-American to perform at the White House. After she was denied the use of Constitution Hall for a performance in 1939, First Lady **Eleanor Roosevelt** arranged for her to sing at the **Lincoln Memorial,** a performance that drew an audience of 75,000 people.

In 1955, Anderson became a permanent member of the **Metropolitan Opera**—she was the first African-American to sing there. During the first year that she lived in this house, she was selected as a delegate to the United Nations.

Carpenter, was the childhood home of writer **George Plimpton**. His father, corporate attorney **Francis T.P. Plimpton** and mother **Pauline Ames**, were the first occupants of the duplex penthouse numbered 14D when the building opened in 1926. George was born on March 18, 1927. His father later became the country's United Nations ambassador.

18/Clarence Day
1170 Fifth Avenue at 98th Street (northeast corner).

Clarence Day, a stockbroker and author, lived in this luxury apartment building during the last years of his life. It was his home from 1928 to 1934. He developed crippling arthritis in his mid-twenties and eventually became an invalid who was forced

MIDTOWN
EAST
OF FIFTH AVENUE

From East 40th Street to East 60th Street
and between Fifth Avenue and the East River

MIDTOWN EAST, as described in this book, can be divided roughly into two areas. The first, between Fifth Avenue and Third Avenue was once largely a neighborhood of mansions and brownstones—a development that took place as the most affluent New Yorkers moved uptown between the Civil War and the turn of the century. The very wealthiest made Fifth Avenue up to Central Park the original Millionaires' Row. Today almost all of those old residences on Fifth are gone, replaced by a mix of modern commercial buildings and luxury apartments; many of the brownstones east of that great avenue, however, still exist.

The second area, between Third Avenue and the East River, had become, by the late nineteenth and early twentieth century, a section of middle class homes and working class tenements with the exception of the landscape that stretched along the river which was dominated by slaughterhouses and breweries. This neighborhood has retained its residential character today although the commercial buildings and the homes of the poor near the waterfront have been replaced by luxury buildings. After World War II, the United Nations building replaced the blight along the East River between 42nd and 48th Street. Midtown East, with such wonderful neighborhoods as Turtle Bay, Beekman Place, Tudor City, and Sutton Place, has been the home for a number of important and colorful New Yorkers.

TOUR 1

1/Sherry-Netherland Hotel
781 Fifth Avenue between 59th and 60th Street.

The luxurious **Sherry-Netherland**, built by restaurateur and ice cream maker **Louis Sherry** and opened in 1927, has hosted a mix of permanent residents and temporary guests over the years.

Many people prominent in the motion picture industry made it their headquarters when they traveled to New York. **Harry Cohn**, head of **Columbia Pictures**, had rooms in the hotel. **Jack Warner,** an original **Warner Brother**, once occupied the penthouse while comedians **Danny Kaye** and **George Burns** lived in apartments below him. **Francis Ford Coppola** lived here; his daughter **Sophia** grew up in the hotel.

For a number of years in the 1940s and 50s, **Howard Hughes** kept a suite here and made it his headquarters when he visited New York. Columnist **Earl Wilson** once wrote that the late actor **Spencer Tracy** shocked the guests of the Sherry one night by turning up in the lobby drunk and stark naked, searching for a drink.

On December 13, 1934, *Time* magazine editor **Henry Luce** came to the glamorous journalist **Clare Boothe's** six-room apartment on the sixteenth floor of the hotel and proposed marriage to her. Luce had met Boothe only a few days earlier and had immediately fallen in love with her, even though he was married at the time. After Boothe finally accepted, Luce divorced his first wife, **Lila,** and married Boothe in November 1935.

Ernest Hemingway was fifty years old in November 1949 when he stayed at the Sherry with his fourth wife, **Mary Welsh**. He was on the way to Europe at the time and busy writing his next novel, *Across the River and Into the Trees*. He spent the winter in France and Italy and hated the prospect of returning to New York—a place he referred to as "that damned chicken-shit cement canyon town." But he returned to the city in the spring of 1950 and spent time again at the Sherry, revising his manuscript before returning home to Cuba. *Muppets* creator **Jim Henson** had a three-bedroom apartment at the Sherry and it was his last home. Henson died of pneumonia in June 1990 while he in was residence here. He was only fifty-three years old.

2/The Beatles
502 Park Avenue at 59th Street (northwest corner).

Built in 1928, this thirty-two-story building was known for many years as the **Hotel Delmonico. Ed Sullivan**, the newspaper columnist and television personality, lived on the eleventh floor from 1944 until his death in 1973. Sullivan is probably best known today as the host of the long-running Sunday night CBS television show on which the **Beatles** made their first appearance in America in February 1964. When the British group returned to New York in August of that same year during their first North American tour, they stayed in a sixth-floor suite here at the Delmonico. Crowds of up to

East 60th

East 59th

East 58th

East 57th

Fifth Avenue

Madison Avenue

Park Avenue

Lexington Avenue

Midtown East
Tour 1

1. Sherry-Netherland Hotel

2. The Beatles

3. Philip Barry

4. Stieglitz-O'Keeffe

5. Toots Shor and William Paley

6. Janet Flanner

7. Audrey Hepburn and Hedy Lamarr

8. Doris Duke

9. Ritz Tower

10. David Merrick

11. Bertolt Brecht

12. Adele Astaire

5,000 gathered across the street and as the lads moved through the lobby on the first day, a hysterical group of girls attacked them and ripped a St. Christopher's medal off **Ringo's** neck. After the performance of their last show at the **Forrest Hills Tennis Stadium** on August 28th, they returned to the hotel where they were introduced to **Bob Dylan**. That night, Dylan introduced the Beatles to the pleasures of marijuana.

Lorenz Hart, the lyricist of the **Rodgers and Hart** songwriting team, made the Delmonico his home during the last year of his life. Hart's alcoholism had destroyed his health by this time and he was no longer working with Richard Rodgers. He was found unconscious in his apartment here on November 17, 1943 and died in the hospital a few days later.

Lucille Ball and her husband, **Desi Arnaz**, lived at the Delmonico for six months in 1946 while she took a break from her movie career and he performed with his orchestra at the **Copacabana** nightclub. It was five years before they began their groundbreaking television sitcom, *I Love Lucy*.

Robert Harrison, founder of the infamous 1950s scandal magazine *Confidential*, was a Delmonico resident. He died here of a heart attack on the afternoon of February 17, 1978 while sitting at his desk. Harrison had been forced to sell the magazine twenty years earlier when a series of libel suits filed by the some of the celebrities that he exposed made it impossible for him to continue publishing the magazine. In its heyday, *Confidential* "named the names" and dished the dirt about

Hotel Delmonico and the Beatles

scores of Hollywood stars and became America's most popular tabloid publication.

3/Philip Barry
510 Park Avenue at 60th Street (southwest corner).

Philip Barry was one of America's most successful playwrights. Comedies like *Paris Bound* and *Holiday,* written in the 1920s, launched Barry on a Broadway career that spanned three decades. His greatest success came in 1939 with *The Philadelphia Story,* which saved the **Theatre Guild** from financial disaster and re-established **Katharine Hepburn** as a major star. She purchased the rights to the play and starred in it both on Broadway and in the movie version.

Barry did most of his writing at his home in France but he lived in New York when his plays were in production and this apartment building on Park Avenue at 60th Street was his last residence. He died here of a heart attack on December 3, 1949 at age fifty-three.

4/Alfred Stieglitz and Georgia O'Keeffe

114 East 59th Street between Park and Lexington Avenue.

In June 1918, **O'Keeffe** arrived in New York from Texas and, at the invitation of **Edward Stieglitz's** niece **Elizabeth**, went to live in a small studio in a brownstone on this site. **O'Keeffe** was suffering from the influenza that was sweeping the country at that time. By then, **Alfred Stieglitz** had fallen in love with the young painter and soon left his wife to live here with O'Keeffe. Her studio, where the **Argosy Bookstore** now stands, consisted of two top-floor rooms and Stieglitz moved his photographic equipment into one of them. O'Keeffe put her bed under the skylight in the other room so that she could look directly up at the starry nights. After she recovered from her illness, she began to paint again. At first, the two strung up a clothes line over which they draped a blanket to separate their beds but, before long, they were lovers.

It was in this studio that Stieglitz began to take his famous photographs of O'Keeffe, posed in various ways. In the spring of 1920, the couple learned that their house was to be demolished and they moved to the residence of Stieglitz's brother on 60 East 65th Street (see Section One, Tour 1, Number 17). Stieglitz and O'Keeffe were married in 1924.

5/Toots Shor and William Paley

480 Park Avenue at 58th Street (northwest corner).

This large apartment building was the home for many years of famed saloonkeeper **Toots Shor,** whose restaurant and bar at 51 West 51st Street was a renowned hangout for New York's most famous athletes, writers, and entertainers for over three decades. Shor, in his role as host, spent much more time at his famous watering hole than he did at his home. He would arrive at his 51st Street joint in the early afternoon and usually stayed until the early hours of the next morning, only returning home to sleep and later to spend a few hours with his family before departing again. Shor shared the twelve-room duplex apartment here on Park Avenue with his wife, **Marion**, and their three children. He died in 1977, not long after he had moved away.

William Paley, president of CBS, lived in a large apartment at the top of 480 Park from 1930 to 1932. Its entertaining and sleeping rooms were decorated at a total cost of $10,000 per room, an unheard-of amount during the early years of the Great Depression. Paley installed eight radios in his place so that he could continuously monitor the programming of both his own station and that of his competition.

Boss **Frank Hague,** mayor of Jersey City, New Jersey for over three decades and the man who ruled the state's politics with an iron hand from 1917 to 1949, maintained an apartment in this building and died here on January 1, 1956 at the age of seventy-nine.

6/Janet Flanner

40 East 58th Street at Madison Avenue (southeast corner).

In the early 1940s, this five-story brick building was the home of **Natalia Danesi Murray**, a woman who worked as an Italian language broadcaster for NBC radio. In July 1940, Murray met **Janet Flanner,** the writer who covered current events and culture in Paris as correspondent for *The New Yorker*. Flanner had recently returned to New York from Europe after the Nazis invaded France.

Before long, Murray and Flanner fell in love and Flanner moved into Murray's apartment here, where the two lived together with Murray's mother and son. While in residence, Flanner wrote profiles for the magazine on **Thomas Mann, Betty Davis,** and **Marshall Petain.** But she missed Europe and, in 1944, she returned to France as one of *The New Yorker's* war correspondents.

7/Audrey Hepburn and Hedy Lamarr
50 East 58th Street between Madison and Park Avenue.

The old **Blackstone Hotel** is gone now, replaced on this block in the early 1990s by the plush **Four Seasons**, designed by **I.M. Pei.** In the 1950s, the Blackstone, with its Continental flavor, was a favorite stop of European travelers to Manhattan.

The young actress **Audrey Hepburn** came from London to live here in 1951 while she performed in the Broadway version of *Gigi*. For $125 a week, she rented a small suite consisting of parlor, bedroom, kitchenette and bath and furnished with a television on which she watched American movies until the wee hours of the morning. Actor **David Niven**, another Blackstone resident, lived next door to Hepburn. One night, a body crashed against Hepburn's window—an apparent suicide. In terror, Hepburn pounded on Niven's door and, after she calmed down, the two began a friendship that lasted for many years.

Former Hollywood movie queen **Hedy Lamarr** lived at the Blackstone in the late 1960s, long after her glamorous screen career was over. She was in her fifties by then and existed on a modest income. When she left New York for California in 1971, she was forced to auction off furniture and clothes to pay her back taxes. Before Lamarr died in Florida in January 2000 at the age of eighty-six, she was forced to support herself on a monthly Social Security check and a small actor's pension.

8/Doris Duke
475 Park Avenue at 58th Street (southeast corner).

This large building was the last New York home of tobacco heiress **Doris Duke**. She owned a penthouse here which was only one of the many residences she maintained in this country; the others were in Somerville, New Jersey, Newport, Rhode Island, Hawaii, and California.

Duke was considered for years to be the richest woman in the world; when her father **James Buchanan Duke** died in 1935, he left her $100 million, in the middle of the Depression. She passed away at her home in Beverly Hills, California on October 28, 1993 at the age of eighty.

9/Ritz Tower

465 Park Avenue at 57th Street (northeast corner).

Designed by famed New York architect **Emery Roth**, this forty-one-story apartment house was the world's tallest residential building when it opened in 1926 and one of the most luxurious. It supplied its tenants with all kinds of amenities including hot meals delivered in electrically-heated dumbwaiters and served by butlers stationed on each floor.

William Randolph Hearst moved into a suite at the **Ritz Tower** in the late 1920s while his main residence—**The Clarendon** on Riverside Drive—was being renovated and it soon became his de-facto home as well as his New York office. When Hearst separated from his wife in 1938 and was forced to sell his huge apartment in the Clarendon, his mistress, **Marion Davies**, moved into the Ritz Tower with him.

Greta Garbo, after retiring from the movies in 1939, moved to a two-room apartment in the Ritz Tower and lived in it throughout the 1940s. Her place, Apartment 26C, was modestly furnished and Garbo lived here like a monk with little except a toothbrush, a piece of soap, and a jar of face cream. She seldom raised her blinds.

French writer-in-exile **Andre Maurois** made the Ritz Tower his home during World War II and later wrote: "I shall miss this tiny New York apartment where there is nothing ugly. In the morning, at sunrise, the soaring towers of New York, amber or rose, take on the smooth luminous softness of walls by Vermeer or Guardi."

Others who have lived at the Ritz Tower over the years include **Arthur Brisbane, Marlene Dietrich, Paulette Goddard,** and **Neil Simon**.

10/David Merrick

119 East 57th Street near Lexington Avenue.

David Merrick, who in his long career made as many enemies as he did hit Broadway plays, lived in several New York apartments during his lifetime. The man who produced such hit shows as *42nd Street, Gypsy,* and *Hello, Dolly!,* lived as a bachelor in this residential apartment building known as **The Galleria** during the 1980s.

Merrick lived unpretentiously and was not known for enjoying the material benefits of his large fortune. His place could have been taken for that of a vagrant—not very clean and with a mattress on the floor. He never slept much and he was seldom at home. But he was in his apartment here one day in February 1983 when he suffered a stroke. Although it left him physically disabled, he recovered and lived for another seventeen years. Merrick died in London in April 2000 at the age of eighty-eight.

11/Bertolt Brecht

124 East 57th Street between Park and Lexington Avenue.

In 1943, German playwright Bertolt **Brecht**, in exile from his native country during the war, was living in Los Angeles and working on a movie script. In February of that year, he traveled to New York to visit his mistress, **Ruth Berlau**, who was renting a fourth-floor walkup apartment in this building. He stayed with her for four months, spending his time visiting fellow exiles, writing, and lecturing. This was the first of five trips that Brecht took to Manhattan from California; each time he stayed here with Berlau. While he was here, he worked on his play *The Caucasian Chalk Circle* with Berlau's help. In 1945, Brecht was living on 57th when he suffered a nervous breakdown; Berlau again aided his recovery by nursing him around the clock. The leftist playwright abruptly fled the United States in 1947 after testifying, nervously, before the House Un-American Activities Committee.

12/Adele Astaire

110 East 57th Street between Park and Lexington Avenue.

Fred and **Adele Astaire,** brother and sister, were Broadway's greatest dancing team of the 1920s. The act broke up in 1932 when Adele, tired of show business, retired and married the British Lord **Charles Cavendish**. She moved with him to Europe. After his death in 1944, Adele married a second time to investment banker **Kingman Douglas** and their last New York home was in this modern white brick apartment building called **The Dorchester**.

Her brother Fred, now a movie star, was a guest on numerous occasions. Adele and her husband lived at this address until his death in 1971. Soon after, she moved to Arizona; she died there in 1981 at the age of eighty-three.

TOUR 2

1/Hotel Lombardy

111 East 56th Street between Park and Lexington Avenue.

This famous residential hotel was built during the mid-1920s. It was a popular home for literary and show business personalities. **Ernest Hemingway** and his new wife, journalist **Martha Gellhorn**, stayed here during the month of January 1941 as they prepared to travel to China as war correspondents. While he was here, Hemingway received a check for $100,000 for the movie sale of his novel *For Whom the Bell Tolls*. He also received a typhoid shot, which kept him sick in bed for a week.

In the winter of 1934, **Dashiell Hammett** set himself up at the **Lombardy** while he awaited the publication of his new novel *The Thin Man*.

In 1929, actress **Louise Brooks** lived here soon after returning from Germany, where she had performed in the silent film that made her famous, *Pandora's Box*.

Author **Edna Ferber** lived on the nineteenth floor of the Lombardy from 1930 to 1935 and while in residence co-wrote the hit play *Dinner at Eight* with **George S. Kaufman**. Ferber became upset when Broadway composer **Richard Rodgers** rented the apartment next door in 1930 because she didn't want to live near a noisy songwriter. When she returned from a trip to find that Rodgers had filled her living room with flowers, she changed her mind and the two became lifelong friends.

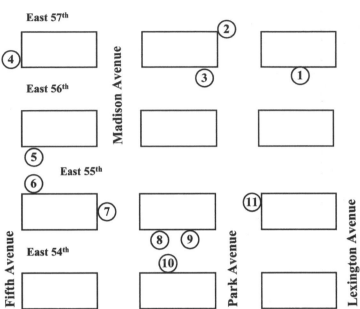

East 57th

East 56th

East 55th

East 54th

Madison Avenue

Fifth Avenue

Park Avenue

Lexington Avenue

Midtown East
Tour 2

1. Hotel Lombardy

2. Jerome Kern

3. Lillian Gish and
   Howard Hughes

4. Trump Tower

5. E.H. Harriman

6. St. Regis Hotel

7. Robert Benchley and
   Charles MacArthur

8. Lillian Russell

9. Alfred Stieglitz and
   Georgia O'Keeffe

10. Hotel Elysée

11. George Gershwin

Rodgers and his wife, **Dorothy**, moved out in 1931, soon after the birth of their first child. Their place was taken by Rodgers's inlaws and in October 1931, Dorothy's father, **Benjamin Feiner**, fell to his death from the nineteenth floor here, probably a suicide.

George Burns and **Gracie Allen** lived briefly at the Lombardy before moving to Hollywood in 1935. **Sinclair Lewis** lived alone here in 1939 and 1940 after breaking up with wife, **Dorothy Thompson**. **Henry Fonda** made the Lombardy his home in 1947 while he starred on Broadway in the play *Mr. Roberts.*

2/Jerome Kern

450 Park Avenue at 57th Street (southwest corner).

Jerome Kern, one of America's greatest songwriters, collapsed in front of the building here at 450 Park Avenue at noon on Monday, November 5, 1945, the victim of a cerebral hemorrhage; he was standing at the southwest corner of Park and 57th, waiting for the light to change. Kern, the composer of such standards as *Ole Man River, Smoke Gets in Your Eyes,* and *The Last Time I Saw Paris,* had come to New York from California to co-produce a revival of his hit musical *Showboat* and was staying at the **St. Regis Hotel** (see Number 6 below). After the accident, he was rushed to Doctor's Hospital where he died six days later. Kern was sixty years old.

3/Lillian Gish and Howard Hughes

444 Park Avenue at 56th Street (northwest corner).

The twenty-one story Drake Hotel-now called the **Drake Swissotel**—was designed by **Emery Roth** and opened in 1927. It was home to silent film star **Lillian Gish** from 1946 to 1949. She had moved to New York permanently in 1929 and lived in this neighborhood for the rest of her life. While she lived at the **Drake,** she performed on stage in **Dostoyevsky's** *Crime and Punishment* opposite **John Gielgud** and appeared in **David Selznick's** epic western film *Duel in the Sun,* both in 1947.

On July 13, 1938, **Howard Hughes** landed his airplane in New York, completing an around-the-world air flight for which he set a new world record. Exhausted, Hughes escaped the mob that had assembled to greet him and secretly turned up here at the Drake seeking a suite. He carried no cash or identification with him but the manager recognized him, paid for his cab and placed a do-not-disturb sign on the door of his suite. Hughes slept for sixteen straight hours. The next day, he and his flight crew were given a ticker-tape parade attended by an estimated 1,500,000 spectators.

Restaurateur **Toots Shor,** who ran one of New York's most famous eating and drinking places at 51 West 51st Street for many years, lived at the Drake during his last years. Shor died in 1977.

Edith Rockefeller, the fourth child of **John D. Rockefeller, Sr.**, lived at the Drake during the last years of her life. Her bohemian lifestyle and carefree spending habits left her alienated from her conservative father and she had to manage on a tight budget while she lived here. She died in her hotel suite on August 25, 1932 at age sixty.

Just west of the Drake at 79 East 56th Street, there once stood a brownstone—long ago demolished—where the elderly parents of **Humphrey Bogart** lived in their last years. From 1925 to 1934, the once-wealthy **Belmont Bogart**, a physician, and his wife, **Maude**, a magazine illustrator, existed here on a diminished income after the family fortune was lost to a bad investment in Michigan timberlands.

4/Trump Tower
725 Fifth Avenue at 56th Street (northeast corner).

This sixty-six story giant glass tower, built by real estate entrepreneur **Donald Trump** in 1983, is a mix of commercial spaces at the bottom with residences at the top, beginning on the thirtieth floor. Among the celebrities who have enjoyed luxury quarters here are **Johnny Carson, Dick Clark, Sophia Loren, Martina Navratilova,** and **Steven Spielberg.**

5/E.H. Harriman
1 East 55th Street at Fifth Avenue (northeast corner).

Harriman, the financier and railroad baron, lived in a large house on this corner beginning in 1895. His son, **Averill,** the future governor of New York and advisor to presidents, was just an infant.

In those days, this stretch of Fifth Avenue was the original Millionaire's Row—a neighborhood top-heavy with families listed on the Social Register. The Harrimans were surrounded by the houses of the **Huntingtons, Vanderbilts, Astors,** and **Whitneys. Joseph Pulitzer** lived directly across the street (see Number 6 below).

Harriman did little to attract attention, staying away from the costume balls and formal dinners that were constantly being given by the neighbors. On the evenings of such events, the Harrimans could be found in their parlor playing parchessi or backgammon. By the time that Harriman died in 1909, the family had moved uptown to 1 East 69th Street (see Section One, Tour 3, Number 14).

6/St. Regis Hotel
2 East 55th Street at Fifth Avenue (southeast corner).

The elegant **St. Regis,** built by **Colonel John Jacob Astor** and opened in 1905, has been called "the best European hotel in the United States." It stands on the site of the four-story mansion where journalist millionaire **Joseph Pulitzer** lived from 1887 until 1900.

In that latter year, on January 9th, Pulitzer's home was destroyed by a fire. His wife and children, barefooted and in their nightclothes, were lucky to escape but two of Pulitzer's seventeen servants lost their lives. The St. Regis was built on the spot of the fire in 1904. It soon became one of New York's most famous luxury hotels.

In 1939, artist **Salvador Dali** was hired to design a window display at the fashionable **Bonwit Teller** store at Fifth Avenue and 56th Street, where the **Trump Tower** now stands.

Dali lived here at the St. Regis, his favorite New York place, while he worked on the project. The artist's surrealistic display—which included a stuffed buffalo head and a bathtub from which rose three wax arms holding mirrors—horrified the chic ladies of Fifth Avenue and the store replaced it immediately. Dali, in a rage, overturned the bathtub and smashed the plate glass of the display window.He was promptly arrested and spent a night in jail.

Orson Welles moved into a room at the St. Regis in the summer of 1938 because the air conditioning relieved his hay fever and living at the hotel allowed the married actor to discretely carry out his many love affairs. Welles was directing the play *Too Much Johnson* at the time and, after he filmed some of the scenes, he had a moviola machine installed in his suite at the hotel so that he could edit the footage. Welles sat here working for hours, surrounded by thousands of feet of film. It was the moment that he discovered a new passion — filmmaking. Welles was staying at the St. Regis when he produced the infamous radio version of *The War of the Worlds,* which made him a national celebrity overnight.

Alfred Hitchcock stayed at the St. Regis during his first trip to the U.S. in 1937 and he enjoyed the place so much that he made it his New York headquarters for the rest of his life. In his suite here in 1944, he worked on the script for his **Cary Grant** and **Ingrid Bergman** film *Notorious,* which he co-wrote with **Ben Hecht**.

In the summer of 1953, film director **Elia Kazan** and his screenwriter **Budd Schulberg** holed up here in producer **Sam Spiegel's** suite, rewriting the script for their movie *On the Waterfront,* which ended up winning eight Academy Awards.

In 1954, **Marilyn Monroe** and husband **Joe DiMaggio** stayed at the St. Regis while she filmed scenes of the movie *The Seven Year Itch*, directed by **Billy Wilder**. DiMaggio became enraged watching Marilyn perform the famous scene on the sidewalk where her skirt blew high in the air (see this section, Tour 7, Number 17). Later that night, in their eleventh-floor suite here, hotel guests heard them arguing bitterly about it. Less than a month later they announced their divorce.

John Lennon and **Yoko Ono** lived in suites at the St. Regis in 1971-72. **Ernest Hemingway** and his wife, **Mary Welsh,** stopped here frequently during their New York visits.

Others who have stayed at the St. Regis for long periods include **Rex Harrison, Humphrey Bogart,** and **John Huston.**

7/Robert Benchley and Charles MacArthur

536 Madison Avenue between 54th and 55th Street.

In 1924, humorist **Robert Benchley** was employed as a drama critic for *Life* magazine. **Charles MacArthur** was a hard-drinking journalist, playwright, and bachelor man-about-town.

The two friends decided to take an apartment together and they chose a walk-up flat on the fourth floor of this brownstone. Benchley earned an extra $500 per week performing his famous skit called *The Treasurer's*

Lillian Russell

prima donna and internationally famous beauty—lived in this old building during the 1880s. It was the period when she was becoming one of America's greatest celebrities; her clear soprano voice and vivacious personality would make her one of the signature figures of the period which came to be known as "the Gay Nineties."

Russell became an early master of publicity by keeping herself constantly in the public eye—in one season she signed five contracts and broke four of them; in another, she sought an injunction restraining any theater from requiring her to appear in silk tights even though her popularity was connected with the sexual image that she projected.

Nowadays, the ground floor of Russell's former residence here on 54th Street is fittingly occupied by an establishment called **Bill's Gay 90's Cafe.**

9/Alfred Stieglitz and Georgia O'Keeffe.
59 East 54th Street between Madison and Park Avenue.

This was the famous photographer's last New York City home. **Alfred Stieglitz**, age seventy-eight, moved into a small apartment in this building in early 1942 with his wife, **Georgia O'Keeffe.** The flat was only a block away from his studio and gallery called **An American Place**, located on the seventeenth floor at 509 Madison Avenue. O'Keeffe furnished the apartment sparingly; the only ornaments were a plain Steuben glass bowl and a few plants. Stieglitz suffered a massive stroke

Report at a Broadway theater. He had a wife and two children in Scarsdale, New York and visited them on weekends but he caroused with his roommate MacArthur continuously from Monday through Friday while they lived here.

The two were fond of women, speakeasies, and practical jokes; **Helen Hayes**, who later married MacArthur, said that "singly, each was an urbane and witty man; together they became a menace to society." The pair lived here together for three years and parted when MacArthur's first play *Lulu Belle* became a success, allowing him to afford more sumptuous quarters.

8/Lillian Russell
57 East 54th Street between Madison and Park Avenue.

Lillian Russell—the comic opera

here on the morning of July 10, 1942 and died three days later. O'Keeffe had his ashes scattered near his home at Lake George.

10/Hotel Elysee
60 East 54th Street between Madison and Park Avenue.

The small, elegant **Elysee** has often been the home for Manhattan celebrities over the years. **Dashiell Ham-mett** came here to live in the fall of 1931. The writer was in an alcoholic haze and almost out of money as he labored to finish his last novel, *The Thin Man*. **William Faulkner**, also staying in New York at that time, visited Hammett on a few occasions; the two would spend long nights drinking and Faulkner would be present in the morning asleep on the couch. Hammett's companion, **Lillian Hell-man**, often joined the meetings. In 1934, Hellman was living at the Elysee alone and nearly broke when her new play, *The Children's Hour,* opened on Broadway. It received excellent reviews and launched Hellman on a major career as a dramatist.

Joe DiMaggio made the Elysee his Manhattan home from 1948 to 1951. While he lived here, he played his last four years with the *Yankees* before retiring. His friend and constant companion, **George Solotaire**, rented a suite here and DiMaggio shared it with him, letting his friend wait on him almost hand and foot. While he was here, DiMaggio got to know actress **Lillian Gish** and her sister, **Dorothy,** who also lived at the hotel in those days.

Tennessee Williams stayed at the Elysee frequently during the last twelve years of his life. His suite in 1971 was the same one formerly used by actress **Tallulah Bankhead**, who lived here permanently between 1931 and 1938. In the winter of 1983, the playwright, who was by then suffering from severe depression, secluded himself in his room, refusing food and almost all company. He was found dead in his bedroom on the morning of February 25, 1983 of a drug overdose. Williams was seventy-one.

11/George Gershwin
417 Park Avenue at 55th Street (southeast corner).

This large apartment building was the 1920s and 30s home of **George Gershwin's** good friend, **Jules Glaenzer**, vice-president of Cartier's, the exclusive jewelry store. Glaenzer was known as the host of some of Manhattan's most glittering parties of that era—gatherings that were a kind of open house for celebrities, businessmen, and society folk. Even though the food was terrible—usually canned corn beef—the supply of champagne was endless and the gifted guests—singers, dancers, composers—entertained the moneyed guests. **George Gershwin** appeared regularly at Glaenzer's parties, always at the piano, and often introducing one of his new songs. Around him would be the likes of **Richard Rodgers, Fanny Brice, Harold Arlen, Johnny Mercer, Fred and Adele Astaire,** or **Noel Coward.**

Gershwin referred to his friend Glaenzer as "one of the most famous

George Gershwin

hosts on two continents." Glaenzer also had a house in Paris, the home base of Cartier's, and entertained there in equally elaborate fashion.

TOUR 3

1/Mickey Spillane
225 East 57th Street between Second and Third Avenue.

This was the New York home of **Mickey Spillane**, the writer of hard-boiled detective stories and the creator of tough-as-nails private detective **Mike Hammer.** Spillane, who was born in Brooklyn, started his writing career scripting comic books but switched to novels in 1946 when, needing $1,000 to buy a parcel of land, decided that the easiest and quickest way was to write a book. Three weeks later, he finished *I, The Jury,* which ultimately registered sales in the millions.

By 1952, he had completed seven

novels with Hammer as his hero and all became best sellers. Spillane rented an apartment in this building and made it his New York headquarters. He also purchased a beach house in South Carolina, where he lived with his first wife and four children.

2/Tennessee Williams
235 East 58th Street between Second and Third Avenue.

Tennessee Williams subleased an apartment in this attractive, three-story white painted brick structure called **The Dux Building** in 1948. He had just won the Pulitzer Prize for his play, *A Streetcar Named Desire,* which was a major success on Broadway. His next play, *Summer and Smoke,* opened in October 1948 to mixed reviews.

One day as Williams was walking along 58th Street, he met **Frank Merlo,** who soon became his lover and moved into Williams's apartment. It was the beginning of the longest and most intimate relationship of the playwright's life.

In 1950, his play, *The Rose Tattoo* opened on Broadway. Williams and Merlo lived in this apartment until 1954 when they moved a short distance east of here (see Number 3 below).

3/Tennessee Williams
323 East 58th Street between First and Second Avenue.

Williams and his companion, **Frank Merlo,** moved the short distance from their previous apartment (see Number 2 above) to a furnished flat on the second floor of this building in 1954. They spent much of their time away from New York in either New Orleans or Key West but Williams created two plays for Broadway during his stay here—*Cat on a Hot Tin Roof* and *Sweet Bird of Youth*. He lived here until 1958.

4/Marcel Duchamp
327 East 58th Street between First and Second Avenue.

Marcel Duchamp, age sixty-three, lived in a fourth-floor walk-up in this old brownstone in 1952. The French artist moved in with his new companion, **Alexina** (nickname **Teeny**) **Matisse**. The apartment had previously belonged to artist **Max Ernst** and his wife, **Dorothea Tanning**. After Duchamp moved in, the nameplate on their doorbell said "Matisse - Duchamp - Ernst." Duchamp lived on practically nothing in those days. He maintained a cheap studio in Chelsea (at 210 West 14th Street) and owned one suit which he cleaned himself. When he visited friends out of town, he never took a suitcase; instead he wore two shirts, one on top of the other, and carried a toothbrush in his jacket pocket. Duchamp and Teeny married in 1954. They lived on 58th Street until the early 1960s.

5/James Farrell
340 East 58th Street between First and Second Avenue.

Writer **James Farrell**, creator of the **Studs Lonigan** novels of the 1930s, lived in this seven-story building beginning in 1941. He had married his companion, **Hortense Alden**, a few months earlier, soon after his divorce from his first wife had become final.

Farrell wrote a novel, *My Day of Anger*, and five volumes of short stories while he lived here and his second son was born in 1947. One day in December 1946, a fire caused by Farrell's cigarette broke out in the building and the writer had to be rescued by a fireman's ladder on the second floor. It would be several months before the family could move back in.

By early 1951, Farrell's marriage was on the rocks and he moved out in April of that year.

6/Ogden Nash
333 East 57th Street between First and Second Avenue.

Ogden Nash, probably America's greatest writer of humorous verse, lived in this building for a decade beginning in 1956. He was fifty-four years old when he moved here with his wife **Frances** and his daughter **Isabel**.

Nash was an established writer by then and, during his years here, twenty volumes of his poems were published. By 1965, his health was in decline and he found New York's smog, traffic, and turmoil too stressful; the family moved to suburban Baltimore where Nash died in 1971.

7/J.D. Salinger and William O'Dwyer
300 East 57th Street at Second Avenue. (southeast corner)

J.D.Salinger rented a small apartment here in July 1951 soon after coming back to New York from a trip

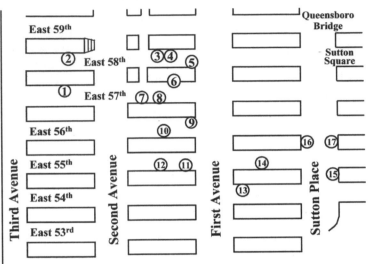

Midtown East
Tour 3

1. Mickey Spillane

2. Tennessee Williams

3. Tennessee Williams

4. Marcel Duchamp

5. James Farrell

6. Ogden Nash

7. J.D. Salinger and
   William O'Dwyer

8. Orson Welles

9. Piet Mondrian

10. Sutton Club Hotel

11. Gore Vidal

12. Norman Mailer

13. Alfred Stieglitz and
    Georgia O'Keeffe

14. Lotte Lenya

15. William Inge

16. Joan Crawford

17. Robert Sherwood

to Europe. While he was gone, his first novel *Catcher in the Rye* had been published to great acclaim and, almost overnight, he found himself to be a famous writer.

His flat on the first floor here was extremely bare; it was furnished with only a lamp and an artist's drawing board. On the wall was one picture of himself in uniform—he had served in the U.S. Army during the Second World War.

Salinger continued to work on short stories while he lived in this place but he grew restless with his life in the city, not knowing how to handle the celebrity which his novel had thrust upon him. In early 1953, he moved to a new home in rural New Hampshire.

Apartment of Orson Welles

300 East 57th Street was the last residence of New York's 100th mayor, **William O'Dwyer.** He was elected in 1945 and again in 1949 on the Democratic ticket, succeeding **Fiorello LaGuardia.** O'Dwyer, one of the city's most controversial politicians, was backed by the Tammany Hall machine and won both of his terms with the secret support of mobster kingpin **Frank Costello.** He abruptly resigned in 1950 amidst charges of corruption in his administration and became **President Truman's** ambassador to Mexico.

O'Dwyer ended up living in a three-room apartment here on 57th Street; he died of a heart attack in November 1964 at age seventy-four.

8/Orson Welles

322 East 57th Street between First and Second Avenue.

Welles had recently shocked America with his *War of the Worlds* radio broadcast when he purchased a duplex apartment here in 1938. The place was huge, outfitted with stained-glass windows, balcony, and a monumental fireplace. He had a living room described as the size of a skating rink and furniture so big that the pieces had to be hoisted by a crane through the front windows—a foreshadowing of the Xanadu home of **Charles Foster Kane.**

Opera singer **Lily Pons** lived in the duplex next door. Welles and his wife, **Virginia Nicolson,** frequently dined at the Swedish restaurant next to his place here. He became busy planning the next **Mercury Theater** production called *Five Kings,* **Shakespeare's** history cycle condensed into five evenings. That project fell through but in 1941 he received an offer from RKO Pictures to direct movies. He moved to Hollywood where he made his first film, *Citizen Kane.*

Sutton Club Hotel

Writer **Stephen Vincent Benet** lived in a house on the site just east of here at 326 East 57th Street in the late 1920s.

9/Piet Mondrian

353 East 56th Street at First Avenue (northwest corner).

Modernist painter **Piet Mondrian** moved from London to the United States in October 1940 and his first home in this country was a tiny apartment on this site (number 353 is gone, replaced by number 345).

The artist's space was on the third floor, facing First Avenue, across the street from the **Sutton Club Hotel.** Mondrian loved Manhattan, especially the skyscrapers which he regarded as a kind of blueprint of the city of the future. Some of his greatest paintings were created here including *Broadway Boogie-Woogie,* which hangs today in the **Museum of Modern Art**.

Mondrian lived at this address until October 1943 when he moved to 15 East 59th Street.He died four months later.

10/Sutton Club Hotel

330 East 56th Street between First and Second Avenue.

The **Sutton Club**was once the temporary home of a number of famous New York writers. It was originally built to accommodate a women's club but when the deal fell through, it was converted into a hotel. **Nathanael West** supported himself as the night manager of the Sutton in the early 1930s while he struggled to complete his novel, *Miss Lonelyhearts.* Because the occupancy rate was low during the early years of the Great Depression, West was able to offer rooms to his needy literary friends at reduced rates. The writers who lived here included **Erskine Caldwell, S.J. Perelman, Edmund Wilson,** and **James T. Farrell.**

Dashiell Hammett and **Lillian Hellman,** low on funds, moved into a small suite of three rooms at the Sutton in September 1932. Hellman hung out with her friend Nathanael West, swam in the pool, and looked for work. Meanwhile, Hammett completely stopped drinking and partying and diligently worked on his new novel *The Thin Man.* Hellman later wrote: "I had never seen anybody work that way: the care for every word, the pride in the neatness of the typed page itself, the refusal for ten days or two weeks to go out for even a walk for fear something would be lost." Hammett finished the book—his last novel— in May 1933. He and Hellman left for Florida soon after.

Jazz guitarist **Eddie Condon's** famous jazz club was located in the Sutton from 1958 to 1967. Condon moved here after his original place at 47 West 3rd Street in Greenwich Village was torn down.

11/Gore Vidal
360 East 55th Street at First Avenue (southwest corner).

In 1956, writer **Gore Vidal** took an apartment in this fifteen-story building with his companion and lover, **Howard Austen**. Vidal's flat was a one-bedroom, fifth-floor walk-up, renting for $175 a month.

Vidal spent some of his time in California working on scripts for MGM Pictures. He lived here on 55th Street for less than a year. In June 1957, he bought a large brownstone not far away at 416 East 58th Street. That house has since been demolished.

12/Norman Mailer
320 East 55th Street between First and Second Avenue.

Mailer and his second wife, **Adele Morales**, rented a beautiful duplex apartment in this old brownstone in 1954. He had recently completed his third novel, *The Deer Park*, which was to be published by Rinehart & Company. At the last minute, the publisher refused to release the book because of its sexual explicitness.

The humiliated and angry Mailer offered it to six other publishers before it was finally accepted by G.P. Putnam's Sons. The Mailers lived in this building until the fall of 1956 when they moved to a farmhouse in Connecticut.

13/Alfred Stieglitz and Georgia O'Keeffe
405 East 54th Street at First Avenue (northeast corner).

In· the fall of 1936, **Georgia O'Keeffe** and **Alfred Stieglitz** rented a three-bedroom duplex penthouse in this building. The previous tenant had been *The New Yorker* cartoonist **Peter Arno.**

O'Keeffe had been recently commissioned to paint a large mural for **Elizabeth Arden** and, to work on it, she needed more space than they had at their previous residence in the **Hotel Shelton** (see this section, Tour 7, Number 12). Here on 54th Street, she painted the walls white, uncurtained the windows, and furnished the place austerely—the only color was in a few Navajo rugs on the floor. O'Keeffe and Stieglitz stayed until 1942.

British actress **Hermoine Gingold** lived in this building for three decades up to her death in 1987.

14/Lotte Lenya
404 East 55th Street between First Avenue and Sutton Place.

The German singer/actress completed a performing tour of Europe in 1960 and, returning to New York, moved into a one-bedroom, rent-controlled apartment on the sixteenth floor of this building. **Lenya** decorated her place in a red and green Chinese motif with one Chippendale cabinet, mock tapestries, and green velvet upholstered chairs. Soon after her arrival, she appeared in the film *The Roman Spring of Mrs. Stone* with **Vivien Leigh** and received excellent reviews. Then, in 1966 she began a three-year run on Broadway in the musical *Cabaret*. Lenya lived in this apartment until 1981, the year of her death.

This building was also **Noel Coward's** last Manhattan residence. The songwriter and playwright died in Jamaica in 1973.

15/William Inge
45 Sutton Place South between 54th and 55th Street.

William Inge was one of America's most notable postwar playwrights with works that included *Picnic, Bus Stop, The Dark at the Top of the Stairs,* and *Come Back, Little Sheba.* During the mid-1950s, he lived at the **Dakota** on West 72nd Street but when he wanted a newer and larger apartment, he moved to this white brick building overlooking the East River.

Inge had a fear of heights so his new place was on the lowest floor of the building. While he lived here, he won an Academy Award for his 1962 screenplay *Splendor in the Grass.* Inge moved to California in 1964, just as public interest in his work began to decline. In 1975, he committed suicide in Los Angeles at the age of sixty-two.

16/Joan Crawford
36 Sutton Place South between 55th and 56th Street.

Crawford was forty-nine years old in 1955 when she married Pepsi-Cola executive, **Alfred Steele.** Soon after the wedding, she moved into his luxury eight-room bachelor apartment in this building. Crawford's four children came with her. Although film offers were becoming scarce for her, she did manage to land roles in *Autumn Leaves* in 1956 and *The Story of Esther Costello* soon after. Before long, Crawford and Steele realized that this Sutton Place house was too small for six people and they moved to a large and plush residence on the Upper East Side in 1957 (see Section One, Tour 3, Number 15).

17/Robert Sherwood
25 Sutton Place South between 55th and 56th Street.

Playwright **Robert Sherwood** lived in a house on this site from the early 1940s until his death. Some of his most important writing was done at this residence. He won two Pulitzer Prizes—in 1941 for his play *There Shall Be No Night* and in 1949 for his biography *Roosevelt and Hopkins.* In 1946, he won an Academy Award for his screenplay of *The Best Years of Our Lives.* Sherwood was living here in November 1955 when he suffered a fatal heart attack. He was fifty-nine years old. The newer building standing here today was erected in 1959.

TOUR 4

1/Mitchell Parish

400 East 56th Street at First Avenue (southeast corner).

Lyricist **Mitchell Parish**, who wrote the words to *Star Dust*, one of America's most popular songs, lived in this large apartment complex during the final years of his life. The melody of *Star Dust* was composed by **Hoagy Carmichael** in 1927; Parish added the lyrics in 1929 but the song remained in obscurity until **Artie Shaw** and his orchestra recorded it. It sold two-and-a-half million records and went on to be recorded almost five hundred times by various artists.

Parish also wrote words to a number of other songs that have become standards including *Deep Purple, Sweet Lorraine, Sophisticated Lady,* and *Stars Fell on Alabama*. He died in 1993 at the age of ninety-two.

2/Jerome Kern

411 East 56th Street between First Avenue and Sutton Place.

The great songwriter was born in a house on this site on January 27, 1885. **Jerome** was the youngest of nine boys. The Kerns lived a comfortable middle-class life; the father earned his living as president of a firm that held a contract with the city to sprinkle the streets with water. Kern's mother, **Fanny**, was an excellent pianist and taught Jerome to play at an early age in the parlor of their house here.

When he was five, the family moved to the Upper East Side (see

Section One, Tour 5, Number 19).

3/Jimmy Cannon

440 East 56th Street between First Avenue and Sutton Place.

Cannon, the syndicated columnist who wrote for the *Hearst* newspapers for over thirty-five years and was probably the city's most popular sportswriter, lived in this large apartment building during the last years of his life. He wrote for the *New York Post* from 1946 to 1959; then he was hired by Hearst's *Journal-American* at a salary of $1,000 a week, making him the country's highest-paid sports columnist.

Cannon was a bachelor who spent most nights at **Toots Shor's** bar on West 51st Street or at the **Stork Club** when he wasn't covering sports events. To gather ideas for his columns, he would walk dozens of blocks in Manhattan every day, observing people and events. Cannon died of a stroke at his apartment here on December 5, 1973. He was sixty-three.

4/Marilyn Monroe and William Saroyan

2 Sutton Place South at 57th Street (southwest corner).

In the fall of 1955, **Marilyn Monroe** moved from the **Waldorf-Astoria Towers** to a small apartment on the eighth floor in this building. It was owned by her friend, **Milton Greene.** Monroe was taking acting classes at the **Actors Studio** and, recently divorced from **Joe Di-Maggio,** had started a relationship with playwright **Arthur Miller.** After

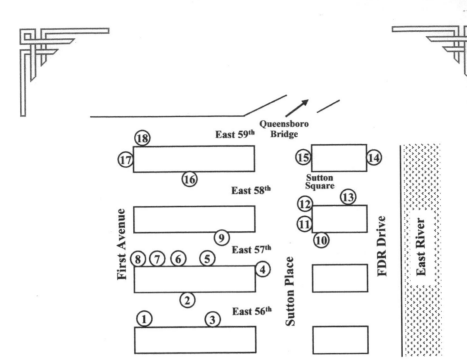

Midtown East
Tour 4

1. Mitchell Parish

2. Jerome Kern

3. Jimmy Cannon

4. Marilyn Monroe and
   William Saroyan

5. Marilyn Monroe and
   Arthur Miller

6. Lillian Gish

7. James Thurber

8. Hammett and Faulkner

9. Tallulah Bankhead

10. J. Paul Getty

11. Anne Morgan

12. Irving Berlin

13. Robert Henri

14. Riverview Terrace

15. John Hersey

16. Ginger Rogers

17. Louise Brooks

18. John Cheever

Monroe and Miller at 444 East 57th Street

5/Marilyn Monroe and Arthur Miller
444 East 57th Street between First Avenue and Sutton Place.

Monroe and **Miller** rented a large apartment on the thirteenth floor of this building in 1956, soon after their wedding. She decorated it in a color scheme of white-white walls, white curtains, pale furniture, and a white piano. She set up a small study for Miller, off the living room. He spent mornings and afternoons writing, emerging only late in the day to walk their basset hound, **Hugo.**

It was in this apartment that Miller wrote the screenplay for *The Misfits*; it was his only produced work during the four years of the marriage. Monroe took two years off from her work before making *Some Like It Hot* in 1958.

By 1960, the marriage had unraveled and, soon after *The Misfits* was filmed, Miller moved back to his old home at the **Chelsea Hotel**. Monroe continued to live here alone after their divorce, in a state of depression and increasingly dependent on drugs.

6/Lillian Gish
430 East 57th Street between First Avenue and Sutton Place.

The great silent film star lived in a stylish apartment in this building during the last years of her life. **Gish** never married and her mother lived with her for many years. In her autobiography *The Movies, Mr. Griffith and Me*, she said that "the Sutton Place area is home to me. I have lived in the neighborhood since 1929 and it is like a village where

she signed a lucrative new contract with Twentieth Century Fox in December, 1955, she went to Hollywood to film *Bus Stop*. On June 21, 1956, Monroe found herself isolated in her apartment here, surrounded by hundreds of reporters and fans outside, after rumors circulated that she and Miller were to be married. The couple managed to secretly escape the premises and retreat to Miller's place in Roxbury, Connecticut. They were married a week later by a justice-of-the-peace in White Plains, New York.

Author **William Saroyan** lived at this Sutton Place address with his wife, **Carol Marcus,** in the 1940s. He moved in soon after he was discharged from the U.S. Army in 1945. While he was a resident, Saroyan published his novel *The Adventures of Wesley Jackson,* which has been called the first anti-war novel of World War II.

everybody knows you." Gish died in her sleep in her apartment here at the age of ninety-nine on February 28, 1993.

7/James Thurber
410 East 57th Street between First Avenue and Sutton Place.

Thurber and his second wife, **Helen Wismer,** moved from their rural Connecticut home to a sublet-apartment in this building in January 1943. The war rationing of heating oil and gasoline made their move to the city necessary. The author was almost totally blind by this time and, in 1944, he became ill with pneumonia and almost died. But, through it all, Thurber continued to write; in 1945, his anthology *The Thurber Carnival* was published and in 1946 he worked here on a screenplay of his classic story *The Secret Life of Walter Mitty,* which became a **Danny Kaye** movie in 1947. The Thurbers lived here on 57th Street until the end of the war.

8/Dashiell Hammett and William Faulkner
400 East 57th Street at First Avenue (southeast corner).

This site, where a modern building now stands, was once the home of husband-and-wife publishers **Alfred and Blanche Knopf.** In the fall of 1931 it was the scene of a notorious incident involving **Hammett** and **Faulkner,** two of Knopf's most important writers, who were living in this neighborhood and often hanging out together, usually in an alcoholic haze. The Knopfs were hosting a for-mal party in their home for author **Willa Cather** and **Hammett** and **Faulkner,** who had been drinking all day, managed to wrangle an invitation. The two showed up at the black tie dinner in casual attire and obviously drunk.Before long, both had passed out on the floor in full sight of the Knopfs' disapproving guests.

In 1935, choreographer **George Balanchine** lived simply in a tiny apartment at 400 East 57th while he directed the **American Ballet** school. The thirty-one-year-old Balanchine was, according to *The New Yorker,* "probably the only man in New York who keeps a grand piano in a one-room apartment."

For relaxation, Balanchine would come home at night and play selections by **Bach** *and* **Stravinsky.**

9/Tallulah Bankhead
447 East 57th Street between First Avenue and Sutton Place.

Actress **Tallulah Bankhead** was sixty years old and in poor health when she moved into a five-room cooperative apartment on the thirteenth floor here in 1962. The building, designed by **Rosario Candela** and opened in 1928, was her home until she died. She made her last notable appearance on the New York stage in 1964 in the play *The Milk Train Doesn't Stop Here Anymore.*

A year later, she had a part in a grade B British movie and she was horrified when she viewed the film and discovered that the camera revealed her once-great beauty to have slipped away. "They used to shoot **Shirley Temple** through gauze," she said. "They should shoot me through linoleum." Her acting career was over but Bankhead lived for another three years. She died in nearby **St. Luke's Hospital** in December 1968.

10/J. Paul Getty
1 Sutton Place at 57th Street (northeast corner).

Multi-millionaire **Paul Getty** ended his fourth marriage in Los Angeles in 1935 and then moved into this four-level Neo-Georgian townhouse, which was to be his New York home for many years. The place had been formerly owned by **Mrs. William K. Vanderbilt,** whose move to this neighborhood in the early 1920s helped to turn it from a working class neighborhood into an exclusive enclave (see Number 11 below). Getty rented the place from **Mrs. Frederick Guest,** socialite and antique collector, and the house was already furnished with the finest eighteenth-century French and English antiques.

"The living room is so big," Getty told his mother, "that when I lent the place to a friend for a dance, he put a twelve-piece orchestra at one end of the room and you could not hear it at the other."

After he moved here, Getty himself became interested in fine art and antiques and began collecting additional objects for his new home on a grand scale. It became a passion that dominated his private life until his death.

In 1936, Getty met **Teddy Lynch**, a nightclub singer; she became his fifth wife and moved into One Sutton Place with him.

11/Anne Morgan
3 Sutton Place near 57th Street.

Until 1920, this Sutton Place neighborhood was mostly a working-class area of factories and tenements strung along the banks of the East River. In that year a group of investors purchased the block of brownstones on the east side of Sutton Place between 57th and 58th Streets and resold the buildings to a group of prominent Manhattan socialites.

One of them was **Anne Morgan,** daughter of banker **J.P. Morgan,** who moved here into Number 3 Sutton Place. Before long, many of the other older houses were being renovated and a number of new private houses were constructed. Once an ordinary street, Sutton Place became one of the fanciest addresses in Manhattan.

In addition to Morgan, this block became home to the likes of **Mrs. William K. Vanderbilt** (see Number 10 above), **Elsie de Wolfe,** and **Robert W. Goelet.** Morgan's house later became the residence of the Secretary-General of the United Nations.

12/Irving Berlin
9 Sutton Place at 58th Street (southeast corner).

Berlin and his second wife, **Ellin Mackay,** moved to this townhouse with its picturesque garden and river view in 1928.They brought their young daughter and new infant son, **Irving Berlin, Jr.** The child died soon after they moved here, on Christmas day, after only twenty-

Irving Berlin

eight days of life, leaving the Berlins devastated. The songwriter experienced a period of declining popularity and low musical productivity while he lived in this house. His own income fell and he witnessed the loss of his millionaire father-in-law's entire fortune in the 1929 market crash.

But Berlin's own fortunes soon brightened in 1932 and 1933 with his two hit musicals *Face the Music* and *As Thousands Cheer.* The Berlins moved to the Upper East Side in 1933 (see Section One, Tour 12, Number 3).

13/Robert Henri
512 East 58th Street (now 14 Sutton Square).

Painter and teacher to a generation of American art students, **Robert Henri** moved to an old four-story brownstone on this site in 1900, overlooking the water. It was his first New York home; he had recently lived in Philadelphia and came here with his new wife, **Linda Craigie.** Henri was the leading advocate of the "Ashcan School" which proclaimed that everyday life was a fit subject matter for the artist.

As a teacher at the **Art Students League,** he sent his pupils into the streets of Manhattan where life in the raw could be recorded. Among those he taught were **Edward Hopper, Rockwell Kent, and John Sloan.** While Henri lived here on 58th Street, he concentrated on painting the city's river traffic and its shore. His wife, **Linda,** described their location as "an ideal place...right on the banks of the East River—and out of both the front and back windows that river is fine [with its] busy little boats hurrying by—and big white steamers."

Henri was crushed in 1905 when Linda died. He stayed here until 1909 when he moved to a studio in Gramercy Park (see Section Four, Tour 1, Number 16).

14/Riverview Terrace
Between East 58th and 59th Street at the East River.

This picturesque, block-long private street, tucked under the shadow of the Queensboro Bridge and facing the East River, is unknown to most New Yorkers. It was developed in 1879 when this waterfront neighborhood was mainly a place of industry. The six residences here are survivors of an original twenty-four, built between 58th and 59th Streets, back to back, with twelve on each side.

Riverview Terrace

Designed by architect **John Sexton,** the original houses were modest dwellings built for middle class people and sold for $8,000 apiece. The other survivors face Sutton Place opposite **Riverview Terrace.**

Number 1 Riverview Terrace was redesigned and turned into a modern-style house in 1941. **Jack L. Warner,** the movie mogul who ran Warner Brothers Studios, lived here from 1952 to 1972. Then it became home to **Clint Murchison, Jr.,** the Texas oil millionaire who owned the **Dallas Cowboys.** Murchison occupied it until he went bankrupt in 1985.

In the 1949 film *The Barkleys of Broadway,* **Fred Astaire** and **Ginger Rogers**, playing a married dancing couple, live in an house on this street (identified as "390 River Terrace") with a view of the Queensboro Bridge out their front window.

15/John Hersey

33 Sutton Place between 58th and 59th Street.

John Hersey, the journalist, novelist, and war correspondent lived in this house in the 1940s. While he was here, Hersey wrote what is, arguably, the most significant and influential magazine article in the history of journalism.It was *Hiro-shima*, written in 1946 as a three-part series for *The New Yorker* but actually published in full in the August 31, 1946 issue of that magazine.The 30,000-word article, which described the effects of the atomic bomb explosion on the lives of its common victims, was immediately acclaimed for its importance—**Albert Einstein** was said to have ordered a thousand copies for distribution.

It was later published as a book by **Alfred Knopf.** Hersey also wrote his best-selling novel, *A Bell for Adano*—which won a Pulitzer Prize in 1945—while living at this address.

John Hersey

16/Ginger Rogers

425 East 58th Street between First Avenue and Sutton Place.

The actress and dancing partner of **Fred Astaire** maintained an apartment in this forty-eight story complex during the last years of her life. The building, called **The Sovereign**, was opened in 1974 and overlooks the Queensboro Bridge.

Rogers stayed at this address whenever business or pleasure took her to New York. She died in 1995.

17/Louise Brooks

1075 First Avenue near 59th Street.

By 1944, the legendary actress, and star of the German silent film classic *Pandora's Box*, had dropped out of the movie business and was living in New York on limited funds. **Brooks,** now thirty-eight years old, moved into a cheap and tiny apartment in this old six-story brick building. She took a job for a spell as a salesgirl at **Saks Fifth Avenue** for $40 a week and later even worked as an evening companion for an escort service.

She could be seen many nights, drinking alone, in the off hours at **Glennon's** bar (now **P.J. Clarke's**) on Third Avenue at 55th Street. Brooks was finally rescued from her financial troubles in 1954 by old friend **William Paley**, CBS executive, who arranged a monthly stipend for her as long as she pursued a career in writing.

In 1954, she left her apartment here and moved to Rochester, New York to be near her close friend, **James Card**, film curator at the **Eastman Museum of Photography.** In Rochester, Brooks settled into a serious writing career and, at the same time, witnessed a renewed public recognition of her greatness as a film actress. She died in Rochester in 1985 at age seventy-eight.

18/John Cheever

400 East 59th Street at First Avenue (southeast corner)

In the summer of 1945, **John Cheever**, with his wife, **Mary**, and infant daughter, **Susan,** took an apartment in this building. Their living room looked out on the Queensboro Bridge across the street.

Cheever, just out of the army, established a daily writing routine. Each morning, wearing a suit and hat, he rode down in the elevator with the other professional men in his building. They, however, got off on the first floor while he rode to the windowless storage room in the basement where he stripped to his shorts and worked at his writing for eight hours. At the end of the day, he put on his suit again for the elevator ride upstairs.

Cheever wrote a number of his best short stories for *The New Yorker* during this time, including *Torch Song* and *The Enormous Radio.*

The Cheevers' son, **Benjamin**, was born in 1948 while they lived here. The family moved to a country house in Scarborough, New York in 1951.

TOUR 5

1/Henry and Clare Boothe Luce
435 East 52nd Street at the East River.

The twenty-six-story **River House** is one of New York's most prestigious addresses. It opened as a cooperative in 1931 and contains only seventy-three apartments.

River House is protected by an ornate iron gate opening onto a cobbled entrance court. The separate **River Club** has quarters within the building with its own entrance and, at its lower levels, a ballroom, tennis courts, and a swimming pool. Prior to the construction of FDR Drive in the early 40s, the building had its own private yacht dock. The typical apartment has twelve rooms, six baths, and two fireplaces.

Time magazine publisher **Henry Luce** and his second wife, **Clare Boothe**, moved into a fifteen-room duplex at River House in 1935, soon after their wedding. The maintenance cost was $7,300 a year and it was furnished with French, English, and Italian antiques. Not long after they moved in, Henry decided to begin production of a new pictorial magazine called *Life,* which first appeared on the newsstands on November 19, 1936. Its first run of 466,000 copies sold out.

In the meantime, Clare wrote a play called *The Women* that opened on Broadway on December 26th and quickly became a great popular and financial success. The Luces lived at River House until 1938.

Edwin Howard Armstrong, one of the genius inventors of the twentieth century, lived here at the end of his life. Armstrong, whose many technical innovations made possible the early development of radio and whose discovery of FM opened the way to send clear signals around the world, found himself in 1954 short of money and heavily involved in unsuccessful lawsuits against corporate giant RCA. On January 31, deeply depressed, the sixty-three-year old Armstrong jumped to his death from his his thirteenth-floor apartment.

Other residents of River House over the years include **Angier Biddle Duke, Cornelius Vanderbilt Whitney, Josh Logan, John Kenneth Galbraith, Henry Kissinger,** and **Marshall Field.**

2/Greta Garbo
450 East 52nd Street at the East River.

The **Campanile**, like its River House neighbor across the street, is one of the city's most elite apartment houses. When it opened in 1927, it also had a private boat dock on the river below. It has the distinction of being the first luxury building in the neighborhood, which at the time of its construction was a working class slum.

The Campanile's most famous resident was **Greta Garbo.** In 1953, she bought a seven-room, fifth-floor apartment with a balcony overlooking the river. The price was $38,000. Her living room was decorated with an assortment of eighteenth century French antiques and numerous valuable paintings including three Renoirs. But, above all, the apartment

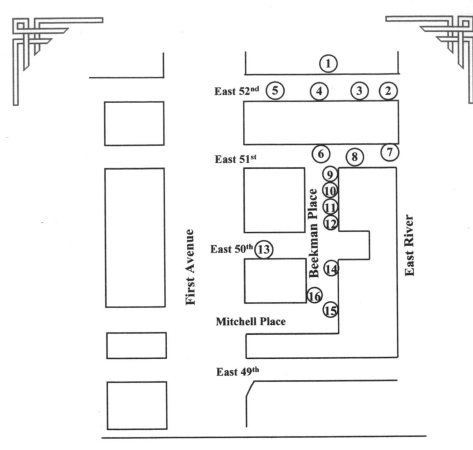

Midtown East
Tour 5

1. Henry and Clare Luce
2. Greta Garbo
3. Dorothy Parker and Clare Boothe
4. Humphrey Bogart and John Lennon
5. Edna St. Vincent Millay
6. Gerald and Sara Murphy
7. Weill and Lenya
8. Max Ernst and Peggy Guggenheim

9. Antoine de Saint-Exupér
10. Billy Rose
11. William Paley
12. Katharine Cornell
13. Walter Huston
14. Irving Berlin
15. John D. Rockefeller 3rd
16. Mary McCarthy

was Garbo's refuge—a place to hide, to eat alone, and a starting point from which to make her daily four-mile walks around Manhattan, usually in disguise. "Sometimes I put on my coat at 10 a.m. and follow people," she said. "I just go where they're going—I mill around." Garbo lived here for thirty-seven years until her death in 1990. Her estate, including the apartment, was valued at $20 million.

Alexander Woollcott was another famous Campanile resident. He entertained his **Algonquin Round Table** companions in his third-floor apartment from 1927 to 1936. His friend, **Dorothy Parker**, dubbed the place "Wit's End."

In the summer of 1938, **Katharine Hepburn** and her boyfriend **Howard Hughes** stayed here in the apartment of her friend, **Laura Harding**, while Hughes prepared for his around-the-world air flight. He completed the trip on July 13th, having set a new world record. After the flight, Hughes and Hepburn stayed here again in secret to avoid the crowds of spectators. Hepburn created a series of disguises to protect them during their solitary walks around the neighborhood.

Actor **Rex Harrison** moved to the Campanile in 1981 with his sixth wife, **Mercia Tinker.** While he lived in New York during the next decade, he starred in three plays. Harrison loved his flat. "I've got a studio there where I can paint, with wonderful light," he said in his autobiography. "It all faces the East River and its very pretty at all times of the day or night, with the bridges and barges and the sense you get in New York of

people working like mad and making their own living." Harrison died of pancreatic cancer in his apartment here in June 1990 at age eighty-two.

Other residents of the Campanile have included **Noel Coward, Ralph Pulitzer,** and **Mary Martin.**

3/Dorothy Parker and Clare Boothe
444 East 52nd Street between First Avenue and the East River.

Dorothy Parker moved into an apartment in this 1929 ten-story building in 1934. Her flat, with its unbroken view of the East River, was located, she said, "far enough east to plant tea." Her companion of that time was actor and writer **Alan Campbell,** who moved in with her.

Clare Boothe lived in a penthouse apartment at 444 East 52nd from 1930 to 1934. She was working as a junior editor at *Vanity Fair* when she moved in but by 1932 she had taken over as the magazine's editor-in-chief. It wasn't until 1934 that she met **Henry Luce** and became the second wife of the *Time* magazine publisher. After their wedding, they moved to River House across the street (see number 1 above).

4/Humphrey Bogart and John Lennon
434 East 52nd Street between First Avenue and the East River.

Humphrey Bogart moved into a shabby apartment here with his second wife, actress **Mary Philips,** in 1932. He was a stage actor in those days and jobs were hard to find because the Depression had killed business on Broadway. The Bogarts befriended two other couples and the six pooled their money for groceries and what entertainment they could afford. Their main pastime was playing bridge or Parcheesi.

Bogart earned a bit of money playing chess as a house player at an arcade, taking on anyone for fifty cents or a dollar. His big career break came in 1935 when he got the role of **Duke Mantee** in the play *The Petrified Forest*. It made him famous and he left for Hollywood in 1936 to begin his movie career.

Edna St. Vincent Millay

In 1973, when **John Lennon** and **Yoko Ono** separated, Lennon began a relationship with **May Pang**, who had been the couple's personal assistant. In mid-1974, Lennon and Pang rented a modest, one-bedroom apartment in this building with views of the East River. It was the scene of many an evening party at which rock stars, fans, producers, journalists, and hangers-on showed up.

One night Lennon was standing naked on the terrace when he thought he noticed a UFO hovering above. Although he was afraid that authorities would be skeptical when he reported the sighting, it turned out that over 400 people called the police that day to report the same thing.

In February 1975, Lennon and Yoko reunited and he moved back into their home at the **Dakota** on West 72nd Street.

5/Edna St. Vincent Millay
400 East 52nd Street between First Avenue and the East River.

During the first few months of 1941, **Edna St.Vincent Millay** mov-ed briefly to Manhattan. She came from her upstate home in Austerlitz, New York and rented an apartment in this large white brick apartment building with her husband, **Eugen Boissevain.**

At the time, Millay was ill and in great pain from injuries suffered in a recent automobile accident.She took medical treatment in New York and soon became addicted to the numerous morphine injections administered to her. While she stayed here on 52nd Street, the poet began to record the readings of her poems for RCA Victor. Millay also witnessed the publication of her new book called *Make Bright the Arrows,* which was a plea to America to abandon its isolation and assist Britain in its fight against the Nazis.

6/Gerald and Sara Murphy
439 East 51st Street between First Avenue and the East River.

The **Murphys**, who played host to a whole generation of writers and artists at their home on the French Riviera in the 1920s and early 30s, came back to live in New York in 1932. In the fall of 1934, they took an apartment in this building facing the East River. They moved in with their two young sons. **Gerald** took over the management of the family's leather goods store Mark Cross, which had fallen into financial trouble in the Depression.

While they lived here, the Murphys suffered two tragic events. In March 1935, their oldest son, **Baoth**, died of spinal meningitis. A year later, the other son, **Patrick**, who had been suffering from tuberculosis, died at the age of sixteen.

7/Kurt Weil and Lotte Lenya

455 East 51st Street at the East River.

Weill and **Lenya** were invited to share an apartment here in September 1936 with its tenants **Cheryl Crawford** and **Dorothy Patten**. It was a generous gesture to the composer and his actress companion who were short of cash after fleeing Nazi Germany to live in the United States. Crawford, one of the founders of the legendary **Group Theater,** also arranged for Weil to write the music for the production of its new anti-war play *Johnny Johnson.* He also obtained the assignment of writing the score for the new play *The Eternal Road* which opened in 1937. Weill and Lenya stayed in Crawford's apartment until late 1937 when their improved financial status allowed them to rent their own apartment on the Upper East Side (see Section One, Tour 2, Number 21).

The Crawford apartment had earlier been occupied by silent film star **Lillian Gish** who lived there with her mother. In her autobiography Gish wrote: "My bedroom...faced the river, and when I awakened in the morning water seemed to ripple on the ceiling and walls, giving me the delightful feeling that I was on a ship. It was the most beautiful apartment we ever had. But the river noises at night disturbed Mother, so eventually we moved."

8/Peggy Guggenheim and Max Ernst

440 East 51st Street near the East River.

Peggy Guggenheim, the wealthy art collector and patron to artists, and **Ernst**, the German Surrealist painter, had met in Europe. They returned to New York together in 1941 after the Nazi occupation of France and she leased this beautiful town house on the East River. The place was called **Hale House** because it was erroneously thought to be the spot where patriot **Nathan Hale** was hanged during the American Revolution (see this section, Tour 6, Number 5).

Ernst had his studio on the third floor. Guggenheim hung her collection of modernist paintings in the living room. They decorated the place with Indian artifacts from the Pacific Northwest and the American Southwest.

For a short time, playwright **Clifford Odets** rented rooms on the top floor of the house and kept the household awake late at night as he loudly rehearsed his newly-written play *Clash by Night.*

Guggenheim's home became a magnet for the expatriate artists community in New York. Her parties and art events drew the likes of **Piet Mondrian, Fernand Leger, Marc Chagall,** and **Yves Tanguy.**

Ernst and Peggy were married in December 1941 but their time together at Hale House was troubled and they separated in 1943. Ernst left New York permanently in 1946 to live in Arizona. He returned to Paris in 1951. Peggy Guggenheim eventually moved to Italy where she lived for the rest of her life.

9/Antoine de Saint-Exupery
35 Beekman Place at 51st Street.

The French pilot and expatriate, with his wife, **Consuelo,** rented a town house here at the end of 1942. The apartment, which at one time had been especially furnished for **Greta Garbo,** had cream-colored, wall-to-wall carpeting, walls of mirror, and an upper-floor library. **Saint-Exupery** cared nothing for this kind of extravagance and gave his dog, **Hannibal,** free rein of the place. The writer was in poor health due to his military services in the European war and depressed because of his separation from his beloved France. According to his biographer **Stacy Schiff,** it was in this house that he wrote most of the book *The Little Prince* "in his usual distracted manner, in long, late night bursts of energy fueled by coffee, Coca-Cola and cigarettes."

In April 1943, Saint-Exupery left New York by boat for Algiers to fight again for the Free French. In July 1944 he failed to return from a reconnaissance mission over southern France. His plane was never found.

CBS executive **William Paley** moved into a town house at 35 Beekman Place in 1932 with his wife, **Dorothy.** They loved the neighborhood so much that in 1934 they tore down another town house just south of here and erected a new home in its place (see number 11 below).

10/Billy Rose
33 Beekman Place near 51st Street.

The Broadway producer, divorced from his latest wife **Fanny Brice,** occupied this house with former Olympic champion swimmer **Eleanor Holm Jarrett** after their wedding in 1939. The place had fourteen rooms and was filled with Rose's expensive collection of paintings and antiques.

The marriage eventually deteriorated. When the couple began a messy divorce and Rose was told by a judge to stay away from the house here where his wife still resided, he went into a rage. Legend has it that, armed with an ax one night, he proceeded to whack down the beautiful front door until he heard Eleanor's voice on the other side announcing that she was holding one of his Rembrandt paintings and that if he smashed through the door, he would destroy the Rembrandt. It stopped him cold and before long the couple made a deal: she got to keep two valuable Renoirs and Rose kept the Rembrandt.

They were divorced in 1952 and Rose moved his residence to an apartment above the Ziegfeld Theater, which he owned.

11/William Paley

29 Beekman Place between 50th and 51st Street.

Paley, the chief of CBS, built this six-story home after tearing down his previous residence in 1934. He and his wife, **Dorothy**, moved here late in 1937; they had been living just up the block at 35 Beekman Place for the past five years (number 9 above). The new residence was designed and furnished with an opulence that seemed out of place in the Depression era—a staircase covered with carpet made of zebra skins, a drawing room brimming with eighteenth-century English furniture, and paintings illuminated by small concealed spotlights and operated by switches on a control panel. After three years, Paley grew tired of the place, saying that "it had no charm or warmth...it was antiseptic."

12/Katharine Cornell

23 Beekman Place near 50th Street.

Legendary stage actress, **Katharine Cornell** came to this five-story house in 1921, soon after her marriage to director **Guthrie McClintic**. They lived in it for thirty-one years until 1952. During that period, this place was the scene of numerous parties attended by show business people, with entertainment supplied by the likes of **George Gershwin, Ethel Waters,** and **Noel Coward.**

The struggling young actor, **Kirk Douglas**, remembers being invited here for Thanksgiving dinner in 1941. "There was champagne. There was caviar. There was **Tallulah Bankhead** looking at me...," he wrote years later. "I had been down on the Bowery and couldn't even get a meal from the Salvation Army. Now here I was in the lap of luxury. And I remember my mother's words: 'America is a wonderful land.'"

13/Walter Huston

406 East 50th Street between First Avenue and Beekman Place

This four-level white stone house was the New York residence of actor **Walter Huston** during the last years of his life. He lived here with his second wife, **Nan Sutherland.** Huston decorated his bar room with photos of all the characters he had played on stage and in the movies during his long career. "I have now about 25 on the wall," he reported at one point. "The only thing wrong with it is it makes me realize how old I am." This was Huston's residence in 1949 when he won an Oscar for Best Supporting Actor in *The Treasure of Sierra Madre*, directed by his son, **John**. Walter Huston died a year later at age sixty-six.

14/Irving Berlin

17 Beekman Place at 50th Street.

This five-story brick house was the songwriter's home for the last forty-three years of his life. He came in 1946 with his wife, writer **Ellin Mackay**, and his three daughters soon after he wrote the music for the hit play *Annie Get Your Gun*. Previously, 17 Beekman Place had been the home of **President Truman's** Secretary of Defense **James Forrestal.**

As he grew older, **Berlin** became a

Irving Berlin

15/John D. Rockefeller 3rd
1 Beekman Place at Mitchell Place.

The philanthropist grandson of the founder of the **Standard Oil Company** lived in this apartment house from 1934 until his death in an auto collision in 1978. During that period, he was director of the **Rockefeller Center** and president of the **Rockefeller Foundation.** His brother-in-law **John Marquand**, the novelist who wrote *The Late George Apley*, also lived at this same address for many years. One Beekman Place was also the home of **Noel Coward** in 1933.

recluse, eventually refusing to see even his closest friends; the telephone became his only link to the outside world. During the last few years of his life, a group of fans would gather outside his home here on Christmas Eve to serenade him. In 1983, as they were singing *White Christmas*, Berlin, who hadn't made a public appearance in fifteen years, impulsively invited everyone in for cocoa. He came into the kitchen in his pajamas, told the group that this was the loveliest Christmas present he had ever received, and gave everyone a hug and a kiss.

The Berlins were married for sixty-two years. Ellin passed away in 1988 soon after suffering a stroke and Irving died in his sleep in this house fourteen months later. He was 101 years old. The Berlin residence now houses the country of Luxembourg's permanent mission to the United Nations.

Berlin's last home at Beekman Place

Sara and Gerald Murphy lived here at 1 Beekman Place for about two years, moving in at the beginning of 1934. One night, the Murphys hosted a party for their friend Ernest Hemingway and one of the guests, neighbor Dorothy Parker (see number 3 above) brought along her two untrained terriers. Another guest, author John O'Hara, reported later that the dogs grew restless during the evening as the group waited for Hemingway to show up.

O'Hara, who felt antagonistic toward Sara Murphy because he suspected that she disliked him, gleefully noted that he "had the pleasure of watching first one dog, then another taking a squirt on Mrs. Murphy's expensive rugs."

16/Mary McCarthy
2 Beekman Place at Mitchell Place.

In 1933, Mary McCarthy was twenty-one years old and a recent graduate of Vassar College when she rented an apartment here with her first husband, playwright Harold Johnsrud. The building, designed by architect Rosario Candela, had opened the previous year. McCarthy supported herself doing freelance writing.

After their divorce in 1936, she lived for a spell in Greenwich Village before moving back here with Philip Rahv, an editor of the *Partisan Review*. Then in 1937, she met forty-two-year-old critic Edmund Wilson and they fell in love. McCarthy left Rahv in 1938 and married Wilson soon after. That union lasted until 1944.

TOUR 6

1/Jack Dempsey
211 East 53rd Street between Second and Third Avenue.

This white brick apartment building called The Hawthorne was the great prizefighter's last home. After years of living in hotel suites, Jack Demp-sey settled into a penthouse here with his last wife, Deanna Piattelli. "She was my fourth," he said. "I wish she had been my first." Late one night in the 1960s, when Dempsey was over seventy, he returned home by taxi from his Broadway restaurant to find two muggers ready to victimize an elderly couple in front of the building here. The ex-champ promptly flattened both assailants while the taxi driver called police. Dempsey lived to age eighty-seven and he died in his home here on May 31, 1983.

2/Claudette Colbert
226 East 53rd Street between Second and Third Avenue.

Actress Claudette Colbert was born in Paris in 1903 but she moved with her family to New York when she was three. They settled into an apartment on the fifth floor of this old red-brick building. Her father took a job as a minor bank official. Colbert always claimed that climbing the stairs in this building every day until the age of eighteen was what made her legs so beautiful.

After high school, she worked as an actress at the Provincetown Playhouse in Greenwich Village and it was in 1923 that she made her

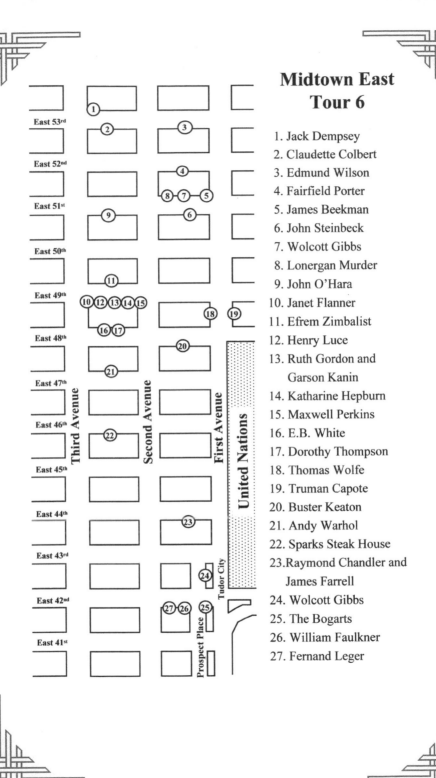

Midtown East
Tour 6

1. Jack Dempsey
2. Claudette Colbert
3. Edmund Wilson
4. Fairfield Porter
5. James Beekman
6. John Steinbeck
7. Wolcott Gibbs
8. Lonergan Murder
9. John O'Hara
10. Janet Flanner
11. Efrem Zimbalist
12. Henry Luce
13. Ruth Gordon and
    Garson Kanin
14. Katharine Hepburn
15. Maxwell Perkins
16. E.B. White
17. Dorothy Thompson
18. Thomas Wolfe
19. Truman Capote
20. Buster Keaton
21. Andy Warhol
22. Sparks Steak House
23. Raymond Chandler and
    James Farrell
24. Wolcott Gibbs
25. The Bogarts
26. William Faulkner
27. Fernand Leger

Broadway debut in a play called *The Wild Westcotts*. She had three lines: "The party was so lovely. The garden is beautiful. I am so hungry."

3/Edmund Wilson
314 East 53rd Street between First and Second Avenue.

After the death of his second wife in 1932, writer and critic **Edmund Wilson**, alone and grieving, moved into a flat in this old building. The wooden house is one of a pair (its twin next door is numbered 312) built together in 1866. Wilson's rent was $50 a month. He worked as a writer for *The New Republic* and soon became leftist in his politics as he traveled around the country reporting on conditions during the Depression.

When he was in New York, Wilson saw few people and scarcely left his apartment here. He sometimes went out to **Rosa's**, a cheap neighborhood restaurant where he ate at a common table with strangers. In 1934 Wilson began writing his book about Marxism and the Russian Revolution, *To The Finland Station*, and in the following year he left New York, traveling to the Soviet Union to do research.

4/Fairfield Porter
312 East 52nd Street between First and Second Avenue.

The painter **Fairfield Porter** bought this four-story brownstone in August 1942 after moving to Manhattan from Winnetka, Illinois. The cost was $13,250. He lived here with his wife, **Anne,** and his three chil-dren for seven years. The house was previously owned by comedian **Eddie Cantor** and during the first years of the Porters' residency, people occasionally came to the door demanding to meet the famous entertainer.

Porter took a studio in Chelsea so that he could continue his painting but, in need of income, he took a wartime job as a draftsman for a naval contractor. The Porters welcomed an array of friends and tenants to stay in their home for long and short periods; the downstairs portion of the building existed as a sort of commune with people coming and going as they pleased. But Porter had always wanted to live in a more rural setting near the ocean and, in 1949, the family moved to Southampton, Long Island.

5/James Beekman Mansion
51st Street and First Avenue (north-west corner).

The plaque on the building at this corner marks the estate of **James Beekman** who owned most of the land in this neighborhood in the late eighteenth and early nineteenth century. His large mansion called "Mount Pleasant" stood on this site from 1763 to 1874, before the area was subdivided into residential blocks.

The Beekman house was used as headquarters by British commander **Lord Howe** during the Revolutionary War because of its commanding view of eastern and southern Manhattan. Patriot **Nathan Hale** was imprisoned and tried on the grounds here and was later executed near the corner of East 66th Street and 3rd Avenue.

John Steinbeck 's home

6/John Steinbeck
330 East 51st Stret between First and Second Avenue.

Not long before his marriage to **Gwendolyn Conger** in the spring of 1943, **John Steinbeck** moved into the lower part of this three-story brick house. The place had two big fireplaces and a small garden.

A few months after he moved in, Steinbeck left for Europe as a war correspondent for the *New York Herald Tribune*. The wartime experience left him depressed and anxious; upon his return to the apartment here, he would be awakened at night by fierce headaches and sweats. A son was born to Steinbeck and his wife here on 44th Street in 1944 and, during

that summer, he spent time writing his next novel *Cannery Row*. The Steinbecks moved out in the fall of 1944, returning to the author's home in Monterey, California.

7/Wolcott Gibbs
317 East 51st Street between First and Second Avenue.

Wolcott Gibbs was a prominent writer and editor at *The New Yorker* magazine for three decades. This house was his last New York residence; he lived here until his death in 1958. Gibbs was one of the magazine's most versatile and talented staff members; he produced short stories, theater criticism, and biographical profiles, and he wrote the weekly *Notes and Comment* feature after **E.B. White** resigned in 1938.

Gibbs did most of his writing in his apartment, wearing a terry-cloth bathrobe and pacing the length of his bedroom with cigarettes burning in ashtrays at either end of the room. This house is now the **Permanent Mission of the Lao Republic to the U.N.**

8/The Lonergan Murder
313 East 51st Street between First and Second Avenue.

This house was the scene of one of the most sensational murders in New York during the last century. It took place on October 23, 1943 when twenty-two-year-old socialite **Patricia Lonergan** was bludgeoned and strangled to death by her estranged husband, **Wayne Lonergan.** His violent act was the result of her threat to divorce him and thus deny him access to the $7 million brewing fortune that she would inherit.

In a strange twist of the story, it was later revealed that Wayne Lonergan had been the onetime lover of Patricia's father.The murder and subsequent trial were the media sensation of 1943 and 1944, even in the middle of World War II. In the end, Lonergan was found guilty of second-degree murder and served twenty-two years in prison. He died in Canada in 1986.

9/John O'Hara
230 East 51st Street between Second and Third Avenue.

John O'Hara, age twenty-seven, lived in a room at this small hotel called the **Pickwick Arms** in 1933 and 1934. He possessed few assets and was barely able to afford the $8 a week rent. It was here that he wrote the novel that made him famous, *Appointment in Samarra.*

O'Hara would start writing at midnight and worked through the early hours of the morning, typing on his bed since his room was too small for a desk.Then, after sleeping until noon, he spent the afternoons at the movies, visiting his friend **Dorothy Parker**, or playing backgammon at **Ira Gershwin's** East 72nd Street apartment.

10/Janet Flanner
212 East 49th Street between Second and Third Avenue.

Janet Flanner, the European correspondent for *The New Yorker* magazine when she lived in Paris during the 1920s and 30s, quickly returned to the United States in 1940 as the German army invaded France. She rented an apartment in this building with her longtime companion, **Solita Solano.**

By 1942, Flanner—whose nom de plume was "Genet"—had fallen in love with **Natalia Danesi Murray**, a radio announcer, and she left her residence here on 49th Street with Solano to move in with Murray and her family (see this section, Tour 1, Number 6)

11/Efrem Zimbalist
225-227 East 49th Street between Second and Third Avenue.

This house, built in 1926, was the residence of renowned violinist **Efrem Zimbalist** and his wife, opera diva **Alma Gluck**. Her daughter, the novelist **Marcia Davenport**, lived here as well.

Zimbalist moved to Philadelphia in 1941 and by the 1950s, this building had been converted into the **17th Precinct Station House** of the New York Police Department. Since then, it has been subdivided into apartments. Note the violin and singing angel carved over the doorway.

TURTLE BAY GARDENS

This quiet block encompassing the south side of East 49th Street (numbers 226 to 246) and the north side of East 48th Street (numbers 227 to 247) between Second and Third Avenues is known as **Turtle Bay Gardens**. It is made up of Italianate row houses that date back to the 1860s.

In 1918, New York socialite **Charlotte Hunnewell Martin** bought the ten houses on each street, renovated them, and tore down all the back fences. Then she proceeded to create a single large Italian garden running down the center of the block which was to be maintained by the individual residents on a cooperative basis. The garden is invisible from the street. Over the years Turtle Bay Gardens has attracted many prominent New Yorkers, including **Judge Learned Hand, Leopold Stokowski,** and **Mary Martin.** Other residents and their houses are described below (numbers 12-17).

12/Henry Luce
234 East 49th Street.

Magazine publisher **Henry Luce,** with his first wife, **Lila,** moved into this town house in 1927. By this time, his *Time* magazine, which he started in 1923, was just beginning to turn profitable—its 1928 circulation doubled from two years earlier to over 200,000 and Luce was on his way to becoming a millionaire.

Luce was a dynamic man with energy to burn—he walked every morning to the offices of the magazine at 25 West 45th Street in fifteen minutes. Luce was living here in 1930 when he launched the glossy business magazine *Fortune,* which became an immediate success.

He and Lila lived at 234 East 49th until 1932, when they moved to grander quarters on the Upper East Side at 4 East 72nd Street (see Section One, Tour 4, Number 14).

13/Ruth Gordon and Garson Kanin
242 East 49th Street.

Gordon and **Kanin** lived in this house for almost forty years, beginning in 1951. It was their friend and next-door neighbor, **Katharine Hepburn,** who arranged for them to buy it; they paid $58,500.

While they resided here, Kanin and Gordon collaborated on the screenplay *Pat and Mike,* a Hepburn-Tracy vehicle, which won an Academy Award nomination in 1952. Ruth Gordon won an Oscar for Best Supporting Actress in 1968 for *Rosemary's Baby.* Kanin, in addition to his prolific writing, directed a number of plays on Broadway including *The Diary of Anne Frank* and *Funny Girl.* After Gordon died in 1985, Kanin continued to occupy the house until 1990, when he remarried.

Whenever Gordon and Kanin were absent from here for extended periods, they rented it to others. Film director **Mike Nichols** installed an intercom system while he lived here. **Tyrone Power** stayed in the house while he was performing on Broadway in 1954. **Mary Tyler Moore** used the top floor study as a dance studio. **Franco Zeffirelli** planned his **Metropolitan Opera** projects during his stay.

14/Katharine Hepburn
244 East 49th Street.

After **Hepburn** finished making *Little Women* in Hollywood in 1932, she returned to the New York stage to star in a play called *The Lake.* She rented this house for $100 a month and moved in with her husband,

Ludlow Smith. They separated soon after but Hepburn loved the place and continued to live here; she finally purchased it for $27,500 in 1937. It was her New York home for more than sixty years.

Late one winter night, when her neighbor, songwriter **Stephen Sondheim** (see number 15 below), was disrupting her sleep by playing his piano, Hepburn decided to pay him a suprise visit. She walked barefoot across the garden in the snow to his window and, draping herself against it, stared at him like an evil angel. Sondheim saw her and froze. Hepburn claimed that she never heard another late night sound from him.

By the late 1990s, the actress, in failing health, decided to leave 49th Street and live permanently at her family home in Connecticut.She died there at the age of ninety-six in June 2003. A few months later her house here was put on the market at a price of $4.9 million.

Katharine Hepburn's Manhattan home

15/Maxwell Perkins
246 East 49th Street.

This was the onetime home of the legendary editor at the publishing house of Charles Scribner's Sons who nurtured such writers as **F. Scott Fitzgerald, Ernest Hemingway,** and **Thomas Wolfe. Maxwell Perkins** moved to Turtle Bay Gardens from New Canaan, Connecticut in 1932 and stayed until 1938. When he was editing Wolfe's mammoth manuscript *Of Time and the River* in 1934, the two men would work together condensing the huge half-million word novel, starting at 8 p.m. every night

here in Perkins's study. Then just before midnight, they would end the day by going out for a stroll and a drink before Wolfe took his long walk home across the Brooklyn Bridge.

Songwriter **Stephen Sondheim** has lived in this house since 1960. In 1995, it underwent extensive renovation after a devastating fire.

16/E.B. White and Katharine Angell White
Numbers 229, 239, and 245 East 48th Street.

The **Whites,** both mainstays of *The New Yorker* magazine almost since its beginning in 1925, lived at three different addresses on this block during a twenty-two-year span. They

E. B. & Katharine White

first moved to Turtle Bay Gardens in 1935 to live at number 239 after having outgrown their smaller apartment in Greenwich Village. A year later, they took up residence three doors east at number 245.

White was unhappy there. "I had never felt really at home in the house we were renting," he wrote. "The rooms were always too hot and dry. I fell asleep every night after dinner." In 1938, he persuaded Katharine to leave New York to live on a farm in North Brooklin, Maine. He accepted an offer from *Harper's* magazine to write a monthly column while she continued to do part-time editorial work from their new home.

The Whites returned to Manhattan in 1945, renewing their connection with *The New Yorker*, and they eventually returned to Turtle Bay, leasing the house here at 229 East 48th Street. E.B. White was living here

when his children's novel *Stuart Little* became a popular success and he wrote *Charlotte's Web* in 1949 during his occupancy in this house. The Whites made 229 their winter home for eleven years, continuing to stay in Maine in the summers. In 1957, they moved permanently to their Maine farm.

17/Dorothy Thompson
237 East 48th Street.

The plaque on the front wall of this house reads: 'Dorothy Thompson "the intrepid girl reporter" lived here from 1941-1957.' The globetrotting journalist bought the place after her divorce from novelist Sinclair Lewis. Thompson's home had a fireplace in every major room, a library with some three-thousand books, a living room with an eight-foot couch and a studio that featured nine telephones and, according to her biographer Marion Sanders, "walls papered with maps, an illuminated globe, and a short-wave radio [that] enabled her to follow the progress of the war on land, sea, and air." Thompson moved away from Turtle Bay in 1957 after she remarried. She died in Portugal in 1961.

18/Thomas Wolfe
865 First Avenue between 48th and 49th Street.

Thomas Wolfe came back to New York from Europe in 1935 and began a search for an apartment with a view of the East River. He found it on the fourteenth floor in this old building, across from where the United Nations Plaza now stands. The rent was

$80 a month which he thought was outrageously expensive but it had a large bedroom and living room and, most important to him, a view of the barges on the river along with the wonderful sounds of the tugboats at night.His editor at Scribner's, **Maxwell Perkins**, lived only two blocks away (see number 15 above) and Wolfe visited him there frequently, practically becoming a member of the family. But by 1937, Wolfe dropped Scribner's as his publisher and when he became short of funds, he moved away from First Avenue to live in a string of inexpensive places including the **Chelsea Hotel.**

19/Truman Capote and Johnny Carson

870 United Nations Plaza (First Avenue between 48th and 49th Street).

Capote moved to a large apartment on the twenty-second floor of this building near the **United Nations** headquarters in 1965. It was just before his bookl *In Cold Blood* was published. The two-bedroom apartment cost $62,000, considered high in 1965, but it didn't deter Capote because money was finally coming in—he had recently sold the film rights to *Breakfast at Tiffany's* for $65,000.

He began to enjoy his celebrity status, becoming a regular on **Johnny Carson's** late night show. He lined the spare room of his apartment with copies of an Interview magazine cover with **Andy Warhol's** silk screen portrait of him. Capote lived here until his death in 1984; he died at the home of **Johnny Carson's** ex-wife **Joanna** in Los Angeles. Earlier, the Carsons were neighbors of Capote here; the late-night entertainer had moved in with his second wife, **Joanna Copeland,** in 1966, four years after he had started hosting *The Tonight Show* in New York. The Carsons divorced in 1972.

Robert Kennedy made 870 United Nations Plaza his New York home beginning in 1964. He had moved to the city to establish residency in his bid to become the state's U.S. Senator. He was elected in November of that year. Truman Capote's good friend **Katharine Graham**, owner of the *Washington Post,* also lived here.

20/Buster Keaton

318-320 East 48th Street between First and Second Avenue.

In the spring of 1917, the twenty-one-year-old **Buster Keaton** had come to New York to work in a stage variety show for which he was to be paid $250 a month. Before rehearsals began, he ran into silent-film star **Fatty Arbuckle,** who persuaded him to visit the studio where he was making his latest movie. Keaton followed Arbuckle to this building on 48th Street—now a five-story parking garage—which housed the production company called **Colony Studio.** By the end of the day, Keaton had acted in his first silent film, a two-reeler called *The Butcher Boy.* Keaton became immediately fascinated with every aspect of moviemaking; he asked Arbuckle to lend him a camera which he took to his rooming house that night and dismantled, piece by piece. The next day he quit his theater job and signed on with Arbuckle to make movies at a salary of $40 a week. He made seventeen short films with Arbuckle. By 1923, he was making his own features and was world-famous.

21/Andy Warhol
231 East 47th Street between Second and Third Avenue.

Warhol moved his art operations to a building on this site in November 1963. The place had previously been a hat factory and now, associated with Warhol, it became known simply as The Factory. The place quickly attracted artists, students, celebrities, and the city's lowlife. It became a cultural mecca of the 1960s that, according to Warhol's biographer, Victor Bockris, functioned as a "Salvation Army for all the artists and would-be artists who couldn't find shelter elsewhere." It was here that Warhol began making the unstructured films which ultimately produced temporary "superstar" celebrities like Baby Jane Holzer, Viva, and Edie Sedgwick.

In early 1966, Warhol brought the rock band called The Velvet Underground, with singer Lou Reed, into the Factory to perform in its underground theater and two months later he produced their first album. But by 1968, the Factory's open-door policy was flooding the place with too many freaks and Warhol decided to move the studio downtown to 33 Union Square West (see Section Four, Tour 3, Number 1). The Factory building was demolished soon after and replaced by the plaza and garage of the modern residence here today at 1 Dag Hammarskjold Plaza.

22/Paul Castellano
210 East 46th Street between Second and Third Avenue.

Sparks is known as one of the finest steak restaurants in New York. It was also the scene of one of organized crime's most notorious assassinations. On December 16, 1985, Paul Castellano, head of the powerful Gambino crime family, came here to Sparks for a lunch meeting and was gunned down—along with his driver, Tommy Bilotti—as the boss emerged from his black Lincoln in front of the restaurant.

The victims were killed instantly by the four hitmen who then trotted to Second Avenue into waiting cars and sped away. John Gotti, who soon after became head of the Gambino family, was later convicted of ordering the killing. He was given a life sentence.

23/Raymond Chandler and James Farrell
310 East 44th Street between First and Second Avenue.

Raymond Chandler, the creator of detective character Raymond Marlowe, was seventy years old and near the end of his life when he traveled to Manhattan from his home in La-Jolla, California in March 1959 and stayed here at the Beaux Arts Hotel. He had come to accept the presidency of the Mystery Writers of America at a party in his honor. From New York, he planned to travel on to London.

After a short stay, Chandler, in poor health to begin with, developed a bad cold in New York's blustery weather and decided to return to California. He soon developed pneumonia and died at the Scripps Clinic in LaJolla on March 26, 1959.

From 1958 to 1966, the Beaux Arts Hotel was home to writer **James Farrell**, the creator of the **Studs Lonigan** trilogy. He came after separating from his wife, **Dorothy**, and his stay here was a time of financial and literary difficulties. His last novel *The Face of Time,* published three years earlier, hadn't sold well and he was almost a forgotten artist. But he continued to write, sometimes sitting at his typewriter for days at a time, dressed in dirty pajamas, the room littered with paper and the remains of old, cheap meals scattered about. Farrell began his new series of novels called *A Universe of Time* while he lived here.

In 1960, at a neighbor's party in the hotel, he met **Cleo Paturis**, twenty-three years his junior, and she became his companion for the rest of his life. Farrell and Paturis moved a few blocks from here to an apartment in Tudor City in 1966.

TUDOR CITY

Tudor City is a self-contained, multi-building residential complex which opened in the late 1920s. It extends from East 40th Street to East 43rd Street between First and Second Avenues. Built by developer **Fred F. French** on the site of a shanty-town called **Goat Hill**, it was New York's biggest housing development up to that time with twelve buildings, 2,800 units, and 4,500 residents. Tudor City was designed to have its own private parks, restaurants, shops, and post office, all in Tudor Style.

French's vision was to provide better living conditions to the white-collar workers in the new office buildings that had shot up around **Grand Central Station.** Everything here faced inward toward the private open space created by the developers and away from the surrounding tenements, slaughterhouses, and generating plants that made up this neighborhood in the days before the United Nation building was constructed in the 1940s.

24/Wolcott Gibbs
45 Prospect Place (Tudor City Place).

Here on **Tudor City's** main street—now named **Tudor City Place** but called Prospect Place when it was first laid out—is number 45, the main building in the complex.

Wolcott Gibbs, the famous *New Yorker* magazine writer and editor moved here with his second wife, **Elizabeth,** soon after their wedding in 1929. On March 31, 1930, she committed suicide in their apartment. Gibbs told police that his wife had become obsessed with a play that they had seen recently, *Death Takes a Holiday*, a fairy-tale drama that ends when the heroine runs away with the figure Death. Gibbs and Elizabeth were discussing the play when she calmly walked to a bedroom window and jumped out. Gibbs spent time under psychiatric care before being able to return to his editorial duties. He later remarried for a third time.

25/Maud and Belmont Bogart
25 Prospect Place (Tudor City Place).

Humphrey Bogart's parents were living a comfortable middle-class existence in 1900 when he was born—his father was a prominent physician, his mother was a well-known magazine illustrator. But by the 1920s, when Humphrey was still a poor young actor, the fortunes of the elder Bogarts had declined due to bad investments and a diminishing medical practice.

By 1934, as Dr. Bogart's health deteriorated, the couple moved into inexpensive separate apartments in this building. "There was no formal separation," their son later wrote. "But they just couldn't stand being together for long." **Maud** cooked breakfast for **Belmont** every morning and was with him for dinner. But she returned to her own flat every evening. In early September 1934, Belmont became critically ill; he died in his son Humphrey's arms in the hospital. Not long after, although he was still grieving and drinking to excess, the actor was chosen for the part of **Duke Mantee** in the play *The Petrified Forest*. It made him a star and led to his first screen role.

26/William Faulkner
320 East 42nd Street between Second Avenue and Tudor City Place.

In November 1931, **William Faulkner** arrived in New York from Oxford, Mississippi for a six-week visit. His latest novel *Sanctuary* had attracted a lot of attention and he was suddenly courted by a host of publishers who wanted the rights to his next book. He moved into an apartment here on the twenty-eighth floor at **Woodstock Tower** in Tudor City and, while visiting friends such as **Dashiell Hammett, Lillian Hellman,** and **Nathanael West**, went on a series of drinking binges. But he also managed to work, spending his mornings in the apartment writing his next novel, *Light in August*.

On some days, when Faulkner missed rural surroundings, he would get on a commuter train to Connecticut, get off at some station which had woods nearby and walk by himself for a few hours. In early December, the author moved to a room at the **Algonquin Hotel** where his wife, **Estelle**, joined him. They returned to Mississippi on December 14th.

27/Fernand Leger
304 East 42nd Street at Second Avenue (southeast corner).

French modernist painter **Fernand Leger** was one of the many European artists and intellectuals who would spend the war years in exile in the United States. He arrived in New York from France on November 12, 1940 and a month later came to live here at the **Tudor Hotel** (now called the Crown Plaza), staying with the artists **Herbert** and **Mercedes Matter**. It was Leger's home until the spring of 1941 when he moved to the **Beaux Arts Building** at 80 West 40th Street near the New York Public Library. Leger came back to the Tudor Hotel in October 1944 and stayed for another six months. He returned to his native France after the war.

TOUR 7

1/Hotel Commodore
109 East 42nd Street at Lexington Avenue (northwest corner).

The thirty-five story **Grand Hyatt**, just up the street from **Grand Central Station**, was known as the **Hotel Commodore** until it was remodeled in 1980.

F. Scott and **Zelda Fitzgerald** moved into a suite in May 1920, a month after their wedding at St. Patrick's Cathedral. They came after being evicted from the **Biltmore Hotel** (just a few blocks away at 43 East 43rd Street—it no longer exists) where their exuberant lifestyle had disturbed the other guests. Fitzgerald's first novel *This Side of Paradise* had become a best-seller and the couple continued to celebrate. They rode down Fifth Avenue on the top of a taxi, danced on people's dinner tables, and here at the Commodore were seen spinning in the revolving door for half an hour.

In July 1925, young Swedish actress **Greta Garbo** arrived in the United States with her director **Maurice Stiller**, on their way to California to make American movies. They stayed at the Commodore for two months while they wrangled over their contract with MGM Studios. New York was suffering from a heat wave at the time and Garbo spent many hours in her room taking cold baths. When MGM's **Louis B. Mayer** received the stunning publicity photographs of Garbo taken by photographer **Arnold Genthe**, he immediately gave in to her new salary demands and she headed for Hollywood.

Zelda and F. Scott Fitzgerald

In May 1927, the Commodore hosted the official dinner of the City of New York with aviator **Charles Lindbergh** as the guest of honor. He had recently completed his historic transatlantic flight and the hotel bragged that the dinner was the largest ever given to an individual in modern history: "3700 guests feasting on 6,000 pounds of chicken, 2,000 heads of lettuce, 125 gallons of peas, and 800 quarts of ice cream."

The Commodore was the scene of a dramatic meeting that led to the trial of **Alger Hiss**, the U.S. diplomat accused in 1948 of having been a communist spy. His accuser was one-time Soviet agent **Whittaker Chambers,** who claimed, against Hiss's

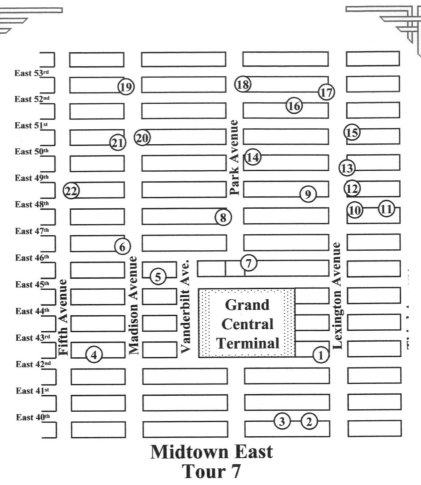

Midtown East
Tour 7

denials, that they had committed espionage together in the 1930s. **Richard Nixon** of the House Un-American Activities Committee arranged to have the two men meet here in Room 1400 of the Commodore. Although Hiss continued to proclaim his innocence, he identified Chambers as a man he had known a decade earlier, thus opening the door to one of the most sensational court trials of the last century in which Hiss was finally convicted of perjury. He served forty-four months in prison beginning in 1950.

Dwight D. Eisenhower stayed at the Commodore on the night of the 1952 presidential election as he awaited the returns that would show that he had beaten **Adlai Stevenson.** At 1:30 AM on November 5, the president-elect made a victory speech before his Republican supporters in the ballroom here.

2/Josephine Baker

118 East 40th Street between Lexington and Park Avenue.

Josephine Baker had become a huge star in France by the time that she returned to the United States in October 1935 to perform in the **Ziegfeld Follies**. She immediately encountered the racial prejudice of that time as she tried to find a residence that would accept blacks, finally registering here at the more liberal **Hotel Bedford,** which housed mainly artists, actors, and newspaper people. Baker took a penthouse with a terrace and, in a mood to celebrate, began to spend a fortune on toys, dolls, and electric trains.

Photographer **Robert Capa** usual-ly made the Hotel Bedford his home during New York visits, beginning in 1937 when he signed a contract with *Life* magazine. He was in the habit of leaving the door of his room open every morning so that friends could come in and kibbitz with him while he soaked in his bathtub.

Soon after the Second World War, Capa spent time here with actress **Ingrid Bergman,** with whom he had a long love affair. On Friday nights, even though he was in financial difficulty, he took part in the poker games here at the Bedford. They were attended by professional cardsharps and Capa rarely won.

The Bedford was also a temporary home of writer **Thomas Mann** and his family in the late 1930s. They had come to New York as exiles from Nazi Germany. Mann moved to California in 1940 where he lived for the next twelve years.

3/James Gould Cozzens

114 East 40th Street between Park and Lexington Avenue.

The novelist, with his wife, **Bernice Baumgarten**, took an apartment in this building in 1938. He was busy writing his ninth book, *Ask Me Tomorrow.*

Early in that year, he had taken a job as associate editor for *Fortune* magazine at a salary of $15,000, a generous figure in those Depression days. **Cozzens** and his wife lived here during the winter months and commuted to his job from his country home in New Jersey during the rest of the year.

4/Sigmund Freud
19 East 42nd Street between Fifth and Madison Avenue.

Freud made one visit to the United States in his lifetime. He came from Austria in August 1909 to receive an honorary degree from **Clark University** in Massachusetts and to deliver a series of lectures. For the first week of his visit, he stayed in the **Hotel Manhattan** on this site. The rate of $2.50 a night was paid by his hosts.

Freud was accompanied on his trip by associates **Carl Jung and Sandor Ferenczi** and they enthusiastically explored Manhattan, getting glimpses of Central Park and Columbia University, Chinatown and Coney Island, and inspecting Greek antiquities at the **Metropolitan Museum.** After his official visit to Clark University, Freud returned to Vienna on September 21st.

5/Guy Lombardo
45 East 45th Street between Madison Avenue and Vanderbilt Avenue.

The **Roosevelt Hotel**, built in 1924, has long been a popular New York stopping place because of its proximity to **Grand Central Terminal** (the underground passage connecting the two buildings is now closed). It was also famous because it was the chief venue of one of America's most popular big bands—**Guy Lombardo and his Royal Canadians.** They performed at the **Roosevelt Grill** here for what was probably the longest continuous engagement in music business history—from 1929 until 1963, interrupted only when Lom-

bardo saw fit to go on the occasional tour.

On December 31, 1929 Lombardo inaugurated what was to become an American institution when he welcomed in the New Year on his network radio show which originated live from the hotel. From that date until his death in 1978, Lombardo hosted the arrival of the New Year for vast numbers of radio listeners and, later, television viewers around the world.

6/Ritz Carlton Hotel
374 Madison Avenue at 46th Street (northwest corner).

One of the landmark luxury hotels of the last century, the old **Ritz Carlton,** stood on this site for forty-one years. It opened in 1910 and a number of famous New Yorkers made it their residence.

Al Jolson always kept a suite here in the 1920s. The *New Yorker* editor **Harold Ross** lived in the hotel as a bachelor after his divorce from **Jane Grant** in 1929. He came back again to live with his third wife, **Ariane Allen,** from 1940 to 1943.

Gambler and underworld fixer **Arnold Rothstein** lived in a deluxe suite in the mid-1920s. **Cole Porter** resided here in 1932 when he wrote one of his trademark songs *Night and Day*, sung by **Fred Astaire** in the musical *Gay Divorce.*

The Ritz Carlton was demolished in 1951 to make way for the more modern building which stands at this location today. A new **Ritz Carlton** opened in the 1950s on the west blockfront of Madison Avenue from 61st to 62nd Streets. More recently, in 1982, the hotel (at least in name) relocated to the former **Navarro** hotel building at 112 Central Park South.

7/Salvatore Maranzano
230 Park Avenue at 46th Street.

By 1931 **Salvatore Maranzano** had become the "boss of bosses" of New York organized crime after he arranged the murder of his chief rival **Joe Masseria.** Surrounded by bodyguards and ensconced in his offices here on the ninth floor of the **Grand Central Building** (now the **Helmsley Building**), Maranzano thought himself secure.

But on September 10, 1931, four killers, identifying themselves as federal agents, got past his office guards and trapped him in his private office. Minutes later, after a violent struggle, he lay dead with six stab wounds and four bullets in his head and body. The murderers had been hired by **Lucky Luciano**, a younger mob chieftain who soon took over as the new crime boss of New York and became the architect of the modern five-family organized crime system that endured in the city until recent years.

8/The Marguery
270 Park Avenue between 47th and 48th Street.

The **Marguery** was an elegant twelve-story apartment hotel that stood on this site from 1918 until the 1960s. During that time it was a residence of many prominent New Yorkers.

Legendary film star and author **Louise Brooks** moved here in 1925 during the time she was working as a dancer in the **Ziegfeld Follies.** She lived in a large room, she wrote, "that looked down on three fine spruce trees crooning peacefully in the courtyard." She was in residence when she acted in her first movie called *Street of Forgotten Men*, filmed at a studio in Astoria, Long Island.

Charles Lindbergh came to New York on June 13, 1927, soon after his historic transatlantic flight, to be honored at a ticker-tape parade which was the largest in the city's history up to that time. He was proclaimed a hero and was mobbed by well-wishers wherever he went. During his five-day stay in Manhattan, Lindbergh and his mother lived in an apartment at the Marguery, loaned to them by a friend of **Mayor Jimmy Walker** for the duration of their stay.

During the early 1920s, **David O. Selznick**, the motion picture producer best known for his film *Gone With the Wind*, lived here as a teenager with his family. His father, **Lewis**, owned a movie company and they rented a twenty-two-room apartment complete with servants and chauffeured Rolls Royce. By 1926, the elder Selznick had lost most of his fortune and David, without money, moved to California to begin his own movie career.

Film directors **John Huston** and **Frank Capra** were busy making documentary war films for the U.S. Signal Corps in 1942. On a long stay in New York, they were loaned the apartment of the wealthy **Norman Winston** at the Marguery and they couldn't believe their luck. The place was full of paintings by Matisse, Picasso, and Braque, had a fully stocked bar, four servants, and the best food, all during the wartime shortage. It was too good to last—the Army eventually reassigned them to Great Britain.

In 1929, **Thomas Wolfe's** lover, **Aline Bernstein**, lived at the Marguery with her husband. Wolfe, who had become a literary celebrity with the publication of his novel, *Look Homeward, Angel,* was a frequent visitor.

One extraordinary night in 1930, the Bernsteins hosted a party here at which one of the guests, sculptor **Alexander Calder,** performed a special entertainment with miniature circus figures that he had constructed. Near the end of the night, a fire broke out in the apartment building and as all the occupants evacuated the premises, Wolfe distinguished himself by rushing into one of the female servant's quarters and carrying the woman to safety.

9/Ernest Hemingway
111 East 48th Street between Lexington and Park Avenue.

The fourteen-story building standing at this location today is the **Hotel Inter-Continental** but it was once called the **Hotel Barclay** and it was a favorite stopping place in New York for **Ernest Hemingway.** He stayed here in 1937 while he finished his novel *To Have and Have Not.* In July 1940, he returned to the Barclay to work on revisions of *For Whom the Bell Tolls,* delivering his book piecemeal by runner to his publisher

Charles Scribner's Sons, which was located a few blocks away.

Eugene O'Neill and his wife, **Carlotta**, lived at the Barclay, in a suite on the eighth floor, for seven months in 1945-46. They had come to New York from their previous home in Sea Island, Georgia. While he was in residence, O'Neill put the finishing touches on his new play *The Iceman Cometh.*

Birth control pioneer **Margaret Sanger** also kept an apartment at the Barclay in the 1940s.

10/Joe DiMaggio and Artie Shaw
511 Lexington Avenue at 48th Street (southeast corner).

Joe DiMaggio had a suite here at the **Hotel Lexington**—now the **Radisson New York Eastside**—and, in the early 1960s, it became his New York headquarters. It was provided to him free of charge by one of his business associates.

After his ex-wife **Marilyn Monroe** separated from **Arthur Miller** in 1961, she and the former *Yankee* spent time together at the Lexington. DiMaggio claimed that he lost nine of his World Series rings here at the hotel in a burglary. "I had a beautiful alligator-covered jewelry box for my rings," he said later. "I went to Alaska for five days and when I got back, everything had been stolen. The only thing they didn't take was a pair of rosary beads." DiMaggio did manage to retain the 1936 ring from his rookie year which he wore until the day he died.

Bandleader **Artie Shaw's** newly-formed band had its first engagement at the Lexington in the summer of

1936. Shaw was only twenty-five years old. His new group was made up of a few friends as well as students he had trained out of music school.

The musician distinguished himself from the other Big Bands of the period by doing something unheard of—he added a string section to a jazz orchestra.

11/Horace Liveright

148 East 48th Street between Lexington and Third Avenue.

Horace Liveright was one of America's greatest publishers—his company, **Boni and Liveright** featured some of the best writers of the twenties, including **Theodore Dreiser, Eugene O'Neill, and Sherwood Anderson.** By 1933, Liveright was down on his luck and living in a small apartment here at the **Hotel Middletown** (now the **Helmsley Middletown**).

When he married a young woman who was the ex-wife of actor **Joseph Schildkraut,** the reception was held in his flat. It was attended by the many famous people who knew Liveright and one of the guests brought a German street band with him, making a loud party even louder.

In the middle of the gathering, a stranger walked up to Liveright, said "I have a message from Joe Schildkraut," and punched the publisher in the face. Although the party continued, the marriage soon fizzled and Liveright eventually ended up alone and broke in a rooming house. He died there on September 24, 1933.

12/Georgia O'Keeffe and Alfred Stieglitz

525 Lexington Avenue between 48th and 49th Street.

Stieglitz and **O'Keeffe** took a two-room suite here at the thirty-four story **Shelton Hotel** (now the **Marriott New York Eastside**) in November 1925. At that time, it was the tallest hotel in the world. It became their New York residence for the next ten years. It was in the Shelton that O'Keefe painted a number of canvases immortalizing the Manhattan skyline.

Their flat was located on the twenty-eighth floor (suite 3003) with spectacular views facing north, east, and south. It had a tiny bedroom and a living room, sparsely furnished, which O'Keefe converted into studio space. Frugal as always, O'Keefe was initially more excited by the low rent of their new quarters than by the breathtaking views.

Tennessee Williams stayed at the Shelton while his play *The Glass Menagerie* premiered on Broadway in 1945. At the same time, he worked on a first draft of another play that later became *Summer and Smoke.* Williams became restless by the end of the year and moved to New Orleans.

Back in the 1920s, **Harry Houdini** staged one of his patented escapes from a steel trunk at the bottom of the large swimming pool in the Shelton's sub-basement. The pool is still there but no longer in use.

13/Dean Martin and Jerry Lewis

541 Lexington Avenue at 49th Street (northeast corner).

This large hotel on the corner of 49th Street and Lexington Avenue used to be the **Belmont-Plaza** (it's now the **W New York**) and one of its claims to fame is tied to the early careers of **Martin** and **Lewis.**

In 1944 and 1945, they were both second-rank entertainers before they knew each other and they lived here separately, on and off, in the hotel. Both of them performed in the hotel's lounge called the **Glass Hat**—Martin as a crooner and Lewis doing a weird comic lip-sync act and doubling as an emcee for other performers. Lewis claims he saw Martin for the first time standing in the lobby here inspecting the billing card that advertised the upcoming show. Not long after, a mutual friend, Sonny King, introduced the two and soon they appeared together for the first time at the **Havana-Madrid** nightclub on 1650 Broadway. It marked the beginning of one of the most popular acts in show business history.

14/Waldorf Astoria Towers

100 East 50th Street at Park Avenue (southeast corner).

The one-hundred-and-twelve luxury suites of the **Waldorf Towers**, just around the corner from the **Waldorf Astoria Hotel's** main lobby on Park Avenue, make up what is considered by many to be New York's ultimate residential hotel. **The Towers,** which opened in 1931, occupies the twenty-seventh through forty-second floors of the hotel. Fifty-one units are leased on a permanent basis; the other sixty-one are transient apartments. They have been the home of numerous prominent Americans.

Cole Porter lived in a suite on the forty-first floor from 1935 until 1964; it was here that he wrote some of the most popular songs of the last century; his piano can be seen today in a room off the main lobby of the hotel. While his wife, **Linda,** was alive, they had adjacent but separate apartments. Porter, who liked to work on his compositions after midnight, had "acoustical mud" placed in the walls to deaden the piano sounds so that he wouldn't disturb his neighbors. He installed his own antique parquet floor from a French chateau in one room and put beautiful oriental rugs in two others.

General **Douglas MacArthur** spent his last years at the Waldorf Towers. He moved here with his wife, **Jean,** in 1951 after he was relieved of his Far East command by **President Truman.** He remained popular even after his dismissal; when he first came here, Waldorf switchboard operators began logging three thousand calls a day from people who wanted to speak to him. The hotel leased him Suite 37A—which normally cost $133 dollars a day—for only $450 a month. MacArthur died in 1964 and his wife continued to live here alone for the next thirty-six years, dying in January 2000.

Charles (Lucky) Luciano, the king of organized crime in New York, resided at the Towers from 1933 to 1936. He stayed in Suite 39C under the alias of Charles Ross and paid $800 a month in rent. It was his last home in America. His reign as the top mob boss ended when prosecutor **Thomas Dewey** sent him to prison for ten years on a morals charge. In 1946 he was exiled to Italy for the rest of his life.

Marilyn Monroe moved into Suite 2728 at the Towers in April 1955. Her small three-room apartment, which she subletted, was decorated in blue and gold and had a dramatic night view. Some observers spotted a lonely **Joe DiMaggio,** her estranged husband, jealous and still in love, outside the Waldorf at night keeping track of her. In those days, Monroe was in a contract dispute with Twentieth Century Fox and was meanwhile studying with **Lee Strasberg** at the **Actors Studio.** By the time that her divorce with DiMaggio became final, she had begun an affair with playwright **Arthur Miller.** Monroe left here when her sublet ended in February 1956 and she married Miller soon after.

Since the Towers opened, every U.S. president has stayed in the **Presidential Suite,** although few were as loyal as **Herbert Hoover,** who not only made Suite 31A his home after his presidency in 1932 but died here in 1964. Suite 42A on the top floor became the home of American ambassadors to the United Nations: **Henry Cabot Lodge** lived here in the 1950s; **Adlai Stevenson** was here from 1961 until his death in 1965.

Frank Sinatra made Suite 33A his New York home for over twenty years beginning in the 1970s. Others who have lived at the Towers include **Henry** and **Clare Boothe Luce, Spencer Tracy, Joseph Kennedy,** **Moss Hart, Elsa Maxwell, Alan J. Lerner,** and the **Duke and Duchess of Windsor.**

15/Eamon De Valera
569 Lexington Avenue at 51st Street (southeast corner).

The plaque inside the door of this mid-town hotel (now the **Hilton Metropolitan DoubleH**) marks the site of the birthplace of Ireland's great statesman who served as that country's prime minister or president every year (except three) from 1932 until 1973. **Eamon De Valera,** whose mother was an Irish immigrant and whose father was Spanish, was born on October 14, 1882 in the **New York Nursery and Child's Hospital,** an institution for destitute and abandoned children that once stood on this block. After living in New York for three years, De Valera was taken by an uncle to Ireland to be raised on a relative's farm in County Limerick. Later, after joining the 1916 Easter uprising against British rule, he narrowly escaped the firing squad.

His newly-formed Republican party won the 1932 election, thus beginning his long career as Irish leader. De Valera died in 1975 at the age of ninety-two.

16/Marilyn Monroe and Gloria Swanson
114 East 52nd Street between Park and Lexington Avenue.

The old **Gladstone Hotel** stood on this site for many years. **Marilyn Monroe,** single again after her divorce from **Joe DiMaggio,** came to

New York from Hollywood in late 1954 and, a month later, moved into a small apartment here.

She was involved in a contract dispute with her studio, Twentieth Century Fox, and had no income; she relied on the generosity of her friends. Photographers and journalists soon found out that she was staying at the Gladstone and often gathered outside the hotel's revolving front door.

One of her neighbors in the hotel was novelist **Carson McCullers;** the two became close friends.

In February 1954, Monroe began taking classes at the **Actors Studio** under the guidance of **Lee Strasberg.** She also began an affair with **Arthur Miller,** who would become her next husband. In April she moved to the Waldorf Towers (see number 14 above).

Legendary film actress **Gloria Swanson** rented a string of three suites at the Gladstone in the 1920s and made them her New York home. She split her time between Manhattan and Hollywood.

17/Marilyn Monroe
Lexington Avenue at East 52nd Street (northwest corner).

It was on this spot, on the night of September 14, 1954, in front of the **Trans Lux** movie theater (since demolished) that the notorious scene from the movie *The Seven Year Itch* was filmed. It is, of course, the one in which the draft from the subway vent blew **Marilyn Monroe's** skirt high above her waist.

The scene, staged by director **Billy Wilder**, was witnessed by a few thousand onlookers, one of which was Monroe's husband **Joe DiMaggio,** who was enraged at his wife's exposure. Their marriage, already troubled, came to an end a few months later. The building on this corner now is called "**600 Lexington**" but the subway vent is still there.

18/Truman Capote and Harold Arlen
375 Park Avenue between 52nd and 53rd Street.

Songwriter **Harold Arlen**, known for such tunes as *Over the Rainbow* and *Stormy Weather*, came from Hollywood in 1954 and lived in a large sublet apartment in a grand old apartment house that stood on this site before it was replaced by the modern **Seagram Building.** Arlen's mother, **Celia,** and brother, **Jerry,** moved in, too.

Arlen had come to New York to work on the score for the musical *House of Flowers* and his collaborator was writer **Truman Capote.** They worked in Arlen's bedroom where his piano had been placed. When the boyish-looking Capote first showed up, he immediately made himself at home and Mrs. Arlen, not knowing who he was, slapped his hand when she caught him with it in the refrigerator.

The Seagram Building, which has stood here since 1958, is the only New York building designed by famed architect **Mies van der Rohe.**

19/Harold Ross and Charles Lindbergh
21 East 52nd Street at Madison Avenue (northwest corner).

The twenty-one story **Berkshire Hotel** (now called the **Omni Berkshire Place**), which was built in 1926, was one of the last residences of **Harold Ross**, founder and first editor of *The New Yorker* magazine. After he separated from his third wife, **Ariane Allen,** in the fall of 1950, Ross vacated their apartment at 375 Park Avenue and took a suite here. He was in failing health by this time and in the early summer of 1951 he was diagnosed with cancer of the windpipe. Ross stayed for a few more months before moving to the **Algonquin Hotel,** which was his home when he died on December 6, 1951. Ross was fifty-nine years old.

The Berkshire was also the hotel where aviator hero **Charles Lindbergh** and his bride, **Anne Morrow,** spent their honeymoon. They were married secretly on May 27, 1929 at the Morrow home in Englewood, New Jersey and came to Manhattan in mid-June after sailing on a private cruiser along the Eastern seaboard. They stayed at the Berkshire for two weeks before embarking on a cross-country air and train trip.

20/Villard Houses
451-455 Madison Avenue between 50th and 51st Street.

In 1882, journalist, railroad promoter, and financier **Henry Villard,** who was married to the daughter of abolitionist **William Lloyd Garrison**, commissioned the architectural firm of McKim, Mead and White to build a set of six linked brownstones here: four surrounding a courtyard on Madison and two facing 51st Street; the aim was to create a single great Italian Renaissance palazzo. Villard moved into the largest house—451 Madison at the corner of 51st—with a plan of selling the others.

His place had a hydraulic elevator, electrical wiring, thirteen flush toilets, and a central heating system that used a ton of coal a day; it was considered a state-of-the-art residence for its day. The cost was nearly a million dollars but Villard didn't enjoy it for long. In 1884 his business empire crumbled, he had a nervous breakdown, and he left his house here house for good. It was purchased by **Mr. and Mrs. Whitelaw Reid,** who published *The New York Tribune.*

By 1943, the last Reid had moved out and the Villard house became the **Women's Military Services Club,** which housed over 250,000 women in the military during the next two years at a rate of fifty cents a night.

After the war, the north wing of the complex was purchased by publisher **Bennett Cerf** as headquarters for his company, **Random House,** which occupied the space until 1969. In 1974, the south wing was taken over by **Harry Helmsley** for his **New York Palace Hotel,** along with the central portion, which had been occupied for years by the **New York Catholic Archdiocese.**

Until 2005, the four-star restaurant **Le Cirque** operated within the space that was originally the entertaining rooms of Henry Villard's house.

21/Francis Cardinal Spellman
452 Madison Avenue at 50th Street (northwest corner).

In his role as Roman Catholic archbishop of New York and later as a cardinal, **Francis Spellman** was New York's most powerful church leader. He lived here in the five-story gothic-style Archbishop's Mansion behind **St. Patrick's Cathedral** during his reign from 1939 to 1967. Spellman occupied a private apartment on the second floor. The residence, built in 1880, was nicknamed "The Powerhouse" because of Spellman's great influence in New York religious and political affairs.

During his long tenure, he built thirty-seven churches, 130 schools, five hospitals, and a number of convents, old-age homes and orphanages. He was friend and advisor to many politicians.

Spellman was the Vietnam War's most vocal religious supporter and when he died in 1967, the embattled President **Lyndon B. Johnson** came to New York to attend his funeral. Although hundreds of antiwar demonstrators had been arrested by police before Johnson's arrival, hundreds more greeting his bulletproof limousine outside St. Patrick's Cathedral chanting, "hey, hey, LBJ, how many kids have you killed today?"

Waiting inside the church was Johnson's nemesis, Senator **Robert F. Kennedy,** soon-to-be challenger for the Democratic presidential nomination who had transformed himself into a leading critic of the U.S. involvement in Vietnam.

22/Preston Sturges
603 Fifth Avenue between 48th and 49th Street.

Film director and screenwriter **Preston Sturges,** creator of a string of popular comedies in the 1940s, was just twenty-six years old in 1927 when he moved to the rear portion of the top floor of this old four-story building.

He came here to live with his mother who had a studio and residence on the second and third floors and operated a business making and selling hand-painted shawls, scarves, and batiks. Sturges had recently separated from his first wife.

He attempted to help his mother with her business but the field of entertainment beckoned to him; after enrolling in a mail-order course on piano playing, he decided to take up playwriting. His first effort, *The Guinea Pig,* opened on Broadway in 1929 and his second, *Strictly Dishonorable,* became a smash hit, making him a celebrity and giving him temporary financial security.

He then married **Eleanor Hutton,** heiress to the Post and Hutton family fortunes in 1931 and they moved out of his cramped quarters here at 603 Fifth Avenue to a large house at 125 East 54th Street.

In 1932 Sturgis traveled to California to begin a new career in the movies, initially to write scripts. He directed his first film *The Great McGinty* in 1940. It won him an Academy Award for Best Screenplay.

MURRAY HILL
AND
SURROUNDINGS

*Section Three of this guide covers the area which includes
the Murray Hill neighborhood and the streets around it.
Its boundaries are East 28th to East 40th Street
and between Third and Fifth Avenue.*

URRAY HILL itself, which is bounded roughly by Madison and Third Avenue and from 34th to 42nd Street, is no longer the destination for the very wealthy that it was earlier in the last century but it is still a comfortable middle class neighborhood with picturesque streets and numerous shops and restaurants. It became very fashionable in the mid-nineteenth century as affluent New Yorkers moved uptown, building mansions along Fifth, Madison and Park Avenues. Murray Hill is named after Robert Murray whose country estate stood at 37th and Park Avenue during the Revolutionary War period. It was there in 1776 that Murray's wife is said to have served tea to the dallying General Howe and his staff while Washington's American troops escaped to the northwest. Although almost all of the great mansions are gone, a number of outstanding brownstones and carriage houses remain, keepsakes of this neighborhood's more elegant days—and reminding us of the fact that Murray Hill was once the home to a number of prominent New Yorkers.

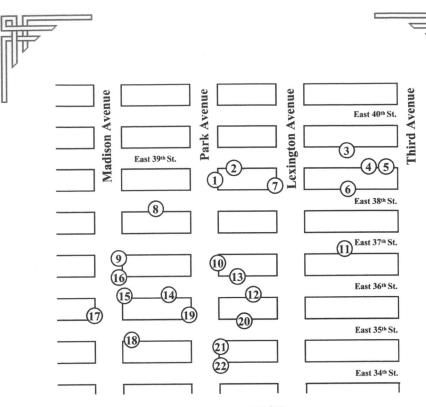

Murray Hill
Tour 1

1. Mrs. George Custer
2. William Shawn
3. F. Scott Fitzgerald
4. Katharine Hepburn
5. James Farrell
6. Dashiell Hammett
7. Dashiell Hammett and Nell Martin
8. Philo Vance
9. J.P. Morgan, Jr.
10. Cornell Woolrich
11. Robert Benchley

12. Ethel Barrymore
13. Franklin D. Roosevelt
14. Ayn Rand
15. Harold Ross
16. J. Pierpont Morgan
17. Sara Delano Roosevelt
18. Charles Addams
19. Kate Smith
20. E.B. White
21. Helen Hayes
22. Anais Nin

TOUR 1

1/Mrs. George Armstrong Custer
71 Park Avenue between 38th and 39th Street.

Elizabeth Custer, the wife of the legendary Indian fighter and Civil war general, lived in this twelve-story apartment building during the last years of her life. Her husband had died in the massacre at **Little Big Horn** on June 25, 1876 and she was a widow for the next fifty-seven years.

Mrs. Custer was a familiar figure here on Park Avenue as she took her daily leisurely strolls around the neighborhood. She died in her apartment on April 4, 1933, at the age of ninety.

2/William Shawn
120 East 39th Street between Park and Lexington Avenue.

The sixteen-story **Tuscany**, now a cooperative, used to be one of the finer hotels in the city. **William Shawn** moved here with his wife, **Cecille**, in 1939 after he was named a managing editor of *The New Yorker* magazine.

Shawn was thirty-two at the time and had been at the magazine since 1933 when he joined the staff as a *Talk of the Town* editor. In 1952, after the sudden death of the publication's first editor and founder, **Harold Ross**, Shawn was made the new editor-in-chief. It was a position he held until 1988 when the magazine changed ownership and he was forced to resign.

F. Scott Fitzgerald

3/F. Scott Fitzgerald
143 East 39th Street between Lexington and Third Avenue.

On February 11, 1920, soon after he finished writing his first novel *This Side of Paradise*, **F. Scott Fitzgerald** moved into a room in this building, known then as the **Allerton Hotel.** He had come to New York after spending a month in New Orleans working unsuccessfully on a second book.

He and **Zelda Sayre** of Montgomery, Alabama, had recently become engaged and while he waited for her to join him in Manhattan, he continued to write. Here at the Allerton, Fitzgerald began work on two of his best-known short stories, *The Jelly Bean,* and *May Day.*

On April 3rd, he and Zelda were

married in the rectory at **St. Patrick's Cathedral**; there were only four other people present.

This building on 39th Street is now numbered 145 and its name is the **Ten Eyck Troughton**.

4/Katharine Hepburn

146 East 39th Street between Lexington and Third Avenue.

In 1928, **Katharine Hepburn** married **Ludlow Ogden Smith** and she moved into his apartment in this five-story residence. She was acting as an understudy in the Broadway production of *Holiday*—a play that would be turned into a successful motion picture starring herself with **Cary Grant** in 1938.

Here on East 39th Street, Hepburn and Smith first lived in the rear apartment on the second floor, then moved to the entire top floor, with double the space. The building had a dumbwaiter shaft, which allowed the couple to have food sent up from downstairs.

In 1932, Hepburn received wonderful reviews for her performance in the play *The Warrior's Husband*. This led to movie offers and eventually to her first film *Bill of Divorcement*, co-starring **John Barrymore**.

When Hepburn returned to New York from California in 1933, she was a famous actress with several films to her credit; she and her husband moved from this apartment to a new place on East 49th Street (see Section Two, Tour 6, Number 14).

5/James Farrell

150 East 39th Street between Lexington and Third Avenue.

Writer **James Farrell** was fifty years old when he moved to an apartment here in the **Hotel Dryden** (now the **Dryden East**) in 1954. He was short of money at the time and struggled to cover the expenses of this well-furnished Murray Hill residential hotel—he had previously been living at the **Hotel Chelsea** with its more modest rates. Soon after he moved to the Dryden, he sold the movie rights of his famous *Studs Lonigan* trilogy and the transaction helped relieve some of his financial problems. Farrell had recently reestablished a relationship with his first wife, **Dorothy,** and in the fall of 1955, the couple remarried and moved together to a new address at 285 West 85th Street.

6/Dashiell Hammett

133 East 38th Street between Lexington and Third Avenue.

In the spring of 1931, writer **Dashiell Hammett** returned to New York from California, where he had been working as a screenwriter. Broke, fed up with Hollywood, and drinking heavily, he took an apartment in this attractive building. His book, *The Glass Key,* was published that April.

Hammett stayed here until the end of the year, working sporadically on a new novel that would later become *The Thin Man* when it was finally completed in 1933. During the previous winter, he had met **Lillian Hellman** while working in Hollywood and, by the end of 1931, the two were living together at the **Hotel Elysee** on East 54th Street (see Section Two, Tour 2, Number 10).

7/Dashiell Hammett and Nell Martin

318 Lexington Avenue between 38th and 39th Street.

This narrow brownstone was the residence of **Nell Martin**, a novelist who at one time had also been an actress, law student, migrant worker, and taxi driver. In 1929, she was also the lover of **Dashiell Hammett.** They first met in San Francisco that year and traveled to New York, renting an apartment at 155 East 30th Street (see this section, Tour 2, Number 5).

They lived together there, then separated, but they remained friends and in 1936 when Hammett returned to Manhattan from Hollywood, broke and sick, he stayed here at Martin's apartment on Lexington Avenue where she attempted to nurse him back to health. He was suffering from tuberculosis made worse by his alcoholism and venereal disease. His writing days were mostly over by then.

8/Philo Vance

38th Street between Madison and Park (south side).

Followers of the classic American mystery novel will know this neighborhood. Somewhere on the south side of this block stands the townhouse of detective **Philo Vance,** who in the 1920s and 30s was one of the most famous characters in popular fiction. Created by writer **S. S. Van Dine**, Vance is a rich, smug, cynical bachelor who, as an art student and connoisseur, spends his time in scholarly pursuits when not solving murder cases. His apartment occupies the top two floors of a beautiful brownstone and is filled with objects of ancient and modern art.

Vance's popularity, based on such best-selling novels as *The Benson Murder Case* and *The Canary Murder Case*, made this fictional residence on 38th Street at one time as recognizable in America as **Sherlock Holmes's** Baker Street flat.

J. Pierpont Morgan

9/J. P. Morgan, Jr.

231 Madison Avenue at 37th Street (southeast corner).

The banker son of **J. Pierpont Morgan** lived in this beautiful four-story townhouse from 1905 until his death in 1943. The one-time forty-five-room house now serves as the northern wing of the newly-refurbished **Morgan Library and Museum.** It is the last of three brownstones built in a row here on the east side of Madison Avenue between 36th and 37th Street in the year 1853.

J. P. Morgan, Sr. purchased all three houses at different times, moving into number 219 himself in 1882 (see number 16 below), demolishing the center house (number 225) for his garden a few years later, and then giving his son this house (number 231) in 1905. After Morgan, Jr. died in 1943, the **Lutheran Church in America** bought his house and used it for offices over the next forty years. The Morgan Library at 219 Madison Avenue purchased the house in 1988 and ultimately at-tached it to the library by building a modern, glass-enclosed connection.

10/Cornell Woolrich

45 Park Avenue at 37th Street (southeast corner)

Cornell Woolrich, the prolific writer of suspense novels and stories—he is probably most remembered today as the author of the story *Rear Window* that became a popular **Hitchcock** film—moved alone into this hotel called the **Sheraton Russell** in 1965. He had recently recovered from eye surgery.

Woolrich was a man who had lived in hotel rooms for most of his life and this one would be his last. He lived on the second floor at the north front of the building. Every night between six and midnight, he would sit in the lobby and look out at the street, saying nothing, doing nothing. The writer's productive days were over—he wrote a few short stories

while he lived here but mostly he would drink, either in his room, or at **McSorley's Tavern** in the East Village (see Section Five, Number 8).

Woolrich suffered a stroke here at the Russell on September 19, 1968 and died soon after. He was sixty-four years old.

11/Robert Benchley

154 East 37th Street between Lexington and Third Avenue.

Writer **Robert Benchley**, age twenty-six, moved to Manhattan from Massachusetts in January 1916 to begin a job with the *New York Tribune*. For two months, while he worked as a general reporter for the newspaper, he lived alone in a furnished room in this four-level brownstone; his wife and baby son were still living in Cambridge.

In the meantime, Benchley's colleagues at the newspaper—**Franklin P. Adams, Heywood Braun,** and **George S. Kaufman**—took the young writer under their wing, treating him to meals and free show tickets. When the Benchley family was finally reunited in March, they moved to an apartment near Gramercy Park (see Section Four, Tour 2, Number 10).

12/Ethel Barrymore

128 East 36th Street between Park and Lexington Avenue.

In 1930, **Ethel Barrymore** leased an apartment in this brownstone for three years. The actress had recently completed a run in the role of **Lady Teazle** in *School for Scandal*.

Ethel Barrymore

Always a spendthrift, she soon realized that she was running out of money and quickly fell behind in her rent payments. In 1932, when MGM made a lucrative offer, Barrymore suppressed her contempt for Hollywood and accepted. She starred in a movie called *Rasputin and the Empress* with her brothers **Lionel** and **John.** It was her first talking picture and she collected a salary of $57,000 for it, even though she incurred expenses of $65,000 during her California stay.

When she returned to New York in 1933, she was sued by the landlord, **William Adams Delano**, for back rent of over $10,000. Barrymore's response was to pack her bags and flee the city to her other home on Long Island.

13/Franklin and Eleanor Roosevelt
125 East 36th Street between Park and Lexington Avenue.

The newly-wed **Roosevelts** moved into this beautiful five-story brownstone in 1905, after returning from their honeymoon tour of Europe. In 1907, **Franklin** completed his last two years at Columbia University Law School and began his law practice. In the meantime, **Eleanor** spent much of her time with her mother-in-law, **Sara,** who lived just three blocks away at 200 Madison Avenue (see number 17 below).

Every day the two women took a carriage ride up Fifth Avenue and through Central Park. Sara, a domineering person, persuaded Eleanor to discontinue her volunteer work on the Lower East Side because she feared that her daughter-in-law would bring the diseases of the slums into her household.

While they lived here on 36th Street, Franklin and Eleanor's first two children, **Anna** and **James**, were born. The family moved to the Upper East Side in the fall of 1908 (see Section One, Tour 1, Number 16).

14/Ayn Rand
36 East 36th Street between Madison and Park Avenue.

Author **Ayn Rand** and her husband, **Frank O' Connor**, moved from California to New York in 1952 and rented an apartment in this large red-brick and white stone building across from the Morgan Library. She turned a tiny 8 x 12-foot room in the flat into an office, jammed with file cabinets; it was here that Rand worked, driving herself under a merciless schedule—she usually wrote seven days a week and often until midnight. The writer completed her hefty novel *Atlas Shrugged* in 1957 while she lived here.

15/Harold Ross
22 East 36th Street at Madison Avenue (southeast corner).

The *New Yorker* editor-in-chief moved into an apartment in this building with his second wife, **Frances Elie,** in 1934, soon after they were secretly wed. He was forty-one years old, she was twenty-three. They immediately had the place redecorated at great expense. Ross's only child, **Patricia**, was born while they lived here. This was an important period in Ross's professional life because, during the Great Depression, *The New Yorker* became not only a financial success but also an artistic and cultural success due to the excellence of its journalism, fiction, and humor. Ross and Elie were divorced in 1939. Their apartment stands directly across from the Morgan Library.

16/J. Pierpont Morgan
219 Madison Avenue at 36th Street (northeast corner).

The **Pierpont Morgan Library** is probably Murray Hill's most notable landmark. On this northeast corner, where the southern wing of the library now stands, was the home of the famous financier, **J. Pierpont Morgan.** It was a three-story brownstone mansion, built in 1853, and Morgan moved into it with his family in 1882. He later purchased the two houses just north of him on Madison Avenue, demolishing one to make room for his garden and giving the other one, at 231 Madison, to his son (see number 9 above).

When he was at home, Morgan Sr.

Former Morgan Mansion

enjoyed domestic life. On Christmas Eve for many years, he dressed up as Santa Claus and drove around the city in his carriage delivering gifts to friends and relatives.

Morgan's house here was the first private residence in New York to be entirely illuminated by **Thomas Edison's** electric lights. One night in the fall of 1883, while the family was attending the opera, faulty wiring in the library set Morgan's desk, carpet, and other furniture on fire. The problem was soon solved and Morgan was so satisfied with the new system that he gave a reception for 400 guests to showcase the new lighting.

Morgan lived at number 219 until his death in 1913 and left an estate of $68 million. He had built his original library next to his mansion at 33 East 36th Street in 1906.

Morgan's son, **J.P. Morgan, Jr.** had the mansion demolished in 1928 to make way for the new annex of the library. This addition contains Morgan's entire private collection of books and art which was originally located on the first floor of the old mansion.

17/Sara Delano Roosevelt

200 Madison Avenue at 35th Street (northwest corner).

Franklin D. Roosevelt's mother, **Sara,** lived in a rented brownstone on this site from 1904 until 1908. She spent much of her time at the family estate in Hyde Park and made this Madison Avenue place her Manhattan home.

When son Franklin began his studies at Columbia University Law School in 1904, he lived here with his mother. He had recently become engaged to his distant cousin **Eleanor** and FDR continued to live with Sara until his wedding in 1905. He and Eleanor stayed briefly in this house just before they embarked on their European honeymoon tour.

Sara lived here alone until 1908, when she built houses at 47 and 49 East 65th Street both for herself and for her son and daughter-in-law (see Section One, Tour 1, Number 16).

18/Charles Addams

20 East 35th Street at Madison Avenue (southeast corner).

This thirteen-story apartment building was the longtime home of cartoonist **Charles Addams.** He was famous for his macabre and hilarious drawings which were mainly featured in *The New Yorker* magazine where he worked from 1932 until his death in 1988. During that time, he created over 1200 cartoons and seventy-five front covers for the publication.

The decor of the Addams apartment seemed to fit the man—half of one wall was covered with ancient crossbows and a headsman's axe, a human skeleton under glass stood on a living room table, there was a skull on the dressing table in the bedroom, and the liquor bottles on his shelves shared space with other containers labeled "arsenic."

On September 29, 1988, Addams was seating himself in his car on the street here outside his building when he suffered a fatal heart attack. His wife, **Tee Miller,** said later that, because Addams enjoyed a lifelong passion for cars, the manner of his death seemed an appropriate one.

19/Kate Smith

20 Park Avenue at 35th Street (northwest corner).

Kate Smith, one of last century's most popular singers, and the woman who the made **Irving Berlin's** song *God Bless America* an unofficial national anthem, lived in a penthouse apartment in this large building for many years. During that time, she had a successful radio show, then switched to television where her *Kate Smith Variety Hour* continued her fame. During her long career, she recorded over 3,000 songs—over 100 of them made the **Hit Parade.** Kate Smith died in 1996 in Raleigh, North Carolina.

20/E.B. and Katharine White.

115 East 35th Street between Park and Lexington Avenue.

The Whites had moved to Maine in 1938 after **E.B. White** resigned from the staff of *The New Yorker.* But in the fall of 1943, he returned to New York and rejoined the magazine as editorial writer. He and **Katharine** took a furnished apartment in this four-story brownstone.

White poured his energies into covering the war effort and writing editorials that promoted the need for a world government. Katharine continued her job as an editor of the magazine. The Whites vacated this apartment in November 1944 to live in Greenwich Village.

21/Helen Hayes
15 Park Avenue at 35th Street (southeast corner).

In 1925, **Helen Hayes**, then an unheralded young actress, was living in a three-room apartment in this building with her mother. She was in rehearsal for the play *Caesar and Cleopatra*.

In her memoirs, Hayes recalled the afternoon that she attended a party at artist **Neysa McMein's** studio on West 57th Street. One of the guests, playwright **Charles MacArthur** introduced himself by offering her some peanuts. "He poured a few in my hand and said, 'I wish they were emeralds.' Right then and there I fell in love." Later that day, MacArthur hired a horse-drawn cab to drive them down to her apartment here on Park Avenue.

They began a three-year courtship that culminated in their wedding, which took place on August 17, 1928, three days after his play, *The Front Page*, co-written with **Ben Hecht**, opened on Broadway to rave reviews. A year earlier, Hayes had achieved her first great stage success in a play called *Coquette*.

22/Anais Nin
7 Park Avenue at 34th Street (northeast corner).

In the spring of 1935, **Anais Nin** rented Apartment 61 in this building with her husband, **Hugo Guiler,** who had recently joined her from Paris. Nin had been living in New York for six months at the **Barbizon Plaza Hotel** on West 58th Street.

Since February of that year, she had been secretly involved in a love affair with fellow writer **Henry Miller,** who was living at the **Roger Williams Hotel** (see this section, Tour 2, Number 16). Nin gave them equal time, moving back and forth between her apartment here on 34th Street and Miller's hotel, five blocks away. During this same period, she worked as a psychoanalyst under the guidance of **Otto Rank,** who had also recently been her lover. When Guiler and Nin returned to France in June 1935, Miller followed in hot pursuit.

TOUR 2

1/Enrico Caruso
4 Park Avenue between 33rd and 34th Street.

This twenty-two-story terra cotta-designed building was once the **Vanderbilt Hotel**, one of New York's most famous stopping places. It was built in 1912 by **Alfred Gwynne Vanderbilt**, great-grandson of **Commodore Cornelius Vanderbilt.** The hotel operated until 1967 when it was converted to mixed office/apartment use.

Alfred Vanderbilt had lived on the top two floors until 1915 when he died aboard the *Lusitania*, sunk by a German submarine off the coast of Ireland. An early promotion stated that the Vanderbilt Hotel was "patronized by the royalty of Europe, the elite of America and the best people everywhere, who appreciate refinement, luxury and an atmosphere of general charm."

Enrico Caruso

It was probably this kind of rhetoric that attracted opera star **Enrico Caruso,** who rented Vanderbilt's old apartment on the top floor in 1920. The Vanderbilt gave the great tenor the privacy that he needed; it also provided a garden for his wife, **Dorothy,** and a playground for their daughter. Caruso and his family stayed here until 1921 when they returned to Italy. He died there soon after.

Willie Morris, editor-in-chief of *Harper's* magazine from 1967 to 1971, rented an apartment on the seventeenth floor of the Vanderbilt in 1970, soon after his divorce. The hotel was conveniently located directly across from the Harper's offices at 2 Park Avenue. During Morris's tenure at the magazine, *Harper's* was

transformed into an important cultural and political voice of the late 60s and early 70s. Morris lived at the Vanderbilt alone and he soon began to lend the use of his apartment to his friends for their afternoon assignations. They included, he reported in his memoir, "a roll call of literary America." The key to his place became," Morris said, "more popular than I myself ever was."

Legendary Notre Dame football coach **Knute Rockne** always stayed at the Vanderbilt when he visited New York.

2/Ayn Rand
120 East 34th Street between Park and Lexington Avenue.

Ayn Rand lived in an apartment in this building with her husband, **Frank O'Connor**, during the last fifteen years of her life. When he died in 1979, they had been together for fifty years. Rand lived here alone after O'Connor's death, continuing her writing and working with the organizations that advocated her philosophy of Objectivism. She died here in her apartment on March 6, 1982 at the age of seventy-seven.

3/Andy Warhol
242 Lexington Avenue at 34th Street (southwest corner).

The artist was twenty-five-years old in 1953 when he rented a fourth-floor walkup in this building (the place is now numbered 230 Lexington). The flat was situated over a nightclub called **Shirley's Pin-Up Bar. Warhol** lived here with his mother, **Julia.** The apartment had a

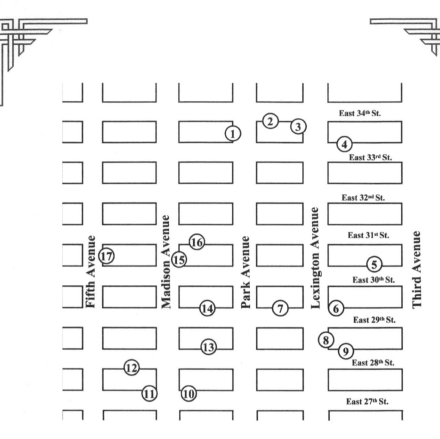

Murray Hill
Tour 2

1. Enrico Caruso
2. Ayn Rand
3. Andy Warhol
4. A.J. Liebling
5. Dashiell Hammett
6. Hadley Hemingway
7. Roy Lichtenstein
8. William Randolph Hearst
9. Anthony Perkins
10. Woodrow Wilson
11. Eugene O'Neill
12. Eugene O'Neill
13. Mark Rothko
14. Louise Brooks and Veronica Lake
15. James Gould Cozzens
16. Henry Miller
17. Alfred Stieglitz

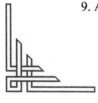

large kitchen that he decorated with a picture of Jesus pointing at his Sacred Heart. Andy and Julia shared a bedroom, sleeping on mattresses thrown on the floor. Their flat was so cluttered with stacks of paper, magazines, photos, and art supplies that Andy had to do his work at a portable desk on his lap. There were as many as twenty cats on the premises and the smell, Warhol's friends said, was indescribable.

4/A.J. Liebling
159 East 33rd Street between Lexington and Third Avenue.

This was the 1930s home of **A.J. Liebling**, one of *The New Yorker's* greatest writers. From 1933 until his death in 1963, his profiles of people, both famous and obscure, were highlights of the magazine. He was also its chief foreign correspondent during World War II. Liebling moved into a walkup apartment in this attractive four-story white brick building in 1935 with his first wife, **Ann McGinn**. A year later, he wrote an expose of African-American preacher **Father Devine** that impressed his editors; after that, he was one of *The New Yorker's* most prominently featured writers. Liebling lived here on 33rd Street until the beginning of the war in 1939, when the magazine sent him to Europe.

5/Dashiell Hammett
155 East 30th Street between Lexington and Third Avenue.

In the fall of 1929, detective writer **Dashiell Hammett** left San Francisco permanently and came to New York with his companion, **Nell Martin**. They lived together in an apartment here while Hammett waited for the publication of his new novel, *The Maltese Falcon*, which he had completed before leaving California. The book soon received rave reviews and made Hammett a literary celebrity. Martin moved out after a few months but Hammett stayed and continued to work on his next book, *The Glass Key*. On February 6th, 1930, he wrote in a letter to a friend: "*The Glass Key*, held back thus far by laziness, drunkenness, and illness, promises to get itself finished somehow by the latter part of next week." He finally completed the novel in one continuous thirty-hour writing session.

6/Hadley Hemingway and James Farrell
129 East 29th Street at Lexington Avenue (northeast corner).

Ernest Hemingway's first wife, **Hadley Richardson**, lived in this apartment building for a short time in the spring of 1927. She had just returned from France, where she had recently divorced Hemingway. Traveling with her was their son **Bumby**, age three. Hadley stayed here on 29th Street with one of her aunts and embarked on a nonstop round of lunches, dinners, and parties with New York friends. A year earlier, Hemingway had fallen in love with **Pauline Pfeiffer**, a wealthy woman from Arkansas who had befriended the couple in Paris—the affair had led to the breakup of the Hemingway marriage. The writer married Pfeiffer in May 1927. Hadley married **Paul Mowrer** in 1933.

Just around the corner from 129 East 29th, at 139 Lexington on the same northeast corner, was the one-time home of novelist **James Farrell**. He lived in an apartment in this four-story building with his companion, actress **Hortense Alden**, from 1935 to 1938. It was a notable time in Farrell's career—his **Studs Lonigan** trilogy, one of the most highly acclaimed and popular works of literature of the 1930s, was published in the year that he moved here.

7/Roy Lichtenstein
105 East 29th Street between Lexington and Park Avenue.

Artist **Roy Lichtenstein**, known as the master of Pop painting, purchased a loft studio in this twelve-story structure called the **Gordon Building** in 1984. He lived and worked here from that year until 1989 when he moved to Greenwich Village. He and his wife, **Dorothy Herzka**, had been living on Long Island for a decade before the move to 29th Street. Lichtenstein's loft had a simple, no-nonsense efficiency and visitors likened it to a factory with its painted image of a Swiss cheese on the elevator doors. The artist worked here on several paintings at once. As a man of habit he kept very precise hours, stopping for lunch every day at exactly one o'clock.

8/William Randolph Hearst and Chester Arthur
123 Lexington Avenue between 28th and 29th Street.

In 1898, **William Randolph Hearst,** the millionaire publisher of

William Randolph Hearst

the *New York Journal*, moved into this four-story house. Hearst, then a bachelor, filled his place with the art objects he had collected from his many European trips. He seldom arose before noon because he worked at the *Journal* offices from late at night until early dawn when the paper hit the streets. In the early evening, he attended the theater and then had dinner with friends before returning to his offices at the newspaper.

Marion Davies, his future mistress, remembered being arrested near here at the age of ten, with other children, for throwing rotten fruit at Hearst's house on a Halloween night.

By 1905, Hearst had a wife, two children, and a very large art collection, and needed larger quarters; he rented a huge apartment on the Upper West Side at 137 Riverside Drive.

Before Hearst lived here on 123 Lexington, this building was the home of the twenty-first President, **Chester Arthur.** He purchased it in 1865. Arthur was serving as Vice President in 1881 when President **James Garfield** was shot by a disgruntled office seeker. On the morning of September 20, soon after Garfield died, Arthur was sworn in as the new president in the first floor parlor of his residence here. After he served his term of office, he returned to his private law practice. Arthur died in his bedroom here on November 17, 1886. There is a memorial plaque inside the door here at the mailboxes.

9/Anthony Perkins
137 East 28th Street between Lexington and Third Avenue.

This building, next to the **Epiphany School**, was actor **Anthony Perkins's** childhood home. He was the son of actor **Osgood Perkins** and his wife, **Jane**, and was born on April 4, 1932, while his parents were living here. It was in that same year that Osgood performed in his most famous movie role as the gangster **Johnny Lovo** in *Scarface*.

The Perkins' two-bedroom penthouse on 28th Street was brimming with books and music and was decorated in an elegant Bohemian style. The Perkins' lived here until young Tony was four when they moved to the Upper East Side (see Section One, Tour 3, Number 7).

10/Woodrow Wilson
39 East 27th Street at Madison Avenue (northeast corner).

Mary Allen Hulbert Peck was an intimate friend of **Woodrow Wilson**. The two met in Bermuda in 1907 while Wilson, who was then president of Princeton University, was on vacation. He was married to his first wife, **Ellen Axson Wilson**, at the time. Wilson soon fell in love with Mary Peck and, subsequently, he began to visit her during 1909 and 1910 at her New York apartment which was located on this corner where the **New York Life Insurance Building** stands today.

Peck's place was on the eleventh floor of the building, in the shadow of the old **Madison Square Garden**, which stood across the street. Wilson, in a fit of guilt, ultimately broke off the affair in February 1910, but the pair remained good friends as long as Wilson lived.

Wilson was elected governor of New Jersey in 1910 before winning the U.S. presidency in 1912. Ellen died in 1914 and Wilson met **Edith Bolling Galt** soon after; they were married in December of 1915. Mary Peck's apartment on this block was demolished in 1928 when the New York Life building was erected.

11/Eugene O'Neill
21 East 27th Street at Madison Avenue (northwest corner).

In 1915, Eugene O'Neill's brother, **Jamie**, moved into a suite in this building, now called the **Madison Hotel** but then known as the **Garden Hotel**. O'Neill's parents had lived here earlier for a short time before moving two blocks away to the **Prince George Hotel** (see number 12 below). Eugene, age twenty-seven, visited the Garden Hotel frequently, sometimes staying with his brother, and often drinking with him in the bar near the lobby. The hotel was a gathering place for fight promoters, circus performers, actors, and gamblers; later it became one of O'Neill's models for the setting of his play *The Iceman Cometh*.

When O' Neill's mother entered a sanitarium, his father James joined his sons here at the Garden Hotel; they lived in rooms on the first floor. An observer remembered a night when he spotted Eugene and Jamie on the sidewalk outside with their arms around each other. "They were talking and kissing each other," he reported, "both as high as kites."

12/Eugene O'Neill
14 East 28th Street between Fifth and Madison Avenue.

O'Neill's parents, **James and Ella**, took an apartment here in the **Prince George Hotel** in the fall of 1913. It became their New York base whenever they were away from their home in New London, Connecticut. Very often over the next decade, their sons **Eugene** and **Jamie**, were living only minutes away at the **Garden Hotel** (see number 11 above). The elder O'Neills lived in an eighth-floor suite at the Prince George and both sons visited here frequently.

Eugene spent much of his time in Greenwich Village, living on next to nothing, and drinking heavily. His father would leave a dollar a day for him with the desk clerk here and often Eugene was physically unable to make the trek up to 28th Street to collect the accumulated cash. A few years later, Eugene became a playwright and it was here, to his parents' suite at the Prince George, that he came on February 4, 1920 to read the favorable reviews of his play *Beyond the Horizon*, the first O'Neill production to open on Broadway.

13/Mark Rothko
29 East 28th Street between Madison and Park Avenue.

Mark Rothko, the abstract expressionist painter lived in this red brick apartment house with his first wife, **Edith Sachar,** from 1940 until 1943. He had escaped from the military draft because of bad eyesight. He worked on his paintings in the back of the loft studio here while his wife produced hand-made jewelry in the front. While he lived in this building, Rothko began to produce the first of his "myth" paintings and, before long, became famous in the New York art world; his first one-man exhibition took place in 1944. Rothko's marriage began to unravel during this time and he moved away from here in 1943.

14/Louise Brooks and Veronica Lake
29 East 29th Street between Madison and Park Avenue.

This upscale hotel called **Thirty Thirty** used to be **The Martha Washington**, the first all-women hotel in the United States. It was a popular choice of students and career girls. In 1924, the young dancer and actress **Louise Brooks** moved here after being kicked out of the **Algonquin Hotel** for dressing improperly. The uninhibited Brooks lived in a room on the top floor of the Martha Washington, but she didn't fit in here, either—most of the other women wore suits and sensible shoes and worked in offices. Brooks was asked to leave when she was discovered, one day, exercising on the roof in flimsy pajamas.

Actress **Veronica Lake**, one of Hollywood's most popular leading ladies of the 1940s, worked as a barmaid at the **Martha Washington** in 1961, over a decade after her acting career had gone into decline. She worked nights in the **Colonnade Room** cocktail lounge and, during the day, slept in a room here that she rented for seven dollars a day. Her last Hollywood film had been *Slattery's Hurricane* in 1949; after that, she received no more movie offers. Lake died in obscurity in Burlington, Vermont in 1973. She was fifty-three years old.

15/James Gould Cozzens
121 Madison Avenue at 30th Street (northeast corner)

Novelist **James Gould Cozzens** moved to a penthouse apartment in this eleven-story red brick building in 1942 with his wife, literary agent **Bernice Baumgarten**. He had recently finished his eleventh novel *The Just and the Unjust,* which achieved both critical and popular success. Cozzens and his wife remained in this apartment during the war while he was assigned to the **Air Forces School of Applied Tactics;** his job was to write manuals and special reports.

16/Henry Miller
28 East 31st Street at Madison Avenue (southeast corner).

Henry Miller occupied Room 1202 here at the **Hotel Roger Williams Apartments** in February 1935. He was in love with writer **Anais Nin,** whom he had met in France and he had traveled to New York to be with her. Although Nin was formally living with her husband, **Hugo Guiler,** only a few blocks away (see this section, Tour 1, Number 22), she spent many hours here with Miller in his small room. By this time, copies of Miller's baudy novel *The Tropic of Cancer* had been smuggled through customs, creating a considerable stir in New York literary circles. During his stay at the Roger Williams, he completed *Black Spring*, the collection of autobiographical pieces that became his second published work. Soon after that, Miller, Nin, and Guiler all returned to France.

17/Alfred Stieglitz
291 Fifth Avenue betwen 30th and 31st Street.

In 1905, photographer **Alfred Stieglitz** opened his famous **"291" Gallery** on the site where the **Textile Building** now stands. The gallery was dedicated to the purpose of displaying the works of those photographers turned down by other New York art houses because they differed from the commercial standards of the time. Stieglitz soon widened the scope of his small gallery, formerly the studio of fellow photographer **Edward Steichen**, to include the works of avant-garde painters and sculptors. Ultimately, the masters of the new art movement in Europe— **Cezanne, Picasso, Matisse, Rodin**—all had their first American representation at the 291 gallery. Stieglitz's place stayed open until 1917. The building that housed it was demolished in 1919 and the Textile Building replaced it in 1921.

GRAMERCY PARK
AND
SURROUNDINGS

*For the purposes of this book, the section covers an area
from East 15th to East 27th Street
and between Broadway and First Avenue.*

G RAMERCY PARK—along with its surrounding streets—is one of New York's most charming neighborhoods and certainly one part of the city that has retained the look and feel of old New York. Change has come slowly here—many of the houses and apartment buildings date from the nineteenth century. Gramercy Park itself is much like a London square. Laid out at the end of Lexington Avenue between 20th and 21st Street in 1831 by lawyer/developer Samuel Ruggles who sold off building lots around the park, it is the city's only private residential square. The park is still beautifully maintained by a board of trustees for the benefit of the residents of the houses facing the square; they are the only ones with keys to its iron gates. Gramercy Park has retained its old world charm—except for the construction done on the north side of the square in the 1920s, there have been relatively few alterations in the last century. Over the years, it has been the home of countless prominent New Yorkers, from artists, writers, and entertainers to politicians and businessmen.

TOUR 1

1/John Garfield
3 Gramercy Park West

This beautiful Greek Revival house with the cast iron veranda, built in 1846, was once the residence of **Iris Whitney**, an actress and interior decorator. On May 21, 1952, the popular actor **John Garfield** came here to visit his friend Whitney, became suddenly ill, and died during the night of a heart attack. He was only thirty-nine years old and had gained fame for his performances in such movies as *The Postman Always Rings Twice* and *Body and Soul*. Garfield began his career on the stage in New York with the **Group Theater** in the early 1930s. It was his performance in a small role in **Clifford Odets's** play *Golden Boy* that gained him the attention that led to his successful Hollywood career. He was starring in a stage revival of the same play, *Golden Boy*, at the time of his death.

2/Edith Wharton and Eleanor Roosevelt
61 Gramercy Park North.

Calvary Church has been located on the corner of Park Avenue and East 21st Street since 1848. In 1875, the thirteen-year-old **Edith Wharton** began coming to the church's rectory which stood on this northeast corner (61 Gramercy Park North) until it was demolished in 1927. She came to visit her new friend **Emelyn Washburn** who, as the only child of the church's rector, lived here.

Edith suffered from acute loneliness in the house that she lived in with her parents on 14 West 23rd Street, just a few blocks from here, and she enjoyed her visits with the Washburn family. The two girls spent many hours perusing classic literature in the rectory library or making use of a new invention—the typewriter owned by Emelyn's father. On warm days, they climbed through Emelyn's bedroom window onto the library's roof and read Dante aloud.

Eleanor Roosevelt's parents were married in Calvary Church on December 1, 1883. Soon after Eleanor was born on October 11th, 1884, she was baptized here. At the ceremony, her uncle, future president **Theodore Roosevelt**, served as her godfather.

3/David Graham Phillips
Gramercy Park North and Lexington Avenue (northwest corner).

David Graham Phillips was a famous novelist and muckraking journalist at the turn of the last century. In 1911, he lived at the **National Arts Club** on the south side of the park here (see number 15 below).

Phillips was unaware that he was being stalked by an unbalanced man named **Fitzhugh Coyle Goldsborough,** who was convinced that the writer had libeled his sister. On the afternoon of January 23rd, as Phillips strolled toward this corner to pick up his mail at the **Princeton Club**, then located near here, Goldsborough approached him, drew a revolver, and fired six shots at him. The assassin then turned the gun on himself, dying instantly. Phillips expired the next night at a nearby hospital.

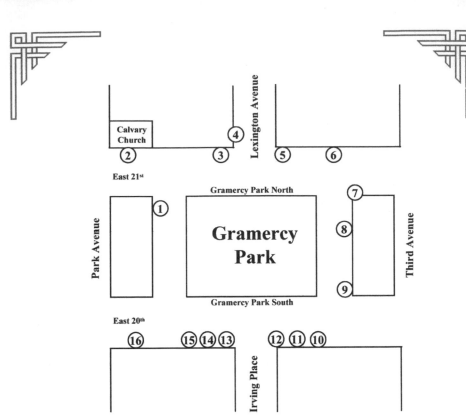

Gramercy Park
Tour 1

1. John Garfield

2. Edith Wharton and
   Eleanor Roosevelt

3. David Graham Phillips

4. Gramercy Park Hotel

5. Cyrus Field

6. Hart Crane

7. John Steinbeck

8. John Barrymore

9. James Cagney

10. Thomas Edison

11. Norman Thomas

12. Ben Sonneberg

13. Joseph Pulitzer

14. Edwin Booth

15. Samuel Tilden

16. Robert Henri

4/Gramercy Park Hotel

2 Lexington Avenue at Gramercy Park North (northwest corner).

Architect **Stanford White** lived in a beautiful house on this corner until his death at the hands of an assassin in 1906. The house was demolished in 1923 and a residential hotel called **Fifty-two Gramercy Park North** (later to be called the **Gramercy Park Hotel**) was built and opened on the site in 1925.

The new hotel had both temporary and permanent residents and it was here that **Humphrey Bogart** married his first wife, **Helen Menken**, on May 20, 1926, in a wedding that took place in the bride's large apartment. Menken's mother and father were both deaf and the preacher, also deaf, translated the ceremony into sign language for their benefit. Bogart and Menken lived here after the wedding but they quarreled constantly and, by the end of 1927, they were divorced.

In 1927, **Joseph P. Kennedy** and his family rented out the hotel's third floor for a number of months before settling in Riverdale, New York. Their son, **John F. Kennedy**, age eleven, could often be seen playing in Gramercy Park.

Another famous troubled couple who lived at the Gramercy was critic **Edmund Wilson** and his wife, writer **Mary McCarthy**. They lived here with their young son in 1944 but each had a separate room. They divorced soon after.

In 1936, **James Cagney** escaped Hollywood and lived in a temporary apartment in the Gramercy with his wife, **Willie.** Cagney was unhappy with how Warner Brothers was man-aging his career and wanted to change employers. He spent many hours with his friends at the **Players Club**, across the park. Cagney loved this neighborhood and later in his life made 34 Gramercy Park East his New York home (see number 9 below). Humorist **S.J Perelman** had an apartment in Room 1621 of the Gramercy and lived alone in it during the last years of his life. He died here in October 1979 at the age of seventy-five. Socialist **Norman Thomas** lived in a small kitchenette apartment here during the last three years of his life; he died in 1968. The plaque in the lobby of the hotel notes that Irish actress **Siobhan McKenna** made the Gramercy her New York home until her death in 1986. **Paul Shaffer, David Letterman's** band leader, had an apartment here for twelve years during the 1980s and 90s while he was a bachelor.

5/Cyrus Field

One Lexington Avenue (northeast corner).

Cyrus Field was a successful paper manufacturer and one of New York's richest men when he built a large house on this site in 1852. Although he was only thirty-four years old at the time, he was able to retire from active business. His house was one of the most elaborately furnished and decorated residences in the city with a large library on the second floor and a greenhouse for his wife. In the stables at the back of the house, the family still kept a cow that grazed in the neighborhood. Field is mainly remembered today as the man responsible for the laying of the first transatlantic telegraph cable in 1858. He died in 1892 and his house was demolished in 1909 and replaced with the grandly self-assured apartment house now on the site.

6/Hart Crane
44 Gramercy Park North.

Poet **Hart Crane** was just seventeen years old and had only recently arrived in New York from his home in Cleveland when he took an apartment in a brownstone on this site in the spring of 1917. He was joined by his mother and grandmother.

While he lived here, he began to see some of his poems published for the first time in small literary magazines. When his mother decided to return to Cleveland, Crane was forced to move to a cheaper place in Greenwich Village. It wasn't until 1930 that he finally finished his masterwork, *The Bridge,* a poem that he worked on for seven years.

7/John Steinbeck
38 Gramercy Park North.

John Steinbeck was a young writer newly arrived from California in 1925 when he rented a small room, infested with cockroaches, in this building which was then called the **Parkwood Hotel.** His home was up six flights of stairs and cost him $7 a week. He obtained a job as a cub reporter for the *New York World,* which supported him temporarily while he worked on his short stories.

After Steinbeck was fired from the newspaper, he holed up in his room here, writing day and night and living on little more than sardines and crackers. After his unsuccessful attempts to publish his stories, Steinbeck, dejected, returned to California in the summer of 1926.

8/John Barrymore
36 Gramercy Park East.

In 1910, soon after their wedding, actor **John Barrymore** rented a tenth-floor apartment in this then-new Gothic-style building with his first wife, **Katharine Harris.** He was acting on Broadway at the time.

"Between engagements, or on Sundays," reported his biographer **Gene Fowler,** "he would appear in old clothes and with a beard-stubble, slouch about Gramercy Park, feed the pigeons there, or enjoy solitary strolls in side streets...He stayed up all night with newspaper men and down-at-the-heel artists. He sometimes forgot his marriage vows."

Barrymore went on intense drinking bouts and, one night, drunk, he picked up a sword in his apartment and chased Katharine into Gramercy Park in her nightgown. She hid in the bushes of the park where she could hear Barrymore pounding door to door, bellowing "I want my wife!"

Eventually, the couple's frequent loud quarrels caused neighboring tenants to write a joint letter of complaint to Barrymore's landlord. But the next day, the now-sober actor and his spouse emerged from their building into Gramercy Park, arm-in-arm, and the letter never got mailed. Barrymore and Harris lived here until they were divorced in 1917.

James Cagney at The Gramercy

9/James Cagney
34 Gramercy Park East.

Built in 1883, this red brick and sandstone Victorian apartment house called **The Gramercy** is the city's oldest existing cooperative. **James Cagney** took an apartment here in 1961 with his wife, **Willie**. The actor always loved this neighborhood and was happy to live near the **Players Club,** which he visited frequently. The fifty-seven-year-old Cagney had recently announced his retirement from the movies although **Billy Wilder** coaxed him back in 1962 to perform in his film *One Two Three.*

Cagney was only one of a number of prominent actors to live at the Gramercy. **Margaret Hamilton**, who played the wicked witch in *The Wizard of Oz* made this her New York home for years. Other residents were *John Carradine* and *Mildred Dunnock.*

For years, the Gramercy maintained its original cable-controlled hydraulic elevator, but its creakingly slow operating system was finally replaced not long ago with a modern one run by electricity—less romantic perhaps, but more reliable and very much faster.

10/Thomas Edison
24 Gramercy Park South.

Thomas Edison was only thirty-four years old but already world-famous when he took a two-year lease on a $400-a-month mansion on this site in the winter of 1881. The inventor lived here with his wife, **Mary**, and their young daughter, **Marion.** At the time, Edison was busy supervising the construction of his first central electrical power system on Pearl Street in downtown Manhattan. He had recently leased a brownstone—just a few blocks south and west of here at 65 Fifth Avenue—for use as his corporate headquarters. After the family moved to Gramercy Park, Mary sent out cards inviting people to tea-and-champagne, though Edison, who detested

Edison & early phonograph

such parties, never appeared at them. The Edisons used their house in Menlo Park, New Jersey as their summer home for the next two years, living here in Gramercy during the other months. Their house was demolished in 1908 and replaced by this modern building.

11/Norman Thomas
20 Gramercy Park South at Irving Place.

Between 1941 and 1945, **Norman Thomas**, the man who ran for president six times as the Socialist Party candidate, lived in a small but elegant apartment here with his wife, **Violet**. Soon after their move to this location, the isolationist Thomas learned of the Japanese attack on Pearl Harbor and announced that the Socialist Party would support America's entry into World War II.

Thomas was living here when he ran for president for a fifth time in 1944; he collected only 80,000 votes. He was evicted from the building in 1945 along with other tenants when **Ben Sonnenberg,** the owner of Number 19 Gramercy Park, took over Number 20 and connected it to his private residence. The Thomases moved to nearby 71 Irving Place (see this section, Tour 3, Number 6).

12/Ben Sonnenberg
19 Gramercy Park South (southeast corner of Irving Place).

Ben Sonnenberg, the businessman who made a fortune revolutionizing the modern public relations business, was one of New York's greatest party hosts.

This five-story red brick townhouse with the mansard roof had been owned by businessman **Stuyvesant Fish** from 1887 to 1899 but fell into decline until Sonnenberg moved here in 1931 (not at first as an owner) and eventually restored it to its former glory, both as a house and as a center of the city's social life. The opulence of his thirty-seven-room mansion was compared by some to Buckingham Palace. Sonnenberg's lavish dinner parties for as many as 150 people mixed the likes of **Greta Garbo, Adlai Stevenson, John Steinbeck, Eleanor Roosevelt,** and the **Rockefellers.** At the top of the house, the host built a fifty-seat movie theater in which he regularly previewed films sent by his friend **Sam Goldwyn.** Sonnenberg died in 1978 and most of his objects of art were sold at auction.

Sonnenberg had paid $85,000 for the house in 1945. By the late 1990s, it went on sale for $18 million.

13/Joseph Pulitzer
17 Gramercy Park South.

In 1883, **Pulitzer**, a St. Louis newspaper owner, bought *The New York World* from **Jay Gould** for $346,000 and moved his family to Manhattan. He leased this red brick house across from Gramercy Park. He immediately turned the *World* into a profitable venture—and in the process, revolutionized the modern newspaper—by combining sensational stories with a crusading zeal, thus laying the groundwork for mass circulation journalism.

Pulitzer was elected to Congress in 1885 while he lived here but found

Joseph Pulitzer

the job so distasteful that he resigned in early 1886. By then, he had moved uptown to a house at 616 Fifth Avenue.

14/Edwin Booth
16 Gramercy Park South.

Edwin Booth, who was the most acclaimed American actor of the nineteenth century and older brother of the man who assassinated **Abraham Lincoln**, was fifty-two years old in 1885 when he left Boston with the idea of founding a New York gathering-place for actors that could also function as his residence. In 1888, he bought this old house, built in 1844, and turned it into a club called **The Players. Stanford White** was commissioned to remodel the building and among its charter members was **Mark Twain** and **William Tecumseh Sherman.** His new residence became a home for actors, as Booth had planned, and the actor himself lived on the third floor. He occupied a sparsely-furnished bedroom facing the park.

On many summer nights, after a supper on the rear porch, Booth would return to his own room, lie on the sofa by the open window, and listen to the sounds from the street. Booth died in his quarters here on June 8, 1893 at the age of sixty. His statue stands across the street inside Gramercy Park.

Samuel J. Tilden's house

15/Samuel Tilden
15 Gramercy Park South.

This brownstone, built in 1845 and remodelled in the Gothic Revival style in 1874, was the home of **Samuel Tilden.** He is best remembered today as the Democratic Party candidate in 1876 who won the popular presidential vote but ended up losing the election in the electoral college to Republican **Rutherford B. Hayes.**

Earlier Tilden had gained fame as the man most responsible for exposing and ejecting from power the corrupt New York City boss **William Tweed.** Tilden then served as New

York governor before running for president.

He died in 1886 and, in 1906, this building became the **National Arts Club.** Founded by *New York Times* art critic **Charles de Kay**, the private-membership institution had a mission of uniting "art lovers and art makers." Among its many prominent members over the years have been **Pierpont Morgan, Henry Frick, Mark Twain, Stanford White, George Bellows, Alfred Stieglitz,** and **Frederic Remington. Woodrow Wilson** was also a member as was **Theodore Roosevelt**, who ate lunch here frequently.

16/Robert Henri
10 Gramercy Park South.

Robert Henri was an influential artist who is best known as a member and chief advocate of the "Ashcan School" in the early part of the last century. Henri, who acted as a teacher and mentor to many prominent American painters, lived here at Number 10 Gramercy Park during the last twenty years of his life. The "Ashcan School" was made up of six artists who moved to New York around 1900 to create art rooted in the real, everyday, life of their time. Henri's studio was on the top floor of this house, built in 1848, and he lived here beginning in 1909 with his second wife, **Marjorie Organ**. Some of his ex-students, such as **Edward Hopper, John Sloan, and Ernest Lawson**, came here to see him.

Anarchist and feminist **Emma Goldman** visited him here when Henri asked her to sit for a portrait. Later she wrote: "His beautiful stu-dio in Gramercy Park, far removed from the dirt and noise of the city, and the sweet hospitality of Mrs. Henri were balm to me." Henri died of cancer in St. Luke's Hospital in 1929. His home became a repository for his works.

TOUR 2

1/Madison Square Garden
55 Madison Avenue between 26th and 27th Street.

The original **Madison Square Garden** once occupied this site where the **New York Life Insurance Company** building now stands. The first Garden was designed by **Stanford White** and opened in 1890. White had a private apartment in its towers. The elegant rooftop theater there was the scene of one of New York's most sensational crimes and it involved White. On June 25, 1906, as the architect watched the performance of a musical review, he was shot to death by Pittsburgh millionaire **Harry Thaw** whose wife, **Evelyn Nesbit**, had carried on a well-publicized affair with White prior to her marriage to Thaw. In one of the most closely-followed trials in U.S. history, Thaw was found not guilty on the grounds of insanity. The old Madison Square Garden was demolished in 1925.

2/James Stewart and Henry Fonda
37 Madison Avenue between 25th and 26th Street.

The old **Madison Square Hotel** was located on this site where an office building now stands. From 1933 to

1935, **James Stewart** and **Henry Fonda**, young and inexperienced stage actors, rented a pair of rooms here. They spent their spare time, among other activities, assembling model airplanes. They struggled at first to get small roles; in December 1933, they both landed parts in the Broadway play *All Good Americans.* Then in the following year, Fonda got his first real notice in the hit play *New Faces* and went on to star in *The Farmer Takes a Wife* in 1935. When he traveled to Hollywood to play the same role in the movie version, his pal Stewart, who also received movie offers, joined him.

During the nineteenth century, at the southeast corner of 26th Street and Madison, adjoining the Madison Square Hotel, there stood the mansion of businessman **Leonard Jerome**. One of his children was **Jennie Jerome,** who lived here with her parents from 1859 to 1867 before her mother took her away to Europe. Jennie married **Randolph Churchill** in England and gave birth to son **Winston Churchill** in 1874.

3/Herman Melville
104 East 26th Street between Park and Lexington Avenue.

Beginning in 1863, **Herman Melville** lived in a one-family brick house on this site with his wife and four children. It was his home for the last twenty-eight years of his life. During that time, the once-productive author was all but forgotten by the public. But Melville continued to write, sitting at a table in his bedroom at night; he wrote *Billy Budd* in this house. Meanwhile, he supported himself and his family by day as a customs inspector in New York Harbor at a salary of four dollars a day. For six months in 1875, his neighbor was **Henry James** (see number 4 below) who rented rooms in a house practically back-to-back with Melville's. James was utterly unaware that he could easily gaze into the back bedroom of the author of *Moby Dick.*

Melville's death in 1891 went almost completely unnoticed—*The New York Times* called him "Henry Melville" in its brief obituary. Melville's house was demolished in 1902.

4/Henry James
111 East 25th Street between Park and Lexington Avenue.

Henry James was thirty-two in January 1875 when he rented two rooms in a house on this site. He had recently returned from Europe. **Herman Melville**, unbeknownst to James, was his back-door neighbor (see number 3 above).

James stayed here for six months, working on his novel *Roderick Hudson* in the mornings and walking in the neighborhood in the afternoons. The author became convinced that New York would turn him into a hack writer and he finally returned to England. His residence was demolished in 1905 to make way for the **Regiment Armory Building.**

5/Fernand Leger
77 Lexington Avenue at 26th Street (southeast corner).

French Modernist painter **Fernand**

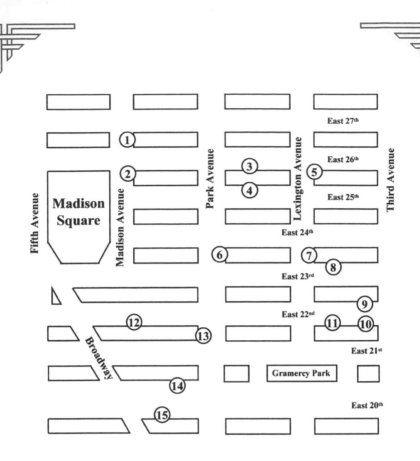

Gramercy Park
Tour 2

1. Madison Square Garden

2. James Stewart and
   Henry Fonda

3. Herman Melville

4. Henry James

5. Fernand Leger

6. Isadora Duncan

7. W.H Auden and
   Christopher Isherwood

8. Nathanael West

9. John Sloan

10. Robert Benchley

11. Cole Porter

12. Edward Hopper

13. Ezra Pound

14. Gilbert and Sullivan

15. Theodore Roosevelt

Leger lived in this four-level building, beginning in April 1945. He had been in exile in the United States since the German occupation of his home country in 1940. While he lived here on Lexington, he created a group of paintings that he called his "Cyclist" series, of which *La Grande Julie*, now exhibited in the **Museum of Modern Art**, was the culmination. Leger's studio in this building was across the street from the **69th Regiment Armory** where, in March 1913, the legendary **International Exhibition of Modern Art** introduced Americans en masse to the world of European modern art. Number 77 Lexington Avenue was Leger's last New York residence; he was homesick for France and returned there after the war in December 1945.

6/Isadora Duncan
303 Fourth Avenue South (Park Avenue) at 23rd Street (northeast corner).

Isadora Duncan lived here at 303 Fourth Avenue South from November 1914 until May 1915. She occupied a studio in the section of the building that comprised the first phase of the structure before it was enlarged to its present configuration.

The avant-garde dancer had recently returned from France, where the outbreak of World War I interrupted the operation of her dance school. Duncan opened a new school in her studio here and brought in a small group of students. She named the place *The Dionysian* and furnished it simply with blue curtains and low divans.But Duncan very soon became disgusted with America's indiffer-

ence to the Allied cause and returned to France, taking some of her students with her.

7/W.H. Auden and Christopher Isherwood
23 Lexington Avenue between 23rd and 24th Street.

The two British writers, **Auden** and **Isherwood**, moved from England to the United States in January 1939 and found a temporary home at the eighteen-story **George Washington Hotel,** which offered cheap rooms to long-staying guests.The place was recommended to them because the manager and many of the guests were British. While here, Isherwood went into a deep depression—he found himself unable to write and he worried about his money running out.

"There is much that is majestic but nothing that is gracious in this city," he wrote, "this huge, raw, functional skeleton, this fortress of capital, this jungle of absolutely free competition." In April, Isherwood and Auden moved uptown to East 81st Street (see Section One, Tour 11, Number 1).

At the end of 1939, **Anais Nin**, escaping the war in Europe with her husband, **Hugo Guiler**, lived here briefly at the George Washington. "It is served entirely by Filipinos," she wrote in her diary. "They give the place a warm, friendly glow."

8/Nathanael West
145 East 23rd Street near Lexington Avenue.

In 1927 and 1928, the author of *Day of the Locust* and *Miss Lonelyhearts* was the assistant manager of this residence called the **Kenmore Hall Hotel**. **Nathanael West** was twenty-four years old at the time and had obtained the job through family connections.He spent his working nights here reading. Before long, he began giving rooms to needy friends, some of them writers—a practice he would continue when he worked at the **Hotel Sutton**, beginning in 1928 (see Section Two, Tour 3, Number 10).

Before the Kenmore was built, this was the site of a building where **Stephen Crane** lived as a young writer. He shared a small studio here in 1893 with three friends.They were so poor that they only had clothes enough for one of them at a time to go out looking for work. Crane wrote part of his novel *The Red Badge of Courage* while he lived here.

9/John Sloan
155 East 22nd Street between Lexington and Third Avenue.

Painter **John Sloan**, with his wife, **Dolly,** took a tiny apartment in this narrow five-level building in 1912. Their former place on West 23rd Street was in a dilapidated structure, and their new place here on East 22nd, although very small, was a definite improvement.Because there was little room to set up an easel, pose a model, or step back far enough from either to get a proper view, Sloan leased a separate studio at 35 Sixth Avenue in Greenwich Village. Both Sloans became involved in leftist causes around this time and joined the Socialist Party. He soon became a staff member for the new radical periodical *The Masses*. By the end of

1912, the couple had moved to larger quarters at 61 Perry Street in Greenwich Village.

10/Robert Benchley
152 East 22nd Street between Lexington and Third Avenue.

In 1916, **Robert Benchley** was writing for the Sunday edition of the *New York Tribune.*After his wife, **Gertrude**, and infant son **Nathaniel**, joined him in Manhattan, they found a cheap, sublet apartment in this building (marked 152-156) across the street from the **Gustavus Adolphus Lutheran Church** and near the Third Avenue elevated train.The flat, which had a dining room, bedroom and kitchen, was a dark and dismal place—all three windows faced brick walls and the fire escape was the only place to go to give the baby fresh air. Gertrude hated the apartment and made no friends in the city.

After only a few months of living here, Benchley decided to find a better place for the family and bought a small house in suburban Crestwood. He worked for the *Tribune* until 1917, when he was fired. His next job was with the magazine *Vanity Fair.*

11/Cole Porter
134 East 22nd Street between Lexington and Third Avenue.

Cole Porter was twenty-three years old and a recent Yale graduate in 1916. In that year, he rented an apartment on this site. He had recently written his first musical comedy to be produced in New York, *See America First*, and it was a flop, closing after fifteen performances. One critic wrote: "Cole Porter is a young man who ought either to give up songwriting or get out of town." Porter realized that he still had much to learn and resumed his musical studies with the distinguished teacher, **Pietro Yon.**

When America went to war in 1917, Porter traveled to France to do volunteer relief work. It wasn't until 1929 that he had his first major Broadway success with the musical *Fifty Million Frenchmen.*

12/Edward Hopper

24 East 22nd Street between Park Avenue South and Broadway.

In 1905, painter **Edward Hopper**—age twenty-three and almost two decades away from his first real success—was growing restless while attending the **New York School of Art** and wanted to earn some money. He landed a part-time job as an illustrator for an advertising agency named **C.C. Phillips & Company.** The business had its offices in this nine-story brick building. Hopper worked here for about a year, mainly producing cover designs for trade magazines. He continued to live at home with his parents in Nyack, New York until the fall of 1906 when he decided to see the works of the great European masters and left for Paris.

13/Ezra Pound

270 Park Avenue South (Fourth Avenue) at East 21st Street (northwest corner).

In 1910, **Ezra Pound** came back to the United States from a long visit to Europe. He was twenty-five years old. He used the vacant apartment of a woman friend in a small building formerly on this site, and stayed until early 1911. During this period, an observer commented on the poet's "cuckoo troubador appearance," which included one tan and one blue shoe and a shiny straw hat with a red polka-dot ribbon. Pound's attempts to get his poetry published gained little success and he quickly grew impatient with New York. In February 1911, he returned to London.

14/Gilbert and Sullivan

45 East 20th Street between Broadway and Park Avenue.

William Gilbert and Arthur Sullivan arrived in New York on November 5, 1879 to produce their popular operetta *H.M.S. Pinafore* for American audiences. In their bags were the unfinished words and music for a new work which they planned to introduce in this country. Two weeks before its scheduled debut, Sullivan realized that he had left the notes for the last act of the new work in England and was forced to rewrite it from scratch. He stayed in this building during that period working around the clock with little thought for the world outside his gas-lit hotel room. Sullivan finished the score on December 28th and, three days later, on December 31, 1879, *The Pirates of Penzance* had its world premiere at the **Fifth Avenue Theater** in New York.

15/Theodore Roosevelt

28 East 20th Street between Broadway and Park Avenue.

Theodore Roosevelt

Theodore Roosevelt, the twenty-sixth President of the United States, was born on October 27, 1858 on the site where this Greek revival house —a replica of the Roosevelt family's original—now stands. He lived here until 1872, when his family took him to Europe to live.

The young Roosevelt had a passionate interest in natural history and gained an impressive knowledge of the flora and fauna around him. His collection of small creatures could be found all over the mansion; houseguests at 28 East 20th Street learned to sit on sofas with caution and to check their water pitchers for snakes before pouring.The Roosevelt house, which over the years had been altered beyond all recognition, was demolished in 1916 and rebuilt to its original specifications in 1923. It's now a public museum, full of period furniture and Roosevelt memorabilia.

TOUR 3

1/Andy Warhol
33 Union Square West between 16th and 17th Street.

Artist **Andy Warhol** moved to the fifth floor of this twelve-story building in 1968. The white-walled loft space was called **The Factory** and housed studios, his office, and a screening room for his films.On June 3, 1968, **Valerie Solanas,** an occasional Factory visitor and sole member of **SCUM** (Society for Cutting Up Men), came to Warhol's office here, pulled a revolver and shot point blank at him, hitting the artist in the chest. Warhol was pronounced dead at the hospital but, miraculously, managed to survive. The crazed Solanas surrendered to the police a few hours after the shooting. She served a three-year sentence and died in 1988. Warhol lived until 1987.

2/Andy Warhol
860 Broadway at 17th Street (northeast corner).

By 1974, **Warhol** had run out of space at his Union Square studio called **The Factory** (see number 1 above) and, in August of that year, he moved across the street to this six-story brick building. The space was located on the third floor and included over 12,000 square feet of offices, storage space, and studios. Always economical, Warhol made it a condition that all visitors to The Factory during the move had to carry at least one item across the street to the new building. Warhol's studio remained here until 1982, when he began to move most of the Factory's enterprises into a disused five-story Con Edison building that was a T-shaped structure with short facades on the west side of Madison Avenue between 32nd and 33rd Street.

3/Edwin and John Wilkes Booth
28 East 19th Street between Broadway and Park Avenue.

Edwin Booth was America's most acclaimed actor during the nineteenth century. During the Civil War, he lived in a house on this site and, frequently, he was visited by his brothers, **John Wilkes** and **Junius,** both also actors.

The Booth brothers appearing in Julius Caesar *in 1864: Left. John Wilkes as* Mark Antony, *(center) Edwin as* Brutus, *and, (right) Junius as* Cassius.

John Wilkes Booth had become violently sympathetic to the Confederate cause and, in August 1864, the brothers quarreled severely about the war during a meeting of the brothers here in the Booth house. In the weeks after his younger brother assassinated **Abraham Lincoln** on August 14, 1865 in Washington, Edwin Booth's life was in danger, even though he had always been a strong Union supporter. Crowds gathered around New York theaters shouting "arrest all the actors." Only at night was it safe for Booth to slip out of his house on East 19th Street and walk the streets disconsolately. He didn't perform again on the stage until January 1866.

4/Horace Greeley
35 East 19th Street between Broadway and Park Avenue.

In 1831, the upstart twenty-year-old journeyman printer **Horace Greeley** came to New York and, ten years later, he became the founder of the daily *New York Tribune*, one of the city's most popular and influential newspapers.

This old three-story building, dating from the 1850s, was one of Greeley's early homes; he lived here soon after he started the *Tribune*. On a typical weekday, he would spend his mornings working here and then walked to the newspaper's offices on Nassau Street around noon, returning here by horse cab after midnight. Greeley had grown up on a farm in New Hampshire and, perhaps to preserve a little of the rural atmosphere he was used to, he kept a goat in the back yard. Greeley operated the *Tribune* for over thirty years. He was the Liberal Republican nominee for president in 1872 against **Ulysses S. Grant** and was defeated in a landslide. He died three weeks after the election. A plaque on the front of the building commemorates Greeley.

5/Ida Tarbell
120 East 19th Street near Irving Place (southwest corner).

Ida Tarbell was the crusading journalist who, beginning in 1904, wrote a series of magazine articles that exposed the ruthless business practices and unscrupulous rise to power of **John D. Rockefeller** and the

Gramercy Park
Tour 3

1. Andy Warhol

2. Andy Warhol

3. Edwin and
John Wilkes Booth

4. Horace Greeley

5. Ida Tarbell

6. Norman Thomas and
George Axelrod

7. Pete's Tavern

8. O. Henry

9. Oscar Wilde and
Elsie de Wolfe

10. Theodore Dreiser

11. Arshile Gorky

12. Charles Dickens

13. Winslow Homer

14. Giuseppe Garibaldi

Standard Oil Trust. Tarbell, who never married, lived in a modest apartment in this four-story brownstone-fronted Italianate rowhouse from 1913 to 1940. Her *History of Standard Oil*, which first appeared in *McClure's Magazine* in nineteen installments helped lead to that company's historic breakup by the U.S. Supreme Court in 1911.

Tarbell was also a prominent biographer of **Abraham Lincoln.** She wrote her autobiography while she lived here on 19th Street. Tarbell died at a hospital near her home in Easton, Connecticut in 1944. She was eighty-seven years old.

6/Norman Thomas and George Axelrod
71 Irving Place near 18th Street.

Socialist Party leader **Norman Thomas** lived on two upper floors of this five-story red brick building with his wife, **Violet**, beginning in 1945. (Number 71 Irving Place is a survivor—along with number 65—of a row of four Late Greek Revival houses that once included 67 and 69 Irving Place.) Violet Thomas owned the building and had operated a tea room on the ground floor in years past. Thomas was devastated in 1947 when Violet died. He ran for the U.S. presidency for the fifth and last time in 1948.

Neighbors would observe Thomas and his dog, **Jester**, as they made their daily hydrant-and-tree stroll around Gramercy Park. In 1954, at age seventy, Thomas moved to Cold Spring Harbor, New York.

Number 71 Irving Place was also the one-time residence of playwright

and Hollywood screenwriter **George Axelrod.** He is probably best known today for such film scripts as *The Manchurian Candidate* and *Breakfast at Tiffany's.* In 1952, while he lived here, he wrote the play *The Seven-Year Itch* which won a Tony Award for its star **Tom Ewell.** The drama takes place "about half a block from Gramercy Park." When the play was made into a movie starring **Marilyn Monroe**, the censors altered parts of Axelrod's original story, making the writer so angry that he decided to move from New York to Los Angeles, where he could more closely monitor the treatment of his scripts.

Pete's Tavern

7/Pete's Tavern
66 Irving Place at 18th Street (northeast corner).

Pete's Tavern, which dates back to 1864, is one of New York's two oldest saloons—along with McSorley's at 15 East 7th Street (see Section Five, Number 8). Pete's was formerly known as **Healy's Cafe** in the early twentieth century, when it was frequented by short-story master **O. Henry**, who lived a block south of here (see number 8 below). The tavern was a goldmine of material for the writer who would arrive here every night around midnight to drink and listen to the stories told by the other colorful customers. He described the place in his story called *The Lost Bend*.

During Prohibition, the joint stayed open by pretending to be a flower shop. In more recent years, the bar became a daytime hangout for the late **John F. Kennedy, Jr.** after he spotted a photo of his parents—also former patrons of Pete's—on the wall.

O. Henry

8/O. Henry
55 Irving Place near 17th Street.

The writer **William S. Porter**, known as **O. Henry,** rented the large parlor, and the alcove above it, in this narrow four-story brownstone from 1903 until 1907 (the plaque in front of the building incorrectly claims he lived here from 1902-1910). O. Henry's main room was on the first floor, just to the left of the front entrance. During the course of the day, he would sit at the window, watch the pedestrians, and then write stories about them. He penned some of his most famous tales while he lived alone here, including *The Gift of the Magi*. The building now houses a restaurant. O. Henry often wrote and drank at **Healy's Cafe**, now **Pete's Tavern**, which stands just to the north of here at Irving Pace and 18th Street (see number 7 above).

9/Oscar Wilde and Elsie de Wolfe
47 Irving Place at 17th Street (southwest corner).

Oscar Wilde completed a lecture tour of the United States in the fall of 1882 and stayed in New York for two additional months before returning to England. The reason for his delayed departure was an attack of malaria which he described as "an aesthetic disease but a deuced nuisance." One of the places where he stayed was here at 47 Irving Place where he rented rooms. In 1892, actress **Elsie de Wolfe** and her companion, literary agent **Elisabeth Marbury**, occupied this house. De Wolfe, who was a pioneer in the profession of interior decoration, used the place to practice her modernist vision of design—she replaced the dark woodwork and wallpaper with plain walls, removed the heavy curtains in the windows, eliminated the carpets, and replaced the old-fashioned furniture with more delicate designs. It was probably de Wolfe and Marbury who invented the inaccurate story that **Washington Irving** had lived here (see the plaque on the north wall of the building).

10/Theodore Dreiser

201 Park Avenue South at 17th Street (northeast corner).

In January 1925, **Theodore Dreiser** rented a small office in the **Guardian Life Insurance Building** across from Union Square while he worked on the completion of his novel *An American Tragedy.* During this period, Dreiser was living in Brooklyn with his companion, **Helen Richardson** and he utilized her, in addition to two other women, to assist him in the typing and editing of the lengthy book. Also residing in the Guardian building was an attorney friend of the author who advised him on the legal aspects of his story based on a real event involving a sensational murder trial. The book was published at the end of 1925 and became a great critical and popular success. After years of financial struggle, Dreiser became rich.

11/Arshile Gorky

36 Union Square East at 16th Street(northeast corner).

Painter **Arshile Gorky** worked on his art in a studio on this site from 1929 until his death in 1948. It was in a three-story building with an entrance on the north side of 16th Street. Gorky was an Armenian born in Turkey who came to New York in 1925. He was poor all of his life; during the 1930s, like many struggling artists, he enlisted in the WPA's Federal Arts Project and also supported himself by teaching. He was one of the few artists of that period with a studio separate from his residence and Gorky treated his working space here as a sacred area—he scrubbed the floor weekly, stocked it with the best materials, and hung life-size photographs of his favorite masters on the wall. Gorky, an early abstract painter who had a deep influence on younger artists, never received the critical acclaim that he deserved during his lifetime. He ran into a streak of bad luck in his last years—he broke his neck in a car crash and also developed rectal cancer. Gorky committed suicide by hanging in Connecticut on July 21, 1948 at the age of forty-eight.

12/Charles Dickens

37 Irving Place at 16th Street (northwest corner).

Charles Dickens made his second visit to America in 1867. He arrived in Boston in November to begin a long series of scheduled readings and, by early December, he was in New York. While he was here, he lived in the **Westminster Hotel** where this municipal government building now stands. Dickens found the hotel almost faultless, offering excellent food and service and providing him with a quiet, private apartment with separate access to the street. Even in the bitterly cold weather, he went out sightseeing, visiting the central police station at three a.m. one morning and taking a long sleigh ride in the country on another. When a fire broke out in the hotel, he enjoyed the spectacle of people turning up in the lobby to help with the fire hoses.

Dickens toured the Eastern United States for almost six months and returned to England in the spring of 1868, in poor health but considerably wealthier.

13/Winslow Homer
128 East 16th Street between Irving Place and Third Avenue.

In 1859, painter **Winslow Homer**, then twenty-three years old, left his native Boston and came to New York City. He decide to make the move after *Harper's Weekly* had accepted some of his drawings; he believed he would have a better chance at success in Manhattan's larger market. Homer took lodgings in this five-story brick house. In 1861, when the Civil War broke out, he became that magazine's military artist, traveling with the Union armies and sketching scenes from the camps and the battle-fields.

14/Giuseppe Garibaldi
24 Irving Place between 15th and 16th Street.

The great Italian patriot and soldier arrived in Manhattan from England in August 1850 after a narrow escape from the European armies that occupied his native country. **Garibaldi** lived for six months in the house of an Italian emigre named **Michael Pastacaldi** on this site.While he stayed here, he worked on his memoirs about the recent fighting in Italy. At one point, Garibaldi expressed the wish to return to his old career as a merchant seaman and even applied

for American citizenship. In October, he moved to a friend's house on Staten Island and worked for a time as a candlemaker. But Garibaldi never felt entirely at home in the United States; he left New York for South America in April 1851 and eventually returned to Italy where he played the leading role in the Italian wars of liberation.

Just a few yards south of this site is 22 Irving Place, where a plaque has been placed to mark the New York home of statesman **Elihu Root** from 1871 to 1878.Root served as **Theodore Roosevelt's** Secretary of State and won the Nobel Peace Prize in 1912.

TOUR 4

1/John Dos Passos
213 East 15th Street between Third Avenue and Rutherford Place.

In November 1920, **John Dos Passos** moved into a small room in this building. He was twenty-four years old and had recently returned to New York from his travels in Europe. He was busy writing essays for various publications including *The Dial*, which had its offices two blocks south of here at 152 West 13th Street.

Dos Passos's first novel *One Man's Initiation: 1917* was published while he lived here on 15th Street and, in early 1921, his second novel, the anti-war *Three Soldiers* was accepted for publication.

Dos Passos, always restless, pulled up stakes here in the spring of 1921 and shipped out to Europe again, this time with his friend, poet **e. e. cummings.**

2/William Dean Howells
241 East 17th Street between Second and Third Avenue.

Novelist **William Dean Howells,** author of *The Rise of Silas Lapham,* lived with his wife and daughter in this well-preserved brownstone in the early 1890s. The house is directly opposite Stuyvesant Square.

Howells was writing for *Harper's* magazine at the time and took the Third Avenue elevated train near his home to work every day. He also took daily walks in the Gramercy neighborhood and his observations of people in all walks of life inspired him to write *A Hazard of New Fortunes* in 1890; it was one of the first novels to offer a realistic view of New York.

3/May Sarton
239 East 17th Street between Second and Third Avenue.

The young poet and novelist **May Sarton** came to New York in 1929 to work as an actor for the **Civic Repertory Theater.** In 1933, she became the director of that theater's offshoot, the **Associated Actors Theater** and, during her tenure, Sarton lived in this attractive white stone house, across from the **Cabrini Medical Center.** Although it operated on a shoestring, this new troupe of performers managed to stay together for three years until it was forced to disband in 1936 for lack of funds.

"It is not a bad thing to have to face total failure at twenty-four," she wrote later."It toughens the spirit and makes one aware that human beings have unquenchable resources within them." It was in 1936 that Sarton made the decision to become a writer.

4/Norman Thomas
221 East 17th Street near Third Avenue.

Norman Thomas was a Presbyterian minister in Harlem in 1918. When his activities as a pacifist and a socialist caused controversy in his church, he was asked to resign. Thomas left Harlem and moved with his wife and five children to this Gramercy Park neighborhood, renting an apartment in this building for $100 a month.

He soon made the decision to enter politics and, before long, became New York's most prominent Socialist Party leader. In 1923, Thomas moved his family a block north of this location to 206 East 18th Street (see number 6 below).

5/Henry Luce
141 East 17th Street between Irving Place and Third Avenue.

Twenty-four year old Yale graduate **Henry Luce,** with his friend **Briton Hadden,** came to New York in 1922 with the idea of starting a new magazine. With that end in mind, the pair rented a small office upstairs in this red building for $55 a month and labored long hours together writing a prospectus to attract the needed investors.

By October, Luce and Hadden had managed to raise $92,000 and then proceeded to create the first issue of *Time* magazine. It appeared on the newsstands on March 3, 1923.

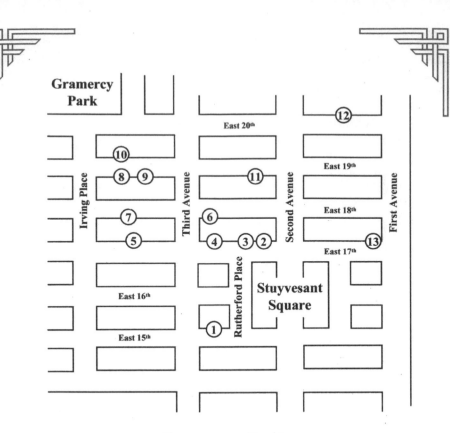

Gramercy Park
Tour 4

1. John Dos Passos

2. William Dean Howells

3. May Sarton

4. Norman Thomas

5. Henry Luce

6. Norman Thomas

7. Elinor Wylie and
   William Rose Benet

8. Theda Bara

9. George Bellows and
   Anne Morrow Lindbergh

10. F. Scott Fitzgerald

11. Max Beckmann

12. Arnold Rothstein

13. Antonin Dvorak

6/Norman Thomas

206 East 18th Street at Third Avenue (southeast corner).

Norman Thomas, the socialist political leader, purchased this four-story house in 1923 and moved in with his wife, **Violet**, and their five children. The residence was next to the elevated railway that ran along Third Avenue in those days. Thomas was the head of the **League for Industrial Democracy** at the time and was soon nominated by the Socialist Party to run as its gubernatorial candidate; he lost badly to **Al Smith** in 1924. The Thomas family lived on 18th Street until 1941 and, during his stay here, Thomas ran for the U.S. presidency three times. His best showing was in 1932 when he received 2 percent of the popular vote.

7/Elinor Wylie and William Rose Benet

142 East 18th Street between Irving Place and Third Avenue.

Poets **Elinor Wylie** and **William Rose Benet** moved into an apartment on this site—where the modern building named **Gramercy Green** now stands—soon after they were married in October 1923. Their building, called the **Stuyvesant**, is one of several possible contenders for the title of the first apartment house in New York City. It was built in 1869 and had four apartments to a floor. Wylie and Benet had a flat on the fourth floor; Benet's three children lived with them. After a year the family moved to Connecticut.

While she was here, Wylie worked on her second novel, *The Venetian Glass Nephew*. The Stuyvesant had no elevators and one of its stairwells was used for a famous scene in the 1948 movie *Kiss of Death*—**Richard Widmark** played the giggling psychopathic killer who pushes an old lady in a wheelchair down the steps.

Other famous Stuyvesant tenants were **Mrs. George Armstrong Custer**, widow of the Indian fighter, and **Calvert Vaux**, one of the designers of Central Park. The apartment building was torn down in 1957.

8/Theda Bara

132 East 19th Street between Irving Place and Third Avenue.

The famous silent screen actress lived in this seven-story studio building between 1916 and 1919. The place was constructed without kitchens because most of the people who lived here were never expected to eat in. **Theda Bara** was almost thirty when she was cast as the **Vampire** in

Theda Bara

a movie called *A Fool There Was*, released in 1915; it made her an overnight star. Bara loved Manhattan and disliked traveling to California to make films. She never got used to the West Coast with its lack of museums, bookstores, good shops, and theater, and, to the end of her life, she kept a New York apartment furnished and ready for a visit.

9/George Bellows and Anne Morrow Lindbergh
146 East 19th Street between Irving Place and Third Avenue.

Painter **George Bellows** purchased this red brick house in 1910. He moved in with his wife, **Emma**, and two daughters, **Anne** and **Jean**. Bellows could be frequently seen in nearby Gramercy Park with his young girls as they skipped rope and played with the other neighborhood children. By the time he moved to East 19th Street, he was one of New York's most successful artists. The painter used the third floor of his house as his studio and, in the winter of 1916, he set up a lithographic press on the premises; he would produce lithographs for the rest of his life. Bellows was only forty-two years old and still living here in January 1925 when he died of a ruptured appendix.

Anne Morrow Lindbergh, age fifty, rented two small rooms in this house beginning in the fall of 1956. Her main home was in Connecticut with her husband, aviator **Charles Lindbergh.** Mrs. Lindbergh had recently begun an affair with psychiatrist **Dana Atchley** and the two met here secretly for a number of years.

The couple spent stolen hours together, eating quiet dinners and hosting occasional breakfasts for their most intimate friends.

10/F. Scott Fitzgerald
131 East 19th Street between Irving Place and Third Avenue.

In the early 1920s, this five-story house was the residence of the Irish critic and essayist **Ernest Boyd,** who was a friend of **F. Scott Fitzgerald**. Boyd's apartment was the scene of a memorable party one night in 1923. **Scott** and **Zelda,** after two days of continuous partying, arrived late, after everyone else had eaten. Soon after they began their meal, the couple fell asleep over their soup. Someone picked up Zelda and put her in a bedroom while Scott slumbered in the living room. Suddenly he awakened and before long had telephoned for an order of two cases of champagne along with a fleet of taxis to take Boyd's guests to a nightclub. It was the kind of behavior typical of the Fitzgeralds in those days.

Zelda and F.Scott Fitzgerald

11/Max Beckmann

234 East 19th Street between Third and Second Street.

Max Beckmann, the German expressionist painter, moved to the United States after the Second World War and lived in a studio apartment in this white stone house from the fall of 1949 until the spring of the following year. He took a teaching position at the **Brooklyn Museum Art School** and continued to practice his art in his flat here.

In October of 1949, Beckmann received first prize at the **Carnegie International Exhibition** in Pittsburgh for his painting *Fisherwomen*. He moved to 38 West 69th Street on the Upper West Side in 1950.

12/Arnold Rothstein

325 East 20th Street between First and Second Avenue.

On this site, where the **Simon Baruch Junior High School** now stands, was the boyhood home of one of New York's most famous and influential figures in organized crime. He was **Arnold Rothstein**, born here on January 17, 1882 in a house owned by his parents **Abraham** and **Essie**. Abraham Rothstein was a prosperous garment manufacturer but his son was attracted to gambling at an early age and it became his lifelong profession. By the early 1920s, Rothstein was considered to be a key power broker in the Manhattan underworld with numerous powerful friends in the **Tammany Hall** political machine and his fingers into a number of illegal activities. Although it was never proved, he is considered by many to be the man most responsible for fixing the **1919 World Series**. He was murdered in a gambling dispute at the Park Central Hotel in 1928.

13/Antonin Dvorak

327 East 17th Street between First and Second Avenue.

The great Czech composer was invited to come to the United States in 1892 to assume the position of director of the **National Conservatory of Music** in New York.

Dvorak arrived in the city on September 27th, with his wife and two daughters and moved into a house on this site. Dvorak loved to visit Central Park and also made an effort to go to the waterfront to see all the large ships leave for Europe, boarding them on sailing days and chatting with the officers.

He wrote and conducted a number of his important works while he lived on 17th Street including *From the New World* in 1893. Dvorak became severely homesick and finally returned to Bohemia in 1895. The site of his home here is now occupied by the **Mapplethorpe House Residence Treatment Facility.**

At 305 East 17th Street, just a few yards west of the Dvorak residence (where the **Beth Israel Medical Center** now stands) was the last residence of **"Boss" Charles Murphy**, one of New York's most powerful political figures in the early years of the twentieth century as the head of the Democratic Party machine of Tammany Hall. Murphy died in the house in 1924.

EAST
GREENWICH
VILLAGE

The East Village represents the eastern extension of the West
Greenwich Village that was covered in Volume One of this work.
It occupies the area from Broadway to the East River and from
Houston to East 14th Street.

I N ADDITION to being the first home to the many immigrant groups that came to New York in the last 150
years, this neighborhood has been a magnet for the
counterculture of the last century, attracting many artists,
writers, poets, musicians, and social radicals.

1/Emma Goldman

210 East 13th Street between Second and Third Avenue.

Emma Goldman

This old brick tenement building, now numbered 208, was the home of anarchist and pioneer feminist **Emma Goldman**. She lived on the top floor from 1903 to 1913. Her bedroom doubled as the office for her journal *Mother Earth,* which she began publishing in 1906.

In that same year, her comrade and lover, **Alexander Berkman**, was released from prison and came here to live with her; he had served fourteen years for his assassination attempt on the life of industrialist **Henry Clay Frick** in 1892.

Goldman's apartment, which was a gathering place for Village radicals and feminists, was also known as "the home for lost dogs" because so many people who had little money and no place to stay often ended up here. In 1977, a fire on the upper floors of the building altered the apartment as Goldman knew it.

2/Willem de Kooning

88 East 10th Street between Third and Fourth Avenue.

Abstract Expressionist painter **Willem de Kooning** was forty-eight years old in the fall of 1952 when he moved to a new studio on the second floor of this old building. His space in the back was long and narrow; the wall where did his painting was in the rear, overlooking an unkempt garden.

De Kooning had been living in poverty until his first one-man show in 1948; after that, his paintings began to sell and he was famous by the mid-1950s. De Kooning's studio was a center of the New York art world in the 1950s; a number of established artists and galleries could be found within a few blocks of this address and de Kooning was sought out and admired as a modern master at work here.

While he lived on 10th Street, he completed one of his masterpieces, the notorious *Woman I,* which hangs today in the Museum of Modern Art. In 1959, de Kooning could afford a better studio and moved to 831 Broadway between 12th and 13th Streets, not far from here.

From 1946 to 1952, de Kooning's studio was located a block north and west of here at 85 Fourth Avenue, across from Grace Church, in a building which has been demolished. The rent was expensive for someone as poor as he was—$35 a month. The unheated space was described by one of his friends as "cold, dingy, and decrepit." While he lived there,

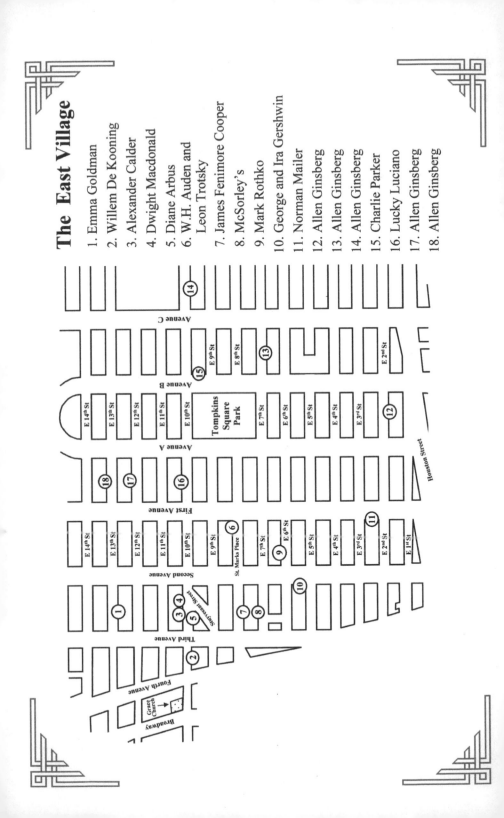

The East Village

1. Emma Goldman
2. Willem De Kooning
3. Alexander Calder
4. Dwight Macdonald
5. Diane Arbus
6. W.H. Auden and Leon Trotsky
7. James Fenimore Cooper
8. McSorley's
9. Mark Rothko
10. George and Ira Gershwin
11. Norman Mailer
12. Allen Ginsberg
13. Allen Ginsberg
14. Allen Ginsberg
15. Charlie Parker
16. Lucky Luciano
17. Allen Ginsberg
18. Allen Ginsberg

de Kooning created a painting called *Excavation*—another of his masterpieces and identified by many critics as one of the greatest paintings of the twentieth century.

3/Alexander Calder
111 East 10th Street between Second and Third Avenue.

In 1923, artist **Alexander Calder**, age twenty-five, came to live with his mother, a painter, and his father, a famous sculptor, in this red brick house.

Alexander had been living a vagabond life for the previous four years; before moving back home here with his parents, he had worked in the boiler room of a passenger ship that sailed between New York and San Francisco via the Panama Canal. After he moved to 10th Street, Calder enrolled at the **Art Students League** to study painting. He found part-time work as a sports illustrator for the *National Police Gazette*.

In 1925, he created the first of his many trademark wire sculptures—a sundial in the form of a rooster on a vertical rod.

4/Dwight Macdonald
117 East 10th Street between Second and Third Avenue.

This Federal-style row house was the home of author and critic **Dwight Macdonald** from 1939 until 1954. He moved into a three-room apartment on the fourth floor with his second wife, **Nancy Rodman.**

Macdonald had joined the staff of the legendary radical journal *Partisan Review* in 1937 and his apartment here soon became a gathering spot for the magazine's staff along with other Village intellectuals. The place became the publication's editorial office in 1940.

In 1951, Macdonald became a writer for *The New Yorker,* where he remained for the next twenty years. He vacated this apartment in 1954 after his divorce from Rodman. He married **Gloria Lanier** and they moved to an apartment on the Upper East Side (see Section One, Tour 14, Number 5).

5/Diane Arbus
120 East 10th Street between Third Avenue and Stuyvesant Street.

In June 1968, the photographer **Diane Arbus** moved to a duplex apartment on the top floor of this brownstone with her teenaged daughters, **Doon** and **Amy.** Their large living room had a skylight and was brick-lined; Arbus painted the bricks white and had a Japanese artist install plaster-of-paris banquettes so that the entire apartment looked like something that had been sculpted. The rent was $275 a month.

Arbus was now at the height of her fame but she was in poor health and continued to suffer from severe depression. During the hot summer nights, when she couldn't sleep, she would go up to the roof and curl up there.

She lived on 10th Street until January 1970 when she moved to the new artists' community at Westbeth on 55 Bethune Street in the West Village—where she would ultimately end her life by suicide.

6/W. H. Auden and Leon Trotsky
77 St. Mark's Place near First Avenue.

W. H. Auden was forty-six years old in 1953 when he rented a walk-up apartment on the second floor of this building. He lived here with his lover, **Chester Kallman.**

The poet was a parishioner at the beautiful old church, **St. Mark's-in-the-Bouwerie**, located a few blocks away at Second Avenue and East 11th Street. Auden said that he liked his apartment on St. Mark's Place better than anywhere else he had lived in New York. The previous tenant had been an abortionist and the poet didn't mind the numerous women who continued to knock on his door, asking for the doctor. He insisted on keeping his telephone number listed over the years even when his fame meant constant interruptions by the young poets who called him. Auden lived here until 1972, when he left the U.S. permanently to live in England. He died there in September 1973.

Seventy Seven St. Mark's Place is noted for another famous resident-the Russian Revolutionist **Leon Trotsky.** While in exile from his native land, he came to New York in 1917 and immediately went to work for the newspaper *Novy Mir*, the voice for international revolutionary propaganda. It was edited and printed in the basement of this building. Trotsky lived with his family in a cheap tenement on 164th Street but came to work on St. Mark's Place every day. He only lived in New York for a few months, returning to Russia after the outbreak of the Revolution to help lead the Bolsheviks to power.

7/James Fenimore Cooper
4 St. Mark's Place near Third Avenue.

Number 4 St. Mark's Place was the home of author **James Fenimore Cooper** and his large family from the spring of 1834 until the spring of 1836.

The author had lived in Europe for seven years before moving back to New York in 1833. His town house here included two drawing rooms, a dining room, and eight bedrooms. Soon after he settled in, his book *A Letter to His Countrymen* was published; it was a bitter attack on American provincialism and earned him the enmity of many of his readers. In May 1836, Cooper moved the family back to his hometown of Cooperstown, New York.

8/McSorley's Old Ale House
15 East 7th Street between Second and Third Avenue.

McSorley's tavern, celebrated by writer **Joseph Mitchell** in his famous story in *The New Yorker*, is claimed by some to be the oldest saloon in New York City, although research has been published to strongly suggest otherwise.

It was supposedly opened by **John McSorley** in 1854 (there is evidence of a later date) who lived in the family flat upstairs and died in 1910 at the age of eighty-seven.Devoted McSorley customers were drawn to the place, said Mitchell, because it was possible to relax there. One of the reasons was its "thick, musty smell that acts as a balm to jerky nerves; it is really a rich compound of the smells of pine sawdust, tap drippings, pipe tobacco, coal smoke, and onions."

The tavern boasts a long list of illustrious customers. Legend has it that **Abraham Lincoln** sat behind the bar when he visited New York to campaign for the presidency in 1860. Artist **John Sloan** and his friends began hanging out here beginning in 1911 and Sloan painted five pictures of the place in his lifetime. It was celebrated in verse by **e.e. cummings**. **Babe Ruth, Will Rogers,** and **Joseph Kennedy** were regulars for years and you can still spot poet **Brendan Behan's** favorite corner near the pot-bellied stove.

9/Mark Rothko

313 East 6th Street between First and Second Avenue.

In the fall of 1938, Abstract Expressionist painter **Mark Rothko** took an apartment in this four-story building with his first wife, **Edith Sachar.** There was a small synagogue in the basement and Rothko said that he often had to hide from its members who wanted him to join the congregation. The artist was then thirty-six years old and still struggling in poverty and obscurity. His fortunes would not change until his paintings appeared in an exhibition at the Metropolitan Museum of Art in 1942. However, Rothko and Sachar were able to move to larger quarters at 29 East 28th Street in 1940 after Edith's hand-made jewelry business improved.

Gershwin home

10/George and Ira Gershwin

91 Second Avenue between East 5th and East 6th Street.

This red brick building with the store front on the bottom level is one of the early homes of **George** and **Ira Gershwin.** Their parents, **Morris** and **Rose Gershwin,** moved here about a month after George was born in Brooklyn in September 1898. Ira was a year old at the time.

Their apartment on Second Avenue was on the second floor above **Saul Birn's Phonograph Shop.** George showed no interest in music as a young boy, preferring activities like roller-skating—he was the Seventh Street champion. But one day in 1910, a van appeared at the front of the building, unloaded a piano, and hoisted it up to the Gershwin flat. It had been purchased by Mrs. Gershwin for her son, Ira. "No sooner had it come through the window and been backed up against the wall than I was at the keys," George recalled. He learned to play it almost immediately and became a serious music student by 1912. Gershwin wrote his first song, *Since I Found You*, a year later.

11/Norman Mailer
41 First Avenue between East 2nd and East 3rd Street.

Norman Mailer left both his home in Vermont and his first wife, **Beatrice Silverman,** in 1950 to start a new life in Greenwich Village. He rented a flat on the top floor of this red brick building; a kosher brewery occupied the ground floor. There were actually two separate apartments available to him and Mailer broke through the wall separating them to create a long, narrow loft. The writer soon began a relationship with painter **Adele Morales,** who would later became his second wife, and after she rented the apartment next door, the two used the adjacent fire escape to enter each other's apartment. Mailer had recently completed his second novel *Barbary Shore* and he wrote a few short stories while he lived on First Avenue. His loft here became the scene of many riotous drinking parties in the early 1950s attended by Mailer's literary and movie friends, including **Marlon Brando** and **Montgomery Clift.** In 1952, Mailer and Adele moved a few blocks south to 14 Pitt Street where he began work on his third book *The Deer Park*, which was published in 1955.

12/Allen Ginsberg
170 East 2nd Street between Avenue A and Avenue B.

Allen Ginsberg and his companion, **Peter Orlovsky,** returned from Europe in 1959 and rented Apartment 16 in this large brick building. It was an inexpensive four-room flat overlooking an all-night Jewish bakery. The two would live here until March 1961 when they journeyed to India.

Ginsberg's mother, **Naomi,** who suffered from paranoia and was in and out of mental hospitals, had died three years earlier and Ginsberg was living on Second Street when he wrote *Kaddish*, an elegy to her that many consider his finest poem. One Saturday morning in November 1959, finding himself suddenly inspired by his memory of her, he sat down at his desk, took up a ballpoint pen and began to write, using sheets of onion skin typing paper. Ginsberg, taking Dexedrine tablets to keep going, wrote the first draft of *Kaddish*—a total of fifty-eight pages—in a single marathon session that lasted thirty-six hours.

13/Allen Ginsberg
206 East 7th Street between Avenue B and Avenue C.

Ginsberg rented a cheap apartment on the third floor in this building from October 1952 until the end of 1953. His place became a center of activity for many of the writers who were associated with the Beat movement.

Ginsberg not only wrote his own poetry here but also worked tirelessly to nurture and promote the works of his friends **Jack Kerouac** and **William Burroughs**. Kerouac visited Ginsberg on Seventh Street frequently and his novel *The Subterraneans* contains scenes that take place in Ginsberg's flat.

After Burroughs moved in with Ginsberg in 1953, the latter helped him to gain a publisher for his novel *Junky*. Burroughs arranged his latest letters to his poet friend into two books entitled *Queer* and *The Yage Letters*.

Ginsberg's stay in this apartment is documented by the many photographs he took of the various friends who visited him. These photos, now in the archives at Columbia University, are a vital record of the Beats during an important period of their existence.

14/Allen Ginsberg
408 East 10th Street near Avenue C.

Allen Ginsberg and his longtime companion, **Peter Orlovsky**, rented an apartment on the fourth floor of this building in the summer of 1965 and made it their New York headquarters for the next decade. As the other key Beat figures faded into the background during this period, Ginsberg became the most prominent voice of the group and he was active on many fronts.

He continued to write poetry, producing important works such as *Wichita Vortex Sutra* and *Wales Visitation* in 1966 and 1967. He was deeply involved in the anti-war movement, going to jail for protesting at the National Democratic convention in Chicago in 1968 and testi-

fying at the trial of the Chicago Seven in 1969.

In the mid-1970s, Ginsberg helped to start a Buddhist University in Colorado, where he taught courses in meditation and poetry. In 1975, he and Orlovsky moved four blocks from here to an apartment at 437 East 12th Street (see number 17 below).

15/Charlie Parker
151 Avenue B between East 9th and East 10th Street.

Legendary alto saxophonist **Charlie Parker** lived in a ground-floor apartment in this building from 1950 to 1954. It was here that his first two children were born to him and his common-law wife, **Chan Richardson**. Parker's brilliant career was in a downward spiral at this time; his heavy use of narcotics prevented him from performing regularly and his erratic behavior got him fired twice from the club named after him, **Birdland**.

One night in 1954, deeply depressed after the death of his young daughter, Parker had a fight with his wife and attempted suicide here by drinking a bottle of iodine. Soon after his release from Bellevue Hospital, he separated from Richardson and moved away from this neighborhood. His last public appearance came on March 5, 1955. Parker died a week later while visiting a friend at the Hotel Stanhope on the Upper East Side (see Section One, Tour 10, Number 5).

16/Lucky Luciano
265 East 10th Street between First Avenue and Avenue A.

Salvatore Lucania, later known as **Charles "Lucky" Luciano**, was eight years old in April 1906 when he came to the United States from Sicily with his parents and four siblings and settled in an apartment in this red brick building. It was a tough, poor neighborhood made up of Italian and Jewish immigrants along with the Irish who had been here longer.

The young Luciano hated school; the truant officer was often at the door of the family's' flat and those visits were usually followed by a beating from Luciano's' father. Lucky quit school at age fourteen after the fifth grade and soon formed a street gang that committed petty crimes. It was the beginning of his long rise toward becoming the top gangster in New York by the early 1930s. That rise was made possible by the advent of Prohibition in 1920, when Luciano began to organize an empire built on the supply of illegal liquor to the speakeasies of Manhattan.

17/Allen Ginsberg
437 East 12th Street between First Avenue and Avenue A.

Ginsberg moved to an apartment in this old tenement building in 1975 with his companion, **Peter Orlovsky**. It would be his New York home for the next twenty-one years. This was an intensely productive period for Ginsberg; he continued to write poetry while maintaining an extensive schedule of public readings and teaching.

He performed with **Bob Dylan** and his *Rolling Thunder Review* tour in 1975. In 1978, he made national headlines when he was arrested as a protester at Rocky Flats, Colorado where the Rockwell Corporation had a nuclear weapons plant. Ginsberg wrote his poem *Plutonium Ode* for that occasion.

Meanwhile, he attempted to organize his huge personal archival collection for future scholars. His apartment on Twelfth Street rapidly filled up with scores of journals, notebooks, manuscripts, letters, and photographs, much of which was stored in shopping bags scattered around the rooms. By 1996, Ginsberg, now age seventy, found it difficult to climb the stairs to his flat here and moved away to 405 East 13th Street (see number 18 below).

18/Allen Ginsberg
405 East 13th Street between First Avenue and Avenue A.

In the fall of 1996, **Ginsberg** and **Orlovsky** moved to a loft, Apartment 5R, in this old building. Although 405 East 13th Street is the official address, the poet's fifth-floor flat here was actually on the north side of this building and faced 14th Street, above the entrance numbered 404 East 14th Street. Ginsberg purchased the place with the money that he received from the sale of his personal archives to Stanford University. This apartment was Ginsberg's last residence. A few months after he came to this address, he was diagnosed with liver cancer; he spent his last days working on poems and saying good-bye to old friends. Ginsberg died in his bed here on April 5, 1997.

ACKNOWLEDGMENTS

I AM GRATEFUL to so many people—friends, family, and colleagues—who offered support in the writing of this book and to mention them all would take up a number of pages. I will confine my thanks to those individuals who had a direct hand in the final result.

This book could not have been completed without the assistance of three key individuals. Walter Vanderborght provided invaluable help with the editing and research and added sound advice and constant encouragement. Andrew Alpern, an architectural historian with an encyclopedic knowledge of New York, edited the text with an eye for detail about the architecture and history of the residential buildings included in this volume. Gary Swanson not only designed the maps but offered invaluable technical support to me every step of the way.

Thanks to Ed Denn, a special friend, who listened patiently to my grumbling, gave me good advice (legal and otherwise) and kept me laughing during our regular breakfasts and walks around Lake Como in St. Paul.

Thanks to Marlin and Loris Bree who run Marlor Press.

Special gratitude goes to Patricia McFadden. She provided not only practical assistance but also generous emotional support. Her help will always be remembered.

SELECTED BIBLIOGRAPHY OF
WORKS CONSULTED

Alleman, Richard. *The Movie Lover's Guide to New York.* New York: Harper & Row, 1988.

Alpern, Andrew. *Apartments for the Affluent: A Historical Survey of Buildings in New York.* New York: McGraw-Hill, 1975.

_____.*Historic Manhattan Apartment Houses.* Mineola: Dover Publications, 1996.
_____.*Luxury Apartment Houses of Manhattan: An Illustrated History.* Mineola: Dover Publications, 1993.
_____.*The New York Apartment Houses of Rosario Candela and James Carpenter.* New York: Acanthus Press LLC, 2001.

Eastman, John. *Who Lived Where.* New York: Facts on File Publications, 1983.

Edmiston, Susan and Linda Cirino. *Literary New York: A History and Guide.* Layton, Utah: Gibbs-Smith, 1991.

Garmey, Stephen. *Gramercy Park: An Illustrated History of a New York Neighborhood.* New York: Balsam Press, 1984.

Gray, Christopher, ed. *Fifth Avenue, 1911.* Mineola: Dover Publications, 1994.
____. *New York Streetscapes: Tales of Manhattan's Significant Buildings and Landmarks.* New York: Harry N. Abrams Inc., 2003.

Jackson, Kenneth T., ed. T*he Encyclopedia of New York City.* New Haven: Yale University Press and New York Historical Society, 1995.

Morgan, Bill. *The Beat Generation in New York: A Walking Tour of Jack Kerouac's City.* San Francisco: City Lights Books, 1997.

Norton, Thomas E. and Jerry E. Patterson. *Living It Up: A Guide to the Named Apartment Houses of New York.* New York: Atheneum, 1984.

Roth, Andrew. I*nfamous Manhattan: A Colorful Walking Tour of New York's Most Notorious Crime Sites.* New York: Citadel Press, 1996.

White, Norval and Elliot Willensky. *AIA Guide to New York City.* New York: Crown Publishers, 2000.

INDEX

250   INDEX

ABOUT THE AU[T

Stephen Plumb has been a refere[
more than forty years. He is curre[
the James Jerome Hill reference L[
Paul, Minnesota, where he has wo[
He also has served as the director[
Legislative Reference Library and [
librarian at the *Minneapolis Star-T*[
author of *Notable New York: The West Side and
Greenwich Village*, and *Notable New York: The East
Side*, as well as *The Streets Where They Lived*.

Visit the author's website
at *www.plumden.com*